Regulating Utilities
New Issues, New Solutions

Regulating Utilities

New Issues, New Solutions

Edited by

Colin Robinson

Editorial Director, Institute of Economic Affairs, London and Professor of Economics, University of Surrey, UK

In Association with the Institute of Economic Affairs and the London Business School

Edward Elgar

Cheltenham, UK • Northampton MA, USA

Published by
Edward Elgar Publishing Limited
Glensanda House
Montpellier Parade
Cheltenham
Glos GL50 1UA
UK

Edward Elgar Publishing, Inc.
136 West Street
Suite 202
Northampton
Massachusetts 01060
USA

ISBN 0–255 36490–3

Printed and bound in Great Britain by MPG Books Ltd, Bodmin, Cornwall

Contents

The authors

John Bridgeman is the UK's Director General of Fair Trading. Prior to becoming Director General in 1995, he was managing director of British Alcan Aluminium plc. He served as a member of the Monopolies and Mergers Commission from 1990 to 1995.

He joined Alcan Industries as a graduate trainee in 1966 and worked in Canada and Australia before becoming a divisional managing director of Alcan Aluminium UK in 1981. From 1992 until 1993 he was director of corporate planning and development for Alcan Aluminium Limited in Montreal, and in September 1993 was appointed managing director of British Alcan Aluminium plc.

Mr Bridgeman graduated from University College, Swansea, with an honours degree in chemistry. He undertook postgraduate training in economics and management studies at Oxford and Montreal and since 1992 has been Visiting Professor of Management at Keele University. He is an Honorary Fellow of University of Wales, Swansea and an Honorary Doctor of Sheffield Hallam University.

Commissioned into the Territorial Army in 1978, Mr Bridgeman is Honorary Colonel of the Queen's Own Oxfordshire Hussars. From 1991 until 1994 he served on the Defence Science Advisory Council as business director on the board of the Military Survey Defence Support Agency. He was appointed to the National Employer Liaison Committee for Reserve Forces in 1992 and appointed its chairman in 1997. He was awarded the Territorial Decoration in 1995.

John Bridgeman was appointed a Deputy Lieutenant of Oxfordshire in 1989 and was High Sheriff of Oxfordshire for 1995/6. He is married and has three daughters.

Martin Cave is Professor of Economics at Brunel University in West London. He holds undergraduate, master's and doctoral degrees from Oxford University.

For the past 15 years he has specialized in regulatory economics – particularly the regulation of utilities – especially in the communications and energy industries. In this field he has published a number of books and articles dealing with regulatory problems in both western economies and economies in transition. A recent book, written with Robert Baldwin of the

London School of Economics, is *Understanding Regulation* (Oxford University Press).

In addition to his academic work, he has advised a number of regulatory bodies, including OFTEL, OFGAS, OFT and DGIV, and consulted for a number of telecommunications operations. He is a member of the Competition Commission.

Howard Davies is Chairman of the Financial Services Authority. He initially became Chairman of the Securities and Investments Board on 1 August 1997, which on 28 October 1997 was renamed the Financial Services Authority, preparatory to taking on broader functions as the UK's single financial regulator in 1998.

Mr Davies had previously served for two years as Deputy Governor of the Bank of England. Prior to that he spent three years as Director General of the Confederation of British Industry. From 1987 to 1992, he was Controller of the Audit Commission. From 1982 to 1987, he worked for McKinsey & Company in London and during 1985-6 was seconded to the Treasury as Special Adviser to the Chancellor of the Exchequer. He had previously worked at the Treasury and the Foreign and Commonwealth Office, including two years as Private Secretary to the British Ambassador in Paris.

Howard Davies was educated at Manchester Grammar School and Merton College, Oxford, where he gained an MA in history and modern languages. In 1979, he was awarded a Harkness Fellowship and in 1980 took an MSc in management sciences at Stanford Graduate School of Business, California.

Mr Davies, who is 49, is married to a journalist. They have two sons and live in London.

David Edmonds is Director General of Telecommunications, the independent telecommunications regulator. He held various posts in the Department of the Environment from 1966 to 1984 and was then appointed chief executive of the Housing Corporation, which became the major instrument for delivering the government's social housing programme. From 1991 to 1997, he was managing director, Group Central Services at NatWest Group and a member of the Group's Top Ten Management Team. He was responsible for co-ordinating work on the Group's preparation for European economic and monetary union. He also chaired the Group's Charitable Foundations and was responsible for creating the Lothbury Gallery in the City.

Malcolm Field was educated at Highgate School and the London Business School. After leaving school he did his National Service in the Welsh Guards, served in Cyprus and Germany, then joined ICI Paints Division working as a personal assistant on the forecasting of demand for industrial paints, working directly to the Paints Director.

He left ICI in 1960 and joined the family business which was subsequently taken over by WH Smith. Most of his working life has been with WH Smith, where he joined the main board in May 1970 as wholesale director, moving to managing director of the Retail Group in 1978 and managing director of the whole group in 1982 and then becoming chief executive when the chairman was appointed as a non-executive chairman.

He retired from WH Smith on 31 December 1995. During the period at WH Smith he was appointed non-executive chairman of the Board of Management of NAAFI in 1986, and subsequently a non-executive director of Scottish & Newcastle (May 1993–October 1998), MEPC (1989–January 1999), The Stationery Office (1996–), Walker Greenbank plc (1997–) and Sofa Workshop Ltd (1998–).

Malcolm was appointed Chairman of the CAA on 1 June 1996 and reappointed on 1 June 1999. He was honoured in the Birthday Honours List in July 1991. Outside of his business career he is a deputy chairman of Highgate School, member of the Council of the Royal College of Art and a director of the English National Ballet School.

His leisure time is spent as a member of the MCC, a keen tennis player and golfer, a collector of modern art and a theatre lover . He enjoys spending time at his house in Devon where he is restoring the garden and an orangery and catching up with his reading.

Dan Goyder is a consultant solicitor with Linklaters & Alliance, with a wide experience of competition and regulatory law. He studied US antitrust law at the Harvard Law School as a Harkness Fellow and co-authored the third edition of Sir Alan Neale's well-known *The Antitrust Laws of the USA* (Cambridge University Press, 1981). After nearly 20 years in full-time practice in London and then in Ipswich, he became a part-time member of the Monopolies and Mergers Commission in 1980 and one of its deputy chairmen from 1991 to 1997. He was awarded the CBE in the 1996 New Year's Honours. He has been a Visiting Professor at King's College, London, since 1991 and a Visiting Fellow at the Centre for European Legal Studies in Cambridge since 1999. He is the author of *EC Competition Law* (3rd edn, Oxford University Press, 1998).

Ian Jones is head of NERA's European Transport Practice. He has directed most of NERA's major transport sector projects, covering rail, road, air and sea transport. Recently, these have included major studies for the European Commission on rail infrastructure charging, barriers to entry in European aviation markets and private financing of transport infrastructure. He has also directed a wide range of projects on regulatory economics, competition policy, labour market issues and policy evaluation. Ian is a former economic adviser to the Department of Transport and the Monopolies and Mergers Commission, and has worked as a senior research officer at the National Institute of Economic and Social Research and as lecturer in economics at the University of Leeds. He also spent two years as a senior research fellow at the London Business School, where he prepared reports for the UK government and the British Railways Board. He has an economics degree from Cambridge University and has published extensively on the economics of transport, training, energy and public policy.

David Llewellyn is Professor of Money and Banking at Loughborough University and at the time of the lecture was a public interest director of the Personal Investment Authority. He has served as a consultant to financial regulatory agencies in other countries, and at the IMF and World Bank. In 1999, he was a special adviser to the Joint House of Lords and Commons Committee on the Financial Services and Markets Bill. He is the president of SUERF, and serves on the international advisory boards of the NCR Corporation and the Italian Bankers Association. He is consultant economist to Garban Intercapital plc.

He has written extensively in the area of banking, financial markets and financial regulation, including as a co-author (with Charles Goodhart and others) of the 1997 Bank of England Central Bank Governors' Symposium, published as *Financial Regulation: Why, How and Where Now?*

He has previously worked at Unilever in Rotterdam, at the UK Treasury in London, and at the International Monetary Fund in Washington.

Callum McCarthy is the first Energy Regulator for Great Britain. He was appointed Director General of Gas Supply on 1 November 1998, and Director General of Electricity Supply on 1 January 1999. Both appointments are effective until 31 October 2003.

A graduate of Oxford University, Mr McCarthy also has a PhD in economics from Stirling University and an MS from the Graduate School of Business at Stanford University (USA), where he was a Sloan Fellow.

On graduating in 1965, he joined ICI as an economist and operations researcher. He moved to the Department of Trade and Industry in 1972 where he held a number of posts, including Principal Private Secretary to Roy Hattersley when he was Secretary of State for Prices and Consumer Protection, and to Norman Tebbit when he was Secretary of State for Trade and Industry.

He left the DTI in 1985, having reached the grade of under-secretary, and joined Kleinwort Benson as director of Corporate Finance. In 1989, he joined

BZW as managing director and deputy head of Corporate Finance. In 1993, he was appointed chief executive officer of Barclays Bank's operations in Japan, where he served until 1996, when he became responsible for their businesses in North America.

Callum McCarthy is married with three children. His wife has a PhD from Sussex University.

Eileen Marshall worked as a stockbroker in the City of London before becoming a university lecturer, then senior lecturer, in industrial economics. Her research specialism was in energy economics and she acted as consultant to many companies and bodies.

Dr Marshall took up the position of Director of Regulation and Business Affairs with the Office of Electricity Regulation (OFFER) in October 1989. In April 1994, she was appointed a chief economic adviser and Director of Regulation and Business Affairs at the Office of Gas Supply (Ofgas). Her responsibilities covered the full range of Ofgas policy issues, including the setting of price controls and the introduction of domestic competition. In January 1997, while retaining her previous responsibilities at Ofgas, Dr Marshall became a part-time economic adviser to OFFER, and from autumn 1997 led the Review of Electricity Trading Arrangements. In January 1998, she was awarded the CBE for services to regulatory policy. In June 1999, the former regulatory offices, Ofgas and OFFER, were merged and renamed the Office of Gas and Electricity Markets (Ofgem). Dr Marshall took up the new position of deputy director general, with particular responsibility for competition and trading arrangements.

Colin Mayer is Peter Moores Professor of Management Studies at the University of Oxford and director of the Oxford Financial Research Centre. He has a professorial fellowship at Wadham College.

Colin Mayer researches in the fields of corporate finance, governance, regulation and taxation. He has worked on international comparisons of financial systems and corporate governance and their effects on the financing and control of corporate sectors. He also researches financial aspects of the regulation of utilities and the regulation of financial institutions.

His publications include *Privatisation and Regulation*, with M.J. Bishop and J.A. Kay (Oxford University Press, 1995); *European Financial Integration*, with A. Giovannini (Cambridge University Press, 1991); *Capital Markets and Financial Integration*, with X. Vives (Cambridge University Press, 1993); *Hostile Takeovers: Defence, Attack and Corporate Governance*, with T. Jenkinson (McGraw-Hill, 1994); and numerous articles on corporate finance, governance, regulation and taxation.

Derek Morris is Chairman of the Competition Commission (formerly the Monopolies and Mergers Commission). He first joined the MMC in 1991 as a member, becoming a deputy chairman in 1995 and chairman in 1998. Having studied Politics, Philosophy and Economics at Oxford from 1964 to 1967, and then for a DPhil in economics at Nuffield College, he took up a Research Fellowship at the Centre for Business and Industrial Studies at Warwick University. Then, from 1970 until 1998, he was fellow and tutor in economics at Oriel College, Oxford.

During this time he wrote numerous books and articles, primarily in the field of industrial economics. Books included *The Economic System in the UK* (three editions); *Unquoted Companies*; *Industrial Economics and Organisation* (two editions); and *Chinese State Owned Enterprises and Economic Reform* (the last three written with D. Hay). Other academic activities included chairmanship of the economics sub-faculty and then the Social Studies faculty at Oxford and editorial board responsibilities for the *Journal of Industrial Economics*, the *Oxford Review of Economic Policy*, *Oxford Economic Papers*, among others.

Other activities have included three years on secondment as economic director of the National Economic Development Council, chairman of Oxford Economic Forecasting Ltd, and as a Governor of the National Institute of Economic and Social Research. He has also been involved for over 20 years in various types of advisory and consultancy work, initially in the field of competition policy but more recently for the Asian Development Bank, in helping to design and implement economic reform measures in China and Central Asia.

Luigi Prosperetti studied at Universit Bocconi, Milan, and at the London School of Economics. He has taught applied economics at the Engineering Schools of Milan and Turin and now holds the Chair of Industrial Economics at the University of Milano-Bicocca.

He is interested in regulation and antitrust, with special reference to telecommunications and energy, has published extensively in the field, and is currently writing a textbook on regulatory economics.

He has been a member of the Italian Price Commission and advised the Italian Government on several regulatory issues.

Colin Robinson was educated at the University of Manchester, and then worked for 11 years as a business economist before being appointed to the Chair of Economics at the University of Surrey in 1968.

Professor Robinson has written more than 20 books and monographs and over 150 papers, mainly on energy economics and policy. For the IEA, he has written 'A Policy for Fuel?' (IEA Occasional Paper no. 31, 1969);

'Competition for Fuel' (Supplement to Occasional Paper no. 31, 1971); 'The Energy "Crisis" and British Coal' (IEA Hobart Paper no. 59, 1974); (with Eileen Marshall) 'What Future for British Coal?' (IEA Hobart Paper no. 89, 1981), and 'Can Coal Be Saved?' (IEA Hobart Paper no. 105, 1985); 'Competition in Electricity? The Government's Proposals for Privatising Electricity Supply' (IEA Inquiry no. 2, March 1988); 'Making a Market in Energy' (IEA Current Controversies no. 3, December 1992) and 'Energy Policy: Errors, Illusions and Market Realities' (IEA Occasional Paper no. 90, October 1993). He has contributed chapters to *Privatisation & Competition* (IEA Hobart Paperback no. 28, 1989) and to four volumes in the 'Regulating Utilities' series. His most recent publication for the IEA, written with John Blundell, the Institute's general director, is 'Regulation Without the State' (IEA Occasional Paper no. 109, 1999).

Professor Robinson became a member of the IEA's Advisory Council in 1982 and was appointed its editorial director in 1992. He was appointed a trustee of the Wincott Foundation in 1993. He received the British Institute of Energy Economists' award as 'Economist of the Year 1992' and the 'Outstanding Contribution to the Profession' award in 1998 from the International Association for Energy Economics.

David Starkie is managing director of Economics-Plus Limited, and director of transport programmes at the Regulatory Policy Institute, Oxford. Apart from a two-year contract with the Western Australian government, when he served as deputy to the Director-General of Transport, he followed a mainly academic career until 1985 and was, latterly, Professorial Fellow at the University of Adelaide.

Since returning to the UK in the mid-1980s, he has been a director of several consultancies and has undertaken work for both private and public sector clients. During his career he has also served on a number of government committees and, between 1972 and 1997, advised select committees of the House of Commons on more than a dozen inquiries covering wide-ranging subjects. A graduate and post-graduate of the London School of Economics, he is a member of the Royal Economic Society and of the Institute of Directors, and an Associate of the American Bar Association. He is the author of many books and papers, including *The Economic Value of Peace and Quiet*, with David Johnson, and *Privatising London's Airports*, with David Thompson, both on the aviation industry, and a seminal paper on rail competition, 'British Rail: Competition on the Network' (in IEA Hobart Paperback no. 28, 1989) first published in *Economic Affairs* in 1984; following its publication he played a major role in the scoping studies leading to privatization of the UK rail industry.

Ralph Turvey is Visiting Professor in Regulation at the London School of Economics where he used to teach before becoming chief economist at the Electricity Council, then deputy chairman of the National Board for Prices and Incomes. He was then a consultant and finally Director of Labour Statistics and Information at the International Labour Office. His published books include *Optimal Pricing and Investment in Electricity Supply* (Allen & Unwin, 1968), *Electricity Economics*, with D. Anderson (Johns Hopkins University Press, 1977), translated into French and Spanish, and *Consumer Price Indexes* (ILO, 1989), translated into Russian and Japanese.

Catherine Waddams Price is Professor of Regulation at the University of East Anglia and was formerly the founder director of the Centre for Management under Regulation at the University of Warwick. Her research has centred on privatization and regulation of utilities, particularly the UK gas industry. Her current work centres on the role of rebalancing tariffs under different regulatory regimes and the introduction of competition to residential consumers; and on the distributional consequences of utility reform, both in the UK and in developing countries. She was a consultant to the Department of Energy in the 1970s, and was appointed adviser to the Office of Gas Supply when it was formed in 1986. She is currently a member of the Office of Gas and Electricity Markets Panel of Economic Experts, and an adviser to the National Audit Office.

Tom Winsor was appointed Rail Regulator and International Rail Regulator with effect from 5 July 1999. He was born in 1957 and brought up in Broughty Ferry, Dundee. He was educated at Grove Academy, Broughty Ferry and then at the University of Edinburgh, where he graduated with an LLB (Scots Law) in 1979. As a solicitor, he qualified first in Scotland, where he is a Writer to the Signet, and subsequently in England and Wales. After general practice in Dundee, he took a postgraduate qualification in oil and gas law at the Centre for Energy, Petroleum and Mineral Law and Policy of the University of Dundee.

In the course of his legal career, Tom Winsor specialized first in UK and international oil and gas law, later adding electricity, regulation, railways and public law. In 1991 he joined Denton Hall as a partner, responsible for the design of the regulatory regime for the electricity industry in Northern Ireland. In 1993, he was seconded to the Office of the Rail Regulator as chief legal adviser and later as general counsel. He returned to his partnership at Denton Hall in 1995 as head of the railways department, part of the firm's energy and infrastructure practice.

Tom Winsor is an honorary lecturer at the Centre for Energy, Petroleum and Mineral Law and Policy of the University of Dundee, where he directed the

UK Oil and Gas Law summer course from 1993 to 1997. He is married, with one daughter, and lives in Kent, travelling daily to his office in London by train.

George Yarrow is director of the Regulatory Policy Institute; visiting professor at Queen Mary College, London, and at Newcastle University; and senior research fellow at Hertford College, Oxford. He is also an economic adviser to the Director-General of Gas Supply.

After studying economics at St John's College, Cambridge, he held appointments at Warwick and Newcastle universities before becoming a Fellow in Economics at Hertford College, Oxford, in 1978. He has also held visiting positions at Harvard University and the University of California at San Diego.

His early research was centred mainly on the economics of the firm, with secondary interests in monetary economics, including theories of hyper-inflation, and environmental policy. During the 1980s and 1990s he published extensively on issues concerning privatization, regulation and competition, including, with John Vickers, *Privatisation: An Economic Analysis* (1988) and, with Piotr Jasinski, the four-volume anthology *Privatization* (1996). Most recently he has extended these interests to analysis of problems surrounding the reform of the welfare state, most notably in the monographs *Welfare, Mutuality and Self-Help* (1996) and *On Welfare Reform* (1997).

Introduction

Colin Robinson

In his Introduction to the published version of the 1998 Lectures in Regulation, the late Michael Beesley argued that the UK system of regulation had become the government's 'primary choice for influencing company conduct in the utilities'. Sadly, the 1999 Lectures had to proceed without Michael, who died just before the series began. Nevertheless, the papers reproduced in this volume – the first produced by Edward Elgar in association with the Institute of Economic Affairs and the London Business School – provide an opportunity to assess whether or not the government is still permitting the regulators to supervise the privatized utilities without the extensive intervention which used to occur under nationalization. Avoiding the politicization of decision making which characterized the nationalized corporations was one of the principal aims of Michael and others who helped formulate the principles on which privatization was based.

The first paper in the 1999 renamed 'Beesley Lectures' was given by Professor Colin Mayer of the Said Business School, University of Oxford who, in the context of the 1999 price review in the water and sewerage industries, produced an ingenious scheme to reformulate the RPI-x price cap devised by Michael Beesley and Stephen Littlechild. Colin argues that, though the water periodic review has been a 'model of process and consultation', it has been complex and has left a significant probability that some of the heroic assumptions made will turn out to be false. The regulator may therefore again intervene between periodic reviews, further undermining the 'credibility of price-cap regulation' and risking a trend towards rate of return regulation. To avoid this unfortunate outcome, Colin proposes to move to 'relative price regulation' (RPR). Under this, at the end of each year the regulatory asset base would be adjusted by the difference between the average rate of return in the industry and the cost of capital. Thus, Colin Mayer argues, RPR 'credibly re-establishes and enhances the incentive properties of price cap regulation'.

The second paper is by Professor David Llewellyn, University of Loughborough, who spoke in a session chaired by Howard Davies, chairman of the Financial Services Authority. David provides an extensive review of the costs and benefits of financial regulation in which he makes some important distinctions and introduces some relevant concepts – notably the 'regulatory regime' and 'regulatory strategy' – the components of which are discussed in detail. Throughout the paper, he emphasizes the 'central importance of incentive structures and the potential for regulation to affect them'. Incentive structures should be aligned to reduce, as far as possible, conflict between the objectives of the firm and those of the regulator. Regulation, though important, is in David's view only one component of the regulatory regime. In the end, it is the responsibility of shareholders, managers and markets to supervise financial firms: managers should not be allowed to 'hide behind the cloak of regulation'.

In his chairman's comment, Howard Davies explains some of the innovative features of the legislation which will establish the Financial Services Authority (FSA) – in particular, its definition of the FSA's statutory objectives. The tasks he sees ahead for the FSA are to explain how its objectives will be implemented and to establish criteria for 'success' or 'failure' in relation to the regulatory regime. He sees David's paper as offering practical help in carrying out these tasks.

Professor George Yarrow, Queen Mary and Westfield College, University of London, examines the shift of emphasis in the new Competition Act towards examination of the effects of competition. He argues that this shift acknowledges the 'significance of decentralized information, discovery and innovation in the market place'. What is now most important, in economic assessments under the Act, is to examine whether certain types of conduct hamper market innovations and restrict economic progress. Short-term market failures are best remedied by market innovations: only 'persistent monopoly' presents problems which are best overcome by public policy. George cautions that poor rules and an inflexible 'rule-making process' can themselves hinder economic progress: the competition authorities should recognize the 'importance of adaptation and innovation in conducting their own activities'.

John Bridgeman, Director-General of Fair Trading when the paper was given, agrees about the need to adapt policy to avoid constraints on economic progress and to concentrate policy on persistent abuse. He expects his new powers under the Act (for example, to levy substantial penalties on companies which breach the prohibitions) to act as a powerful deterrent. The new Act will be a clear 'change for the better'.

In a paper on the New Electricity Trading Arrangements (NETA) and transmission, Professor Ralph Turvey, London School of Economics, describes how the interim new arrangements will deal with transmission losses and transmission capacity costs. He then discusses possible ways of introducing better locational incentives. He bases his conclusions on the view that use of system charges which do not reflect marginal costs should be minimized (subject to recovery by NGC of its allowed revenue), difficult though that will be under NETA. Ralph considers such thorny issues as how transmission problems can be dealt with in ways consistent with the 'NETA approach', how to determine long-run marginal costs and how to establish transmission zones.

Dr Eileen Marshall, Deputy Director-General of Ofgem, in her chairman's comments, finds Ralph's paper 'timely and thought-provoking'. She stresses the importance of governance reform under NETA so that in future changes become easier than they have been in the past. In the cases of both transmission losses and transmission constraints, she points out that some of Ralph's suggestions are close to Ofgem's ideas. In her view, it might be possible to develop a system for dealing with transmission constraints in electricity similar to the new entry capacity regime in gas.

European communications regulation is discussed in a paper by Martin Cave, Brunel University and Luigi Prosperetti, University of Milan: the lecture was given by Martin. The paper is principally concerned with the European Commission's November 1999 Communications Review. The authors argue that, though the review promises some 'welcome adjustments to the existing framework', it does not place as much reliance on competition law as it should. Martin and Luigi are concerned that it does not provide a coherent access policy and that it fails to give incentives for the construction of new broadband networks. Some of the remedies proposed in the review rely too much on 'a regulatory framework which has clearly shown various shortcomings' and too little on 'full deployment of [the Commission's] powers under competition law'.

David Edmonds, Director-General of Telecommunications, in his chairman's comments argues that there is an underemphasis on the consumer as the 'proper object of regulation'. Competition, not regulation, is the best way of protecting consumers, he says. Hence Oftel will be moving to 'the heaviest possible reliance on competition law' and away from sectoral regulation and the use of licence conditions.

The role of on-rail competition in public policy towards the railways is, as Ian Jones of National Economic Research Associates argues, an 'important area of unfinished business'. Ian believes that franchise renegotiation could result in a further reduction in already limited on-rail competition. The Strategic Rail Authority (SRA) should, in his view, look sceptically at proposals to reduce on-rail competition through mergers and at demands for 'exclusivity in return for investment'. There is some evidence that competition on a given rail route has had beneficial effects. Moreover, experience in other transport markets which have been liberalized (such as European air transport) shows that competition stimulates service innovation. The limited extension of open access proposed by the previous rail regulator should therefore proceed.

Tom Winsor, the Rail Regulator, agrees with the case Ian Jones makes for more rail competition. He wants to avoid undue protection for franchise holders. But he is concerned that franchisees may not invest if they are subject to competition from open-access operators. He sees 'little appetite for additional competitive services' at present. He points out also that there is a 'new regulatory agenda' of 'more proactive regulation'.

In a paper on airport regulation, Dr David Starkie, Economics Plus Ltd, continues with a theme emphasized by Michael Beesley in his lecture in the 1998 Regulation Lecture Series: that, in terms of regulation, airports are different. David explains the present regulatory regime for airports and some of its effects, such as the distortions which arise from operation of the 'single-till' principle. In his view, there would be advantages in doing away with the single till. Abolition of price-cap regulation should also be considered seriously now that the Competition Act will give the CAA power to monitor and, if necessary, punish abuse of a monopoly position. Pricing undertakings under general competition law could replace formal price caps.

Sir Malcolm Field, Chairman of the Civil Aviation Authority, comments on David's paper that it makes important contributions in several 'key areas'. He agrees with David's reservations about the applicability of RPI-x to airports. However, he points out that the single till has resulted in reducing real prices to airlines and he questions whether airlines have sufficient market power to counter the market power of airports.

The 'original model of economic regulation' is not well suited to delivering social objectives, argues Professor Catherine Waddams Price, University of Warwick, in her paper on regulatory response to social needs, particularly in the gas industry. But views are changing, she argues, as evidenced by the government's proposals to issue statutory guidance to regulators, *inter alia*, about social measures with significant financial implications. Catherine assesses the plans developed by Ofgem which has, she says, 'embraced the need to address social needs as part of the regulatory process', including asking supply companies to report on their social programmes. She questions how far utility markets should be used to 'deliver social objectives which can be much more effectively addressed through the tax and benefits system'.

In his chairman's response, Callum McCarthy, Director-General of Gas and Electricity Markets, agrees with Catherine that it is difficult to identify those in 'social need'. A central concern of Ofgem, he says, has been to establish a balance between competition promotion and establishing a safety net for sectors where competition is not yet effective. In those sectors where price control remains, it is intended to be a 'complement to competition' rather than to 'bite'.

The final paper, by Professor Dan Goyder of King's College, University of London, examines prospects for the Competition Commission, including the new Appeal Tribunal, which replaced the Monopolies and Mergers Commission in April 1999. He is generally optimistic, but he sees several problems.

He is uncertain whether the new 'open approach', involving public hearings in some cases, will be an improvement; he sees dangers in reducing the use of scale monopoly references; he wonders whether the Appeal Tribunal will have sufficient resources; and he foresees difficulties in the two parts of the Commission working closely together. Professor Goyder also notes the dependence of the Commission on the work of other bodies (especially the Office of Fair Trading and the Department of Trade and Industry).

Dr Derek Morris, Chairman of the Competition Commission, accepts that there is considerable uncertainty about how the new Competition Act will operate. How the Appeal Tribunal will deal with decisions by the Office of Fair Trading, for example, raises difficult issues. Despite the different types of processes represented by the two parts of the Commission, he sees logic in combining them. He thinks the Commission will 'deliver a sound, coherent and transparent approach as competition policy evolves in the future'.

It is clear from the papers in this volume that utility regulation continues to evolve, as it has done since its beginnings in the early 1980s. The regulators and the competition authorities have done much to liberalize markets following privatization schemes which, in many cases, left incumbents with substantial market power. Some of the changes have been remarkable. For example, small consumers now have choice of gas and electricity supplier and those two products are now traded in markets similar to those for other commodities. The flourishing of services in telecommunications is another example of a development which could not have been foreseen at the time of privatization.

But liberalization may no longer be foremost on the agenda. Though the government evidently accepts the benefits of improving efficiency, it also sees a need to pursue social and environmental objectives. It is not clear how the tensions between these different objectives can be reconciled. Similarly, there are signs that ministers are not always comfortable with leaving regulation to the regulators – for example, on the railways, in water and in energy (where coal policy has had consequences for electricity and gas). The roles of the regulators may therefore be changing in ways which, at present, can only be foreseen dimly. It is such changes which will provide ample material for future papers in the Beesley Lectures series.

1. Water: the 1999 price review

Colin Mayer[1]

THE REVIEW

Sixteen years ago, Professors Michael Beesley and Stephen Littlechild advocated that 'the price of a bundle of telecommunications services should not increase by more than X percentage points below the retail price index (the RPI-X) for a period of five years. This could be applied to any set of services, perhaps weighted as the bills of a representative consumer. The level of X would, in practice, be the outcome of bargaining between BT and the government; an exhaustive costing exercise is not called for'.[2]

I will spare you the much quoted reference to RPI-x being a temporary safeguard, not a permanent method of control. But I do need to remind you that 'the one-off nature of restriction is precisely what preserves the firm's incentive to be efficient, because the firm keeps any gains beyond the specified level'.

We are just going through the process of consultation over draft determinations for water and sewerage charges over the period 2000–5. This will culminate with the publication of final determinations on 25 November. Few can complain about the degree of openness and consultation. The document on which the Director-General of Water Services, Ian Byatt, is seeking representation amounts to some 150 pages. This followed a document entitled 'Prospects for Prices' (135 pages) published last October, another five documents consulting on the proposed framework, seeking guidance from the Secretary of State for the Environment and setting out the technical details of efficiency determination and the financial framework (300 pages in total) and several letters to managing and regulatory directors of water companies on levels of service, mergers and the cost of capital. As an exercise in consultation, this periodic review has been exemplary.

It also demonstrates due process. The cost of capital was determined after discussions with institutional shareholders, City analysts, finance academics, banks, bond investors, credit rating agencies and other regulators. The regulator received advice from financial advisers, results of surveys of institutional investors, and he was aware of the academic literature on the subject. How do I know – because he tells us!

The 600 or so pages of consultation compares with a slim volume entitled 'Future Charges for Water and Sewerage Services' of just 58 pages at the last periodic review in 1994. What has happened? Have water and sewerage services become radically more complex? Has the regulator been stung by complaints of rising prices and excessive rates of return of water companies? Is he protecting himself against Competition Commission investigations, judicial reviews and interference from his political masters? Or has the process simply become more sophisticated and accurate?

I will try to answer these questions by focusing on four key areas of debate in this review: (1) environmental standards, water quality and level of services, (2) OPEX and CAPEX efficiencies, (3) incentives, and (4) cost of capital and financial indicators. Improvements in *standards, quality and level of services* are expected to increase bills by just under 10 per cent by 2004/5. Even this is very much at the bottom end of what is likely to materialize, particularly towards the end of the regulatory period. As the Director-General himself notes, 'new quality and environmental directives are on the way. They may increase investment needs considerably and they would need to be allowed for in price limits. ... History has shown that it is likely that further new obligations will be imposed before the next review' (page 17 of OFWAT's consultative draft determination document).

The quality and service level increases that Byatt has allowed are more than offset by anticipated *efficiency savings* of over 10 per cent. Table 1.1 shows

Table 1.1   *Operating efficiency savings of different utilities prior to and after their most recent reviews*

	Annual OPEX grow for each sector	
	Prior to review (actual)	After review (allowed for)
Water industry, real OPEX per unit delivered	−0.2	−2.0
REC distribution, real unit OPEX, net of depreciation	−2.7	−2.0
NIE, real OPEX per customer	−8.5	−5.7
Transco, real OPEX per unit throughput	−5.6	−8.0
BT, real unit costs	−3.4	−3.0 to −4.0
BAA, real staff costs per passenger	−3.8	−4.0 to −6.0
Manchester Airport, real staff costs per passenger	−2.9	−4.6

Source: OXERA calculations.

the differences in efficiency savings achieved by different sectors before their most recent reviews (1994 in the case of the water industry) and the expected savings for the next period (as set in the periodic review). It shows that historically water has had lower operating efficiency savings than other sectors. However, these increased during the last review period and are projected to be in line with those in electricity distribution in the next period.

Table 1.2 shows that there are two components to the anticipated efficiency savings, as outlined by OFWAT in draft determinations. The first is a shift in the frontier of the most efficient firms of 1·4 per cent per annum for base operating expenditure and capital maintenance and 2·1 per cent per annum for operating and capital enhancement. In addition, firms are on average expected to catch up 40–75 per cent of the difference between actual and efficient levels of operation and investment.

Crucial to projections of efficiency savings is an estimate of future productivity improvements. As Table 1.3 records, there is a wide variation in

Table 1.2   Operating efficiency targets set for water services in the next review period

	Frontier	Catch-up	Aggregate
Base OPEX	1.4	0–3.5	1.4–4.9
Capital maintenance	1.4	3–12	7–16
Capital enhancement	2.1	3–19	9–25
Enhancement OPEX	2.1	0–21	2–23

Source: Draft Determinations, OFWAT, 1999.

Table 1.3   Productivity growth in different sectors of the UK economy, 1986–96

Sector	Growth %
Electricity	6.5
Gas	6.5
Water	–0.2
Transport and storage	2.4
Market sector	1.5
UK economy	1.3

Note: The negative TFP estimate for the water sector is biased by the difficulty in measuring a key output in the sector, namely quality.

Source: OXERA productivity database.

estimates of total factor productivity (TFP) growth in different sectors of the economy. Over the ten years from 1986 to 1996, these ranged from –0·2 per cent in water to 6·5 per cent in electricity and gas. There is also a considerable discrepancy in estimates of potential productivity improvements in water. Europe Economics and Professor Nick Crafts[3] have estimated potential operating cost reductions of 1.25 per cent to 1.75 per cent per annum. In contrast, Professors Derek Bosworth and Paul Stoneman[4] have proposed potential reductions of only 0.1 per cent per annum. There is therefore a large margin of uncertainty surrounding (a) the quality of services and environmental improvements that companies will be expected to deliver and (b) the costs of meeting them.

Considerable attention has been given by both water and electricity regulators to the provision of *incentives* for companies to pursue efficiency savings. The perceived advantage of price cap over rate of return regulation is that it has stronger incentive properties. Ian Byatt has stated that 'the incentive framework has delivered substantially greater savings than were anticipated in the 1994 review' (MD145). Its deficiency is that, towards the end of a regulatory period, incentives are weakened by anticipation of a clawback of the gains in the subsequent regulatory settlement. The regulatory regime originally allowed companies to retain outperformance for up to ten years but, following the MMC investigation into South West Water in 1994, this was reduced to five years. To overcome the problem of incentives waning towards the end of the regulatory period, it is proposed that companies should be allowed to retain efficiency savings on a rolling five-year basis. This means that projected rather than actual levels of expenditure will be employed in determining price caps over a five-year period but thereafter actual expenditures will be used. In the case of water it is proposed that this rolling five-year approach should apply to both operating and capital expenditures. In the case of electricity, the rolling five-year approach will apply to capital but not operating expenditures. Shifting to the rolling five-year period overcomes the termination date problem but moves regulation closer to an annual assessment of which expenditures are to be included as efficiency savings. It raises the issue of how costs will be monitored, how efficiency savings will be separated from other factors affecting actual costs, and how an output monitoring system will be developed alongside the cost analysis.

The *cost of capital* continues to be a source of dispute. The capital asset pricing model (CAPM) is firmly established in UK regulation as the basis for determining the cost of capital. But there are disagreements concerning the riskless rate of return and the equity risk premium. The regulator proposes setting the riskless rate close to current yields on long-term index-linked government bonds. Companies argue that these are subject to considerable fluctuation and an average of recent past rather than current rates is appropriate. The water regulator argues that the equity risk premium is in the range of 3-4 per cent and the electricity regulator in the range 3.25-3.75 per cent. In contrast, the MMC used a range of 3.5-5 per cent in the Vodafone case, and historic averages and surveys of investors in the USA are well in excess of this. There is a considerable measure of uncertainty surrounding the equity risk premium.

In addition, both the electricity regulator and the water regulator have introduced a new procedure into their financial analyses. They claim that there is no reason why customers should be required to finance the windfall tax or what may be deemed to be excessive dividend distributions by firms. In computing whether proposed levels of charges satisfy minimum financial requirements to maintain investment grade ratings, they have therefore gone back and rewritten companies' balance sheets to eliminate the windfall tax and assumed excess dividend distributions. This clearly introduces a further degree of discretion into regulation and increases regulatory uncertainty from the perspective of utilities. Whether it satisfies the regulator's duty to ensure that companies can 'finance their functions' is a moot point on which the newly established Competition Commission or the courts may well be asked to adjudicate.

In sum, while the water periodic review has been a model of process and consultation, it has also been extremely complex and detailed. There remains considerable uncertainty about obligations on companies, the costs at which they should be delivered, the incentives that companies will be able to retain, and whether they will earn appropriate rates of return on new investments and existing assets that will allow them to finance their functions. There is a significant probability that at least one of the many heroic assumptions (concerning quality, quantity, productivity, efficiency, riskless rates, equity risk premia or financial ratios) will prove to be false and that companies will end up making unacceptably large profits or will not be able to meet their targets. If so, the regulator will have to intervene once again between periodic reviews to adjust charges or the way in which they are levied. This will further undermine the credibility of price-cap regulation and push us closer towards rate of return regulation. The volume of material produced in this review therefore reflects the fragility, not the robustness, of the process.

To illustrate, there is an active debate about whether the current proposals for charging in water are too draconian. The regulator points to the large efficiency gains made in the past, the overestimation of operating costs and capital expenditures by companies at the last review (often referred to as 'gaming') and current declines in the cost of capital. The companies claim that they have made large savings in the past by implementing demanding efficiency programmes. They argue, however, that they have now wrung all possible savings out of their systems and there are no more to be had, that the

infrastructure will deteriorate on projected expenditures and that movements
in cost of capital are cyclical and will be reversed.

Who is right? I could express my own views on this but I would be as much
crystal ball gazing as anyone else. In any event, while facts are free, you
should not value an opinion for which others do not pay and you should not
hear an opinion for which others do pay. The water companies can point to
such graphs as Figure 1.1, that shows that water companies' returns have

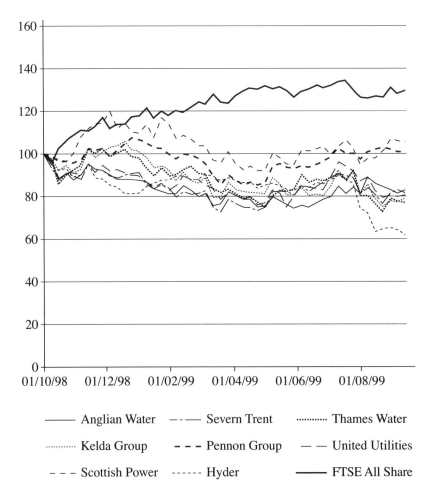

Source: OXERA, UtilityView Finance Database; Datastream.

*Figure 1.1   Total Rates of Return of Water and Sewerage Companies and
the FTSE All Share Index, October 1998 to September 1999*

fallen by 30 per cent over the past year relative to the stock market as a whole since the regulator published his first consultation document. On the other hand, the regulator might retaliate by showing total returns since privatization (as in Figure 1.2) that have still been in excess of those on the stock market as a whole even allowing for recent underperformance and the effect of the windfall tax.

But neither graph is very relevant since high or low returns can be due to

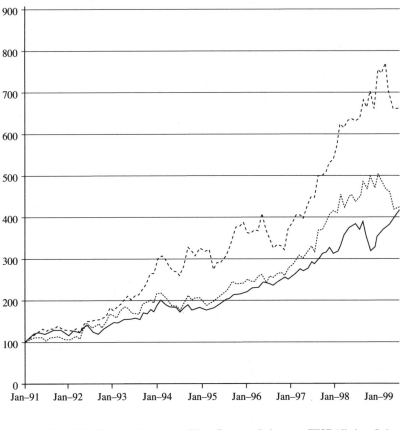

----- Electricity Company Index ·········Water Company Index ——FTSE All-share Index

Source: OXERA.

Figure 1.2 Total Rates of Return of Water and Electricity Company Indices and the FTSE All Share Index, January 1991 to April 1999

either slack (or tight) regulation or efficiency savings over and above those anticipated at the previous review. Past returns therefore do not allow one to identify the source of over- or underperformance. Of more relevance is the market's current assessment of likely future returns relative to the amount that companies should be receiving. This can be measured by comparing the value that the market attaches to utilities (their market capitalization) relative to the value that regulators attach to their assets when setting charges (the regulatory asset base). If anticipated future rates of return are just in line with the cost of capital then this ratio should be equal to unity. If the regulator has been too generous in setting prices or has overestimated the cost of capital then the ratio will be greater than one and if he has been too draconian it will be less than one.

Unfortunately, diversification of utilities out of their core activities has complicated this powerful test. At a previous one of these seminars, Tim Jenkinson and I argued that core utilities should be listed on stock markets separately from the rest of their groups. This is required to allow valuations of regulated businesses and their costs of capital to be determined. It is particularly important where utilities have been acquired by other firms. It is now impossible to obtain any accurate stock market information on electricity distribution companies. The problem exists in water but is less acute. It is nevertheless necessary to make adjustments for the non-core businesses of water firms. Table 1.4 reports the ratio of the market capitalization (market value of equity plus book value of debt) to the sum of

Table 1.4   Ratio of market capitalization (market value of equity and book value of debt) to sum of regulatory asset base of water companies and the book value of the remainder for the groups

Firm	Market capitalization plus book value of net debt	Regulatory asset base (RAB) plus book value of non-regulatory assets (NRA)	Ratio of market cap. plus book value of net debt to RAB plus NRA
Anglian	3386.7	3041.4	1.11
Hyder	2398.8	1999.4	1.20
North West			
(United Utilities)	6360.3	5209.9	1.22
Severn Trent	4503.2	3787.9	1.19
South West (Pennon)	2052.2	1344.5	1.53
Thames	4596.8	3774.7	1.22
Yorkshire (Kelda)	2446.8	2089.8	1.17

Source: OXERA.

the regulatory asset base of utilities and the book value of the remainder of their businesses. It records ratios that are somewhat in excess of, but close to, unity. It is probably an overstatement of the true ratio because the book value of non-regulated businesses has not been restated to current costs. Nevertheless, it suggests that the market believes that current price proposals are not far off those required to yield a normal return on current regulatory asset bases.

WHAT IS GOING WRONG WITH REGULATION?

Given that it is hard to imagine a regulatory review being undertaken with greater care and consideration, why does the process remain so fragile and at risk of collapsing into rate of return regulation? The answer is that it has one serious deficiency. To see what this is, consider the theory that underlies the incentive arrangements described above. Companies are to be given five-year retention periods after which gains are to be passed on to customers. Why? This is thought to replicate competitive markets in which firms gain temporary competitive advantage before entry occurs or competitors react and imitate. There is no particular reason for choosing five years – it is very short in comparison with the lives of many assets in the water and sewerage business and short in comparison with most patent lives. It therefore provides weak incentives for the pursuit of efficiency savings. It is, however, probably long in relation to periods over which costs can be predicted with any measure of confidence and to political cycles over which attitudes to utility profits may change. The five years therefore has more to do with regulatory and political expediency than with economic theory.

Indeed, this is not how competition works at all. Firms operating in competitive markets do not earn a fixed excess return for a specific period and then normal returns thereafter. They earn high returns so long as competitors fail to match their output or costs and until new firms enter into the market. If, as indeed it should, regulation mimics competitive markets then the rolling five-year procedure is not the appropriate system.

Furthermore, it is unlikely to be sustainable. It relies on being able to project normal levels of costs and demand over the five-year period. To the extent that errors are made in these projections, firms have windfall gains and losses imposed on them. That is precisely what has happened since privatization. When Ian Byatt notes the unanticipated efficiency gains in water over the past five years, he is as much describing the inaccuracies in predicting productivity gains as the powerful influence of the regulatory system.

It is the inherent impossibility of making accurate aggregate forecasts over five years that undermines the current system. After all, macroeconomic forecasting over two, let alone five, years is regarded as highly suspect. The provision of abnormal losses or gains for the industry as a whole is neither a necessary nor a desirable feature of an incentive system. It gives rise to precisely the types of calls for profit-sharing arrangements that we have heard powerfully expressed over the past few years. The regulators and the government have quite rightly resisted these. They point to the fact that it is a move in the direction of rate of return regulation and blunts incentives. But that is an inevitable consequence of creating a regulatory process that gives incentives through industry-wide returns. This has nothing to do with the way in which markets provide incentives. As noted above, competitive markets operate through the relative incentives that they provide to companies to earn temporary abnormal returns against the background of average normal returns.

This conflict between stable returns at the industry level and individual firm incentives lies at the heart of the problem with the current regulatory system. The impossibility of accurate forecasting over even a relatively short period of time, combined with the political and commercial unacceptability of abnormal industry-wide profits and losses, means that the current system of price-cap regulation will almost inevitably break down. Whether or not price-cap regulation is formally abandoned in the near future, interventions by the regulator between reviews will undermine the operation of regulation as anything like a pure price cap.

A graph of rates of return in the water industry since privatization published in OFWAT's consultation document illustrates the point very clearly (Figure 1.3). It shows that, at the beginning of the privatization period, water companies were on average earning around 12 per cent post-tax rates of return and even now they are earning 8 per cent. Given that the regulator currently believes that the post-tax cost of capital is under 5 per cent, it is not surprising that there has been a political outcry when the industry as a whole, not individual firms, has been consistently allowed to earn between 50 per cent and 150 per cent more.

But this gloomy prognostication does not mean that price-cap regulation should be abandoned. At each review, regulators regularly go through the ritual of reaffirming their support for price cap regulation. And so they should, because the principle of creating a regulatory system that provides firms with incentives and does not create the gold-plating of rate of return is vitally important. Furthermore, there is no reason why the incentive effects of regulation need be lost. There is a perfectly feasible way of delivering them without either incurring the high costs of the current review or the inevitable political backlash of inaccurate forecasts. But it needs a different approach.

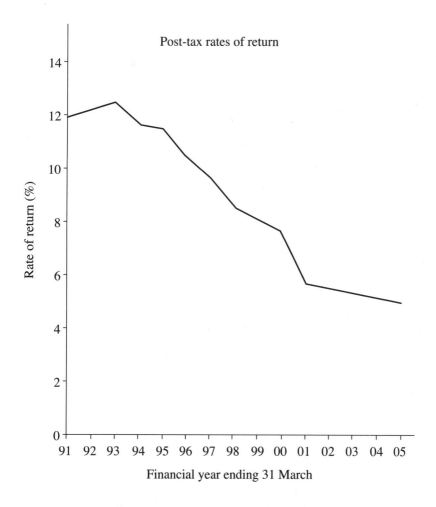

Source: Draft Determinations, OFWAT, 1999.

Figure 1.3

A DIFFERENT APPROACH

The main attraction of rate of return regulation is that it avoids the need to
make prior forecasts of future costs and demand. Prices are simply set to
achieve a particular out-turn return. However, this simplicity is achieved at a
considerable cost in terms of incentives to lower costs. As noted above,

competitive markets achieve these incentives by providing *relative* incentives for firms to outperform each other. A desirable system of regulation would therefore combine the simplicity of rate of return at the aggregate level with the relative incentives of competitive markets.

The way in which this can be done is by setting prices as at present for firms on the basis of projected costs over a five- or ten-year period. The regulatory asset base which is used to determine prices would be rolled forward in relation to projected capital expenditures as at present (together with price revaluations) and prices set on the basis of the cost of capital and projected operating costs. But at the end of each year the regulatory asset base would be adjusted, not only for projected new capital expenditures and changes in the retail price index (RPI), but also for differences between average rates of return in the industry as a whole and the cost of capital.

To take an example, suppose that the average rate of return of water companies is 2 per cent in excess of the cost of capital. Then at the start of the next period the regulatory asset base of all companies will be reduced by 2 per cent. Relative values of the asset base and price levels of companies will be unchanged but the average level will re-establish returns at the cost of capital across the industry as a whole. The attraction of this approach – which I will term 'relative price regulation' (RPR) – is that it combines the best features of price cap and rate of return regulation. It retains incentives for companies to outperform their peers. As noted above, competitive markets create incentives via relative returns for as long as companies have superior performance, not for prespecified periods. That is precisely what RPR does. Companies with costs below average go on earning returns above the cost of capital until competitors mimic their performance.[5]

RPR has the merit of rate of return regulation that, at an aggregate level, prices are set *ex post*. It therefore avoids the fundamental problems noted above of having to make accurate projections over five-year periods of industry-wide levels of demand, productivity growth, and operating and capital expenditures. Aggregate fluctuations in these are simply offset through adjusting out-turn industry-wide rates of return to bring them back in line with the cost of capital.

It also incorporates profit sharing without a diminution in incentives. Customers share in the benefits of outperformance at the industry level through price reductions to bring aggregate rates of return back in line with the cost of capital. Companies retain incentives to outperform their peers by retaining relative returns in excess of the cost of capital. It might at first sight be surprising that incentives are not weakened by clawing back aggregate industry profits. The reason is that the benchmark against which the performance of firms is measured is unaffected by the performance of a particular firm. Thus if $EP_i(X_i)$ is the excess profit of firm i $(P_i(X_i))$

relative to the industry average which is dependent on its efficiency savings X_i, then

$$EP_i(X_i) = P_i(X_i) - \sum_j \alpha_j P_j(X_j)$$

where α_j is the share of firm j of industry assets. Thus the marginal return to firm i of a unit increase in its efficiency savings is

$$EP'_i(X_i) = P'_i(X_i) - \alpha_i P_i'(X_i)$$

where ' denotes a derivative. Provided that the number of firms is large and the share of firm i is small then this is approximately the same as $P'_i(X_i)$ – the incentive of firms with no benchmark adjustment. Even this small diminution of incentives can be eliminated by measuring the benchmark of the industry for firm i as average profits excluding that of firm i; that is, $\sum_{j \neq i} \alpha_j P_j(X_j)$. In that case, $EP'_i(X_i)$ exactly equals $P'_i(X_i)$.[6]

Far from diminishing incentives, RPR intensifies them by allowing excess returns to be retained for longer periods without risks of regulatory intervention. By separating industry-wide and individual firm adjustments, it offers the opportunity of providing more powerful incentives than at present. The need for *ex post* interventions by the regulator will be avoided by the automatic adjustments that occur at the industry level. Regulators will therefore be able to commit themselves credibly to the retention of incentive arrangements, whereas at present they are prevented from doing so by the emergence of unexpectedly high or low rates of return.

RPR therefore eliminates three of the four fundamental difficulties with the current regulatory review recorded above: predicting obligations, forecasting operating and capital efficiencies and providing incentives. RPR also eliminates the fourth problem that is currently being encountered, and that is the determination of the cost of capital. Under RPR, rates of return at the industry level are equal to the cost of capital. While rates of return are unknown for individual firms, they are across the industry as a whole. The cost of capital of all water utilities is therefore known precisely. It is the riskless rate. The reason is that a portfolio comprising all the water companies (weighted together by their regulatory asset base) will earn a rate of return equal to the cost of capital. A portfolio of water companies is therefore riskless even though each individual firm is risky. In terms of Figure 1.3, had RPR been in place since privatization then post-tax rates of return would have been flat throughout at a cost of capital close to the riskless rate and, in looking forward, rates of return can be predicted with confidence to be equal to the cost of capital.

This has two attractions. Firstly, the cost of financing the water industry will be reduced because in aggregate it will be riskless. This will significantly lower charges to customers. Secondly, problems of measuring equity risk premia and beta coefficients will be avoided by making the regulatory cost of capital dependent only on debt and not equity costs of finance. This deliberately overstates the point. In practice, some residual equity risk will remain since rates of return will be adjusted at most annually, but its scale and significance will be considerably reduced.

RPR will not of course eliminate the need to undertake cost comparisons. The cost structures of firms are dependent on a range of factors outside their control (population density, age of inherited capital stock, physical terrain and so on). As at present, price structures across the industry will have to take account of these considerations. However, what RPR does is to focus attention appropriately on relevant relative cost considerations and away from aggregate future changes. As OFWAT has led the way in demonstrating, considerable progress can be made in comparative cost exercises and benchmarking. There is an immense amount of data on which to perform cost comparisons. Over time, as more data accumulate, these models will be further refined. The factors that will drive relative prices are therefore amenable to modelling; those that relate to aggregate movements cannot be modelled with anything like the same precision. Relative cost projections can be updated in a mechanical fashion as new information becomes available, though the more weight that is placed on current as against historic cost data in projecting forward relative costs, the lower will be the proportion of relative performance retained by firms. A balance can therefore be struck between strengthening incentive effects by allowing firms to retain relative outperformance for longer periods than at present, and updating relative cost estimates with current data.

CONCLUSIONS

The periodic review in water has been a very impressive exercise. It continues the principles that OFWAT established from the start, of openness, careful analysis, consultation and discussion. Since economists are rarely praised for their practical competence, it is a pleasure to note that it is an economist who has been at the helm of this process.

I have avoided trying to draw conclusions in this paper as to whether proposed prices are too high or too low. As I noted, both sides can put forward compelling evidence in support of their cases. But the high degree of uncertainty as to who is right is indicative of the nature of the regulatory problem: there are too many issues over which reasonable people can significantly disagree. The regulator may have overreacted to past excess returns and imposed too draconian efficiency assumptions on firms. The cost of capital may have been pushed down too far. OFWAT believes that it has produced convincing evidence in support of its proposals; many people in the industry genuinely believe that this is not the case and that proposed charges will not be adequate to finance their obligations.

The regulatory process simply should not have such a high degree of uncertainty associated with it. We should not, some 15 years after the introduction of price-cap regulation in British Telecom (BT), still be arguing about the fundamental process of price setting. Even if Beesley and Littlechild's aspiration of regulation withering on the vine was a touch optimistic, we should by now have converged on a procedure that is essentially mechanistic in nature. But we have not. We are still debating the very basic issues: cost projections, incentives and cost of capital. Something is fundamentally wrong.

The paper has argued that what is wrong is the incentive mechanism. Providing incentives through price cap as against rate of regulation was a noble objective and should not be lost. But the way in which it is currently being implemented, not just in water but across utilities as a whole, is both inappropriate and unsustainable. It relies on creating aggregate incentives over time instead of relative incentives across firms. It therefore hinges crucially on projections that are inevitably disproved almost as soon as they are made. The regulatory process is, as a consequence, inherently unstable and exposed to regulatory and political interference. In its current form, it seriously risks collapsing into rate of return regulation.

Not only would this be highly undesirable, it is also unnecessary. A system that combines the best features of rate of return regulation (in particular setting prices on the basis of actual rather than projected outcomes) with the incentives of price cap regulation has been described. 'Relative price regulation' involves adjusting the regulatory asset base of all companies for divergences of average industry rates of return from the cost of capital. It is easy to implement, avoids the need for accurate medium-term cost and demand projections at an industry level and focuses attention appropriately on comparative costs. It reduces the cost of capital close to the riskless rate and allows lower charges to be levied on customers. Most significantly of all, by incorporating an element of profit sharing at an industry but not an individual firm level, it credibly re-establishes and enhances the incentive properties of price cap regulation.

NOTES

1. This paper was written for the 1999 IEA/LBS Lectures on Regulation, Series IX. I am grateful to Professor Michael Beesley for the invitation to speak in the series and to Andrew Mack and

James Ryan for research assistance on the paper. I am grateful to Dieter Helm and Cloda Lane for comments on an earlier version of this paper.

2. M. Beesley and S. Littlechild (1983), 'Privatization: Principles, Problems and Priorities', *Lloyds Bank Review*.
3. Europe Economics and N. Crafts (1998), 'Water and Sewerage Industries' General Efficiency and Potential for Improvement', October, prepared for OFWAT.
4. D. Bosworth and P. Stoneman (1998), 'An Efficiency Study for the Water Industry', August.
5. The approach cannot, of course, be applied to natural monopolies, for example national electricity or gas transmission. It emphasizes the advantages of comparators and the costs of mergers in regulated industries.
6. This assumes that there are no direct spillovers of efficiency savings from one firm to another arising from, for example, technical improvements.

CHAIRMAN'S COMMENTS

Colin Robinson

Colin Mayer's paper raises a number of interesting issues about the 1999 price review in water and makes a proposal about modifying RPI-x so as to produce better incentives. To start our discussion, I want to make two general points and then comment on the proposed RPI-x modification.

Openness in Regulation

Colin begins by describing the large number of documents which have been produced in the course of the 1999 price review, which he says has been 'exemplary' in terms of consultation. Most people would probably agree with his statement that 'Few can complain about the degree of openness and consultation'. He estimates that the consultation documents contain about 600 pages, or about ten times the number of pages produced for the 1994 review.

Ofwat has always emphasized the openness of regulation in water. Of course, other things equal, it is a good idea to have open procedures. But I think their value is very much exaggerated. Presumably, taking the extreme case, no one would support a fundamentally misguided regulatory system which was open in its procedures.

The System of Regulation in Water

I would not go so far as to say water regulation is fundamentally misguided, but there are many problems with the present regime. Paradoxically, openness seems to have become a cloak for concealing those problems. The estimates of future general productivity improvements in water are suspect, as Colin says; the system of 'comparative competition' which is central to the regulatory regime is based on econometric models which in my view will not bear the weight which is placed on them; and, as Colin again points out, there is considerable uncertainty about the cost of capital. As he says, so many heroic assumptions are being made that the chances are that company profits will diverge substantially from expectations so that the regulator will intervene again within the five-year period, undermining the credibility of price-cap regulation.

Given the state water regulation is in, two types of remedies are conceivable. One is to try to modify RPI-x or some other aspect of the regulatory system, which is what Colin proposes. The other, which I favour, is to look *ab initio* at this industry and ask to what extent it needs to be regulated. From the beginning, including the privatization legislation, there seems to have been an implicit assumption that water is inherently a 'regulated industry' which should be supervised using old-fashioned 'public sector' economics. Evidently, there are no potentially competitive sectors, as there are in the other regulated utilities, so, it is claimed, there is little scope for real competition: virtually all aspects of the industry must be regulated, using instruments such as comparative competition. Such arguments lead naturally to some curious conclusions, such as that capital markets cannot be allowed to operate freely in water for fear that the number of comparators might be diminished.

My view is that regulation is so unsatisfactory that turning a whole industry over to a regulator is bound to produce the poor results we now see in the water industry, which are in sharp contrast to gas and electricity, where regulatory action has concentrated on promoting competition, and regulation of the traditional kind is being confined primarily to the natural monopoly networks (themselves much diminished, compared with what economists used to believe). Even the smallest consumers are now seeing the benefits. Whether because of its weak duty with respect to competition (to 'facilitate' rather than to 'promote') or for whatever reason, OFWAT has not made great efforts to bring competition into water though, spurred on by the new Competition Act, it is now warning water companies that the Act may necessitate changes in their behaviour.

Regulating a whole industry, without separating out natural monopoly networks, is a recipe for excessive regulatory activity; 60 pages at the 1994 review turned into 600 in 1999: the next review may well see 6000 for all I know. The regulatory game, uninformed by signals from markets, inevitably generates this kind of growth. Regulated companies will always try to find ways round rules set by their regulator, so that he or she intervenes again to close 'loopholes' and establishes yet more rules. But in water, the problem is magnified because the scope of regulation is so wide and, as Colin has explained, the regulator is trying to guess at so many unknowables.

So I would like to see a thorough examination of the scope for competition in water with the aim of significantly reducing the scale and scope of regulation. We now have examples in gas and electricity of industries which people used to think were natural monopolies but which contained large potentially competitive sectors, where competition has been successfully introduced. The companies in the industry used to produce rather similar arguments to those we now hear from some parts of the water industry about why competition is either not feasible or not desirable.

I do not want to underestimate the difficulties of introducing widespread competition into water. Separation of the pipelines would probably be necessary and the powers of the environmental regulators might have to be curbed. But the prize – of moving towards competitive markets like those in gas and electricity rather than relying on rather old-fashioned regulation – is considerable.

The future state of the industry if more competition is not introduced is also worth considering because, like Colin, I doubt whether the present regime is sustainable. Consumers who have choice of electricity and gas supplier will become increasingly restive that there is no choice in water. Moreover, if the trend to increasingly tight regulation continues, as I expect it will, political interference seems certain to grow. Politicians are unlikely to allow so much power to remain in the hands of a regulator and will probably intervene more and more. Thus there will be a gradual reversion to state control (though not state ownership). Managers of water companies, like their predecessors under nationalization, are already unable to manage, in the sense that they have control of few of the key variables that most private companies expect to use. It could become much worse.

Modifying RPI-x

Whatever is done about the boundary between competition and regulation in water, some parts of the industry will remain to be regulated. That is where Colin's proposal to improve RPI-x fits in. The RPI-x regime, which rests on intellectual foundations laid by Michael Beesley and colleagues, has proved remarkably robust. It survived, for example, an examination by the present government which initially seemed hostile towards it,[1] favouring some form of profit sharing. But, like all regulatory mechanisms, there is an arbitrary element about it: why should price changes in a particular industry be linked to some average price change and how can x sensibly be estimated?

Colin's ingenious proposal would try to improve the incentives which the present price cap offers by moving to what he calls 'relative price regulation' (RPR). There would be annual reviews at which the regulatory asset base would be adjusted for differences between average rates of return in the industry and the cost of capital. Thus excess returns would result in a reduction in the regulatory asset base, so the problem of 'excess profits' would no longer be significant. However, company incentives would be preserved because companies would know that, if they were relatively successful in reducing costs, they would be able to earn more than the industry average.

As I understand the proposal, it would not apply to single natural monopolies, since it relies on comparisons between the performance of individual firms and the industry average. Colin has in mind, I think, situations like water (though presumably not only water) where there are several companies and comparative competition.

I can see that the proposed system might be applicable where (say) there are several pipeline or transmission companies operating under a comparative competition regime. But I have a reservation about possible misapplication to potentially competitive sectors of regulated industries, such as production and supply, where there are several companies. The proper approach with such sectors, it seems to me, is to open them up to real competition. But it might be tempting to continue to regulate them under a modified RPI-x system because changing the system of regulation will always seem easier in the short run than introducing competition. In his description of the effects on incentives, Colin says, 'companies with costs below average go on earning returns above the cost of capital until competitors mimic their performance'. His reference here is, I think, to 'comparative competitors': if there were real competitors there would be no need for any form of RPI-x.

As with all proposals for introducing or changing regulatory systems, I find it difficult to assess, except very generally, what the full effects of applying Colin's proposal would be on incentives. I am impressed with the unintended consequences which generally flow from such actions and which make it hard to perceive their eventual impact.

Perhaps people from the industry and from OFWAT, who know more about water regulation, will be able to venture more informed opinions than mine about the effects of such a change. To repeat, I perceive a pressing need to have more competition and less regulation in water, though that should not preclude changes to the price-cap mechanism which are consistent with a move to a more competitive market.

Note

1. *A Fair Deal for Consumers: Modernising the Framework of Utility Regulation - The Response to Consultation*, Department of Trade and Industry, July 1998.

2. Alternative approaches to financial regulation

David Llewellyn

INTRODUCTION AND ISSUES

The objective of this paper is to consider alternative approaches to achieving the objectives that are set for financial regulation. A central theme is that what are often defined as 'alternatives' should in fact be regarded as complements within an overall regulatory strategy. The discussion will be set within the context of what will be termed a *regulatory regime*, which is far wider than the rules and monitoring conducted by regulatory agencies. In essence, the focus will be on how the various components of a regulatory regime are to be combined to produce an optimum overall strategy, rather than as ways of addressing specific regulatory problems.

When a particular regulatory problem emerges, the instinct of a regulator is often to respond by creating new rules. This implies an *incremental approach* to regulation by focusing upon the rules component of the regulatory regime. The paper argues that there are potentially serious problems with such an incremental rules approach in that it may blunt the power of the other mechanisms in the regime and may, in the process, reduce the overall effectiveness of the regime in achieving its core objectives.

Although there is considerable academic debate about whether or not financial firms should be regulated at all, this issue will not be addressed. Some studies (notably those of Benston and Kaufman, 1995) argue that the economic rationale for bank regulation has not been robustly established and that, in some cases, banking problems have their origin in regulatory rather than market failure. In particular, emphasis is given to the moral hazard effects of safety net arrangements. A similar approach is found in Schwartz (1995).

The general economic rationale for financial regulation (in terms of externalities, market imperfections, economies of scale in monitoring, gridlock problems and moral hazard associated with safety nets) and therefore why there is a rational consumer demand for regulation has been outlined elsewhere (Llewellyn, 1999). For purposes of the present paper, the economic rationale for regulation is taken as given and, therefore, that there is a rational consumer demand for it which, within bounds, it is economic to supply.

While this ground will not be repeated, two observations are made at the outset. First, the presence of an economic rationale for regulation, and a consumer demand for it, do not justify everything that a regulator does. Second, the case for regulation does not exclude a powerful role for other mechanisms to achieve the objectives of systemic stability and legitimate (but limited) consumer protection. On the contrary, the central theme of the paper is to emphasize that the various components of the regulatory regime need to be combined in an overall *regulatory strategy*, and that, while all are necessary, none is sufficient. A major issue to consider is the potential danger that the regulation component, if it is pressed too far, might blunt other mechanisms and in the process compromise the impact of the overall regime.

Having briefly set the scene, and to some extent outlined what the paper is not about, the main themes may be summarized as follows. First, debate about regulation is often excessively polarized, with too many dichotomies. A central theme is that what are often posed as alternative approaches are in truth not alternatives but complementary mechanisms. It will be emphasized that the skill in formulating regulatory strategy is not so much in choosing between the various options, but in the way the seven components of the regulatory regime are combined.

Second, regulation needs to be viewed and analysed not solely in the narrow terms of the rules and edicts of regulatory agencies, but in the wider context of a regulatory regime, whose components are as follows:

- the rules established by regulatory agencies (the regulation component);
- monitoring and supervision by official agencies;
- the incentive structures faced by regulatory agencies, consumers and, most especially, financial firms;
- the role of market discipline and monitoring;
- intervention arrangements in the event of compliance failures of one sort or another;
- the role of corporate governance arrangements in financial firms; and
- the disciplining and accountability arrangements applied to regulatory agencies.

Third, regulatory strategy is not to be viewed solely in terms of the rules and supervision that are established by a regulatory agency. In some respects the debate about regulation is often too narrow because it focuses almost exclusively on the first component of the regime, namely rules imposed by the regulator. The real debate should be about how to optimize the combination of the seven components of the regime; strategy needs to focus on optimizing the overall regulatory regime rather than any one component. This is a difficult and demanding mandate, and to the regulator the more effective approach in the short run might appear to be imposing more rules. There is a danger of thinking only in terms of incremental change to regulation, rather than strategically with respect to the overall regime. The objective is to move towards an optimum mix of the components, combined with careful choice of the various regulatory instruments within each. It is not a question of choosing between *either* regulation *or* market disciplines.

Fourth, a key issue for the regulator to consider is not only how its actions can contribute directly to the objectives of regulation, but also how they have an impact on the other components of the regime. Most important is the issue of the way regulation affects incentive structures within firms, and the role that can be played by market discipline and monitoring.

Fifth, all this needs to be set in the context of trade-offs between the various components of the regime. In some circumstances the more emphasis that is given to one of the components (for example, regulation) the less powerful becomes one or more of the others (for example, market discipline on financial firms) and to an extent that may reduce overall effectiveness and efficiency. For instance, an excessive reliance on detailed and prescriptive rules may weaken incentive structures and market discipline.

Sixth, the optimum mix of the components of the regime changes over time as market conditions and compliance culture change. It is argued that, in current conditions, there needs to be a shift within the regime in five dimensions: less reliance to be placed on detailed and prescriptive rules; more emphasis to be given to official supervision; a greater focus on incentive structures; an enhanced and strengthened role for market discipline and monitoring; and a more central role for corporate governance arrangements within financial firms.

Seventh, consumers, financial firms and different types of financial business are not homogeneous, which means that the optimum regulatory approach will be different for different consumers, financial firms and businesses. This has been recognized by the regulatory authorities in the UK with more emphasis being given to a risk-based approach. However, it is argued that there should be yet more differentiation. The skill lies in making sufficient differentiations to reflect the heterogeneous nature of regulated firms, consumers and different types of business, while not unduly complicating the regulatory process to an extent that can cause consumer confusion and also unwarranted inequality of treatment.

Finally, one approach to be considered is what (in a later section) is termed *contract regulation*. In this model, once the regulator has established objectives and a set of general principles, individual financial firms are able to choose their own regulation. Once the choice has been agreed with the regulator, a contract is established between them. If the firm does not deliver on the contract, sanctions are applied in the normal way and the regulator has the option of withdrawing the choice from the regulated firm and imposing its own contract.

This all amounts to emphasizing an overall 'regulatory strategy' rather than focusing on regulation *per se*. A central theme is that regulation is an important, but only one, component of a regulatory regime designed to achieve the objectives of systemic stability and consumer protection. Giving too much emphasis to regulation *per se* has the danger that the importance of the other components are played down, or even marginalized.

SOME INITIAL PERSPECTIVES

Before considering some of the themes in more detail, four initial perspectives are offered which are of relevance to the discussion that follows. First, regulatory agencies can usefully be viewed as supplying regulatory, monitoring and supervisory services to various stakeholders: financial firms, consumers, government and so on. However, complications immediately arise as, unlike most other goods and services, they are not supplied through a market process, but are largely imposed by the regulator even though there may be a process of consultation. This leads to several problems: valuable information is lost about what type and extent of regulation consumers demand, and how much consumers are prepared to pay for regulation. It also reduces the discipline on the regulator. A problem also arises in that consumers are not homogeneous, and yet their different demands cannot be signalled through a market process. Above all, regulation is largely perceived as being a free good as, absent a market for regulation, no market price is generated.

This leads on to a second perspective: if the perception that regulation is costless is combined with risk-averse regulators, there is an evident danger of regulation becoming both overdemanded by consumers and oversupplied by regulators. A major issue, therefore, is how to guard against such demand- or supply-driven overregulation.

Third, potential hazards are created in regulation because, not only is there no market, but regulatory agencies are supplying their services as monopolists. Anticipating a later argument, this further emphasizes why regulation should be viewed as only one among several components in a regulatory regime. The other components need to be strengthened, in part as a restraint on the monopoly power of the regulator.

The fourth perspective is that, in the final analysis, regulation is about changing the behaviour of regulated institutions on the grounds that unconstrained market behaviour of financial firms tends to produce socially sub-optimum outcomes. One of the key questions that arises is the extent to which behaviour is to be altered by way of externally imposed *rules*, or through creating *incentives* for firms to behave in a particular way. Laws, regulations and supervisory actions provide incentives for regulated firms to adjust their actions and behaviour, and to control their own risks internally. They can usefully be viewed as *incentive contracts* within a standard principal–agent relationship where the principal is the regulator and the agent is the regulated firm. Within this framework, regulation involves a process of creating incentive-compatible contracts so that regulated firms have an incentive to behave in a way consistent with the social objectives of systemic stability and investor protection.

THE DANGER OF REGULATORY MONOPOLY

The Financial Services Authority (FSA) has been created as a single, unified regulatory agency taking over the responsibilities of the multiple regulators constructed within the 1986 Financial Services Act. Although several other countries are moving in the same direction, in terms of scope and powers it is likely to become the most powerful financial regulator in the world. It is powerful because of the extent of its remit, the powers the bill confers on it, and the discretion it has in the exercise of those powers. It is effectively a monopolist. There must always be some concern about monopolist regulators.

One approach to reducing the monopoly power of a single regulator is to have more than one agency. Several analysts, including the author, argued this case at the time it was first proposed to establish a single regulatory agency. Others have argued various versions of Twin Peaks and so on. I would now argue that this is not the best approach and that, under modern conditions and market structures, the case for a single regulatory agency is very powerful. The case for a single agency is outlined elsewhere (Goodhart *et al.*, 1998) and most persuasively by the FSA itself (Briault, 1999). It is also unlikely that, in practice, multiple agencies would solve the monopoly problem, largely because they would be operating in different areas.

However, given the way the UK financial system has evolved, and the complex nature of the business of many financial firms, while there is an overwhelming case for a single agency, the problems of monopoly remain, and need to be guarded against. If the multiple agency approach is rejected, what is the alternative? The theme to be developed below is twofold: (a) a more effective and efficient solution lies in strengthening the other components of the regulatory regime, and (b) there needs to be restraining and accountability mechanisms on regulatory agencies. These are likely to be more effective and efficient ways of addressing any monopoly concerns than having multiple agencies.

THE REGULATORY REGIME

The concept of a regulatory regime is considerably wider than the prevailing set of prudential and conduct of business rules established by regulatory agencies. External regulation has a positive role in fostering a safe and sound financial system and consumer protection. However, this role, while important, is limited, and insufficient in itself. Equally, and increasingly, important are the other components of the regime, most especially the incentive structures faced by financial firms, and the efficiency of the necessary monitoring and supervision by official agencies and the market.

Analysis of recent financial crises throughout the world, and in both developed and less developed countries (see, for instance, Brealey, 1999; Corsetti *et al.*, 1998; Lindgren *et al.*, 1996; Llewellyn, 2000) indicates that 'regulatory failures' are not exclusively (or even mainly) a problem that the rules were wrong. Five common characteristics have been weak internal risk analysis, management and control systems; inadequate official supervision; weak (or even perverse) incentive structures within financial institutions; inadequate information disclosure and the failure of markets to impose discipline on banks; and inadequate corporate governance arrangements both within banks and their large corporate customers.

A maintained theme in this paper is that a regulatory regime is to be viewed more widely than externally imposed regulation of financial institutions. In current conditions it would be a mistake to rely wholly, or even pre-dominantly, on external regulation, monitoring and supervision by the 'official sector'. The world of banking and finance is too complex and volatile to be able to rely on a simple set of prescriptive rules for prudent and compliant behaviour. The central role of incentive structures is constantly emphasized. There are many reasons (market imperfections and failures, externalities, 'gridlock' problems, and moral hazards associated with safety net arrange-ments) why incentive structures within financial firms may not be aligned with regulatory objectives (Llewellyn, 1999).

This means that a major consideration for the regulator is the impact its own rules have on regulated firms' incentive structures, whether they might have perverse effects, and what regulation can do to improve incentives. Incentive structures need to be at the centre of all aspects of regulation because, if these are wrong, it is unlikely that the other mechanisms in the regulatory regime will achieve the regulatory objectives. It is necessary to consider not only how the various components of the regime directly affect regulatory objectives, but also how they operate indirectly through their impact on the incentives of regulated firms and others. This is illustrated diagrammatically in Figure 2.1. In many ways, incentive structures are at the heart of the regulatory process.

Trade-offs within the Regime

Within the regulatory regime there are trade-offs at two levels. In terms of regulatory strategy, a choice has to be made about the balance of the various components and the relative weights to be assigned to each. Thus a powerful role for official regulation with little weight assigned to market discipline might be chosen, or alternatively a relatively light touch of regulation but with heavy reliance on the other components. For instance, a given degree of investor protection can be provided by different combinations of rules, supervision, market discipline and so on, and with various degrees of

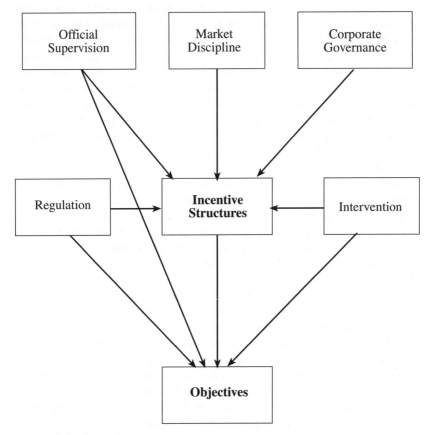

Figure 2.1   Incentive structures

discretion applied by the regulator. The same level of investor protection could be provided by combining a highly detailed and prescriptive rule book with a small degree of supervisory discretion, or by combining a set of general principles with a high degree of supervisory discretion in how those principles are to be translated into action by regulated firms.

The second form of trade-off relates to the way the components of the regime may be causally related. In some circumstances the more emphasis that is given to one of the components (such as regulation) the less powerful becomes one or more of the others (such as market discipline on banks) and to an extent that may reduce the overall impact. Thus, while regulation may be viewed as a response to market failures, weak market discipline and inadequate corporate governance arrangements, causation may also operate in the other direction, with regulation weakening these other mechanisms. For instance, the more emphasis that is given to detailed, extensive and prescriptive rules, the weaker might be the role of incentive structures, market discipline and corporate governance arrangements with financial firms. This has been put by Simpson (2000) as follows: 'In a market which is heavily regulated for internal standards of integrity, the incentives to fair dealing diminish. Within the company culture, such norms of fair dealing as "the way we do things around here" would eventually be replaced by "It's OK if we can get away with it"'. In other words, an excessive reliance on detailed and prescriptive rules may weaken incentive structures and market discipline.

Similarly, an excessive focus on detailed and prescriptive rules may weaken corporate governance mechanisms within financial firms and may blunt the incentive of others to monitor and control the behaviour of banks. Weakness in corporate governance mechanisms may also reflect the fact that banks are monitored, regulated and supervised by official agencies. The way intervention is conducted in the event of bank distress (for example, whether forbearance is practised) may also have adverse incentive effects on the behaviour of banks and the willingness of markets to monitor and control their risk taking.

An empirical study of regulation in the USA by Billett *et al.* (1998) suggests that some types of regulation may undermine market discipline. The authors examine the costs of market discipline and regulation and show that, as a bank's risk increases, the cost of uninsured deposits rises and the bank switches to insured deposits. This is because changes in regulatory costs are less sensitive to changes in risk than are market costs. They also show that, when rating agencies downgrade a bank, the bank tends to increase its use of insured deposits. The authors conclude: 'The disparate costs of insured deposits and uninsured liabilities, combined with the ability and willingness of banks to alter their exposure to each, challenge the notion that market discipline can be an effective deterrent against excessive risk taking'. This type of evidence demonstrates that, under some circumstances, regulation can have the effect of blunting market discipline.

The public policy objective should be to optimize the outcome of a regulatory strategy in terms of mixing the components of the regime, bearing in mind the possibility of negative trade-offs. The key to optimizing the effectiveness of a regulatory regime is the portfolio mix of the seven core components. All are necessary but none alone is sufficient. The skill of the regulator in devising a regulatory strategy lies in how the various components in the regime are combined, and how the various instruments available to the regulator (rules, principles, guidelines, mandatory disclosure requirements, authorization, supervision, intervention, sanctions, redress and so on) are to be used.

The issue of combination also applies to the instruments of regulation. A key choice for regulators relates to the selection of instruments and how they are to be combined. An issue for any financial regulator, as with any policy maker with clearly defined, but multiple, objectives, relates to the selection from the various policy instruments available and the way they are combined to achieve the broad set of objectives. The skill lies not so much in the selection of instruments as in the way they are combined in the overall policy mix. Thus it is not a question of rules *versus* principles but how the full range of instruments is used to create an overall effect.

The optimum mix of components of a regulatory regime and of instruments will change over time. It might, for instance, be argued that the regulation of retail investment business in the UK has been excessively prescriptive and detailed. It might also be argued that, given past experience and the various scandals that had been discovered, this was necessary at the outset in order to 'shock' the industry into a more compliant approach to its business and the way it conducts business with potentially vulnerable investors. If the norms and compliance culture of the industry change, it could become appropriate to rely less on detailed and prescriptive regulation, at least as far as some firms are concerned. The Personal Investment Authority's Evolution Project was designed to consider how regulatory strategy might be modified in the light of changing circumstances.

Neither does the approach and mix of components in the regulatory regime need to be the same for all regulated firms, all consumers or all types of business. On the contrary, given that none of these is homogeneous, it would be sub-optimal to apply the same approach. The key strategic issue in this dimension is the extent to which differentiations are to be made between different consumers, regulated firms and business areas.

Financial systems are changing substantially and to an extent that may undermine traditional approaches to regulation, and most especially the balance between regulation and official supervision, and the role of market discipline. In particular, globalization, the pace of financial innovation and the creation of new financial instruments, the blurring of traditional distinctions between different types of financial firm, the speed with which portfolios can change through banks trading in derivatives and so on, and the increased complexity of banking business, create a fundamentally new (in particular, more competitive) environment in which regulation and supervision are undertaken. They also change the viability of different approaches to regulation which, if it is to be effective, must constantly respond to changes in the market environment in which regulated firms operate.

In the following sections consideration is given to some of the issues that are relevant for each of the dimensions in the regulatory regime, with particular reference to regulatory strategy designed to optimize the overall effect of the total, rather than the component parts of, the regime.

REGULATION

Three particular issues arise with respect to the regulation part of the regime: the weight to be given to formal and prescriptive rules of behaviour, the types of rules established, and the impact that rules may have on the other components of the regulatory regime.

A former US regulator has noted: 'Financial services regulation has traditionally tended towards a style that is command-and-control, dictating precisely what a regulated entity can do and how it should do it … generally, they focus on the specific steps needed to accomplish a certain regulatory task and specify with detail the actions to be taken by the regulated firm' (Wallman, 1999). His experience in the USA also suggests that the interaction of the interests of the regulator and the regulated may tend towards a high degree of prescription in the regulatory process. Regulators tend to look for standards they can easily monitor and enforce, while the regulated seek standards they can comply with. The result is that regulators seek precision and detail in their requirements, while the regulated look for certainty and firm guidance on what they are to do. Wallman suggests: 'The result is specific and detailed guidance, not the kind of pronouncements that reflect fundamental concepts and allow the market to develop on its own'.

Although precise rules have their attractions for both the regulator and regulated firms, there are several problems with a highly prescriptive regulatory regime:

- An excessive degree of prescription may bring regulation into disrepute if it is perceived by the industry as being excessive, with many redundant rules.

- Risks are often too complex to be covered by simple rules.
- Balance sheet rules reflect the position of an institution only at a particular point in time, and its position can change substantially within a short period.
- An inflexible approach based on a detailed rule book has the effect of impeding firms from choosing their own least-cost way of meeting regulatory objectives.
- Detailed and extensive rules may stifle innovation.
- A prescriptive regime tends to focus upon firms' processes rather than outcomes and the ultimate objectives of regulation. The rules may become the focus of compliance rather than the objectives they are designed to achieve. In this regard, such a regime can give rise to a perverse culture of 'box ticking' by regulated firms. The letter of the regulation may be obeyed but not the spirit or intention.
- A prescriptive approach is inclined towards 'rules escalation' whereby rules are added over time, but few are withdrawn.
- A highly prescriptive approach may create a confrontational relationship between the regulator and regulated firms, or alternatively cause firms to overreact and engage in excessive efforts at internal compliance out of fear of being challenged by the regulator. In this sense, regulation may become more prescriptive and detailed than is intended by the regulator because of the culture that a rules-based approach generates.
- Forcing a high degree of conformity on regulated firms causes an information loss. If firms are given leeway to satisfying the regulator's objectives and principles, more may be learned about consumer preferences in regulation, about how different behaviour affects regulatory objectives, and about the properties of different rules and so on.
- In the interests of 'competitive neutrality', rules may be applied equally to all firms, even though they may be sufficiently heterogeneous to warrant different approaches. Treating as equal firms that in practice are not equal is not competitive neutrality, and a highly prescriptive approach to regulation reduces the scope for legitimate differentiations.
- A highly prescriptive rules approach may prove in practice to be inflexible and not sufficiently responsive to market conditions.
- There is a potential moral hazard because firms may assume that, if something is not explicitly covered in regulations, there is no regulatory dimension to the issue.
- Detailed rules may also have perverse effects in that they are regarded as actual standards to be adopted rather than minimum standards, with the result that, in some cases, actual behaviour of regulated firms may be of a lower standard than, without the rule, they would have chosen.

This is most especially the case if each firm assumes that its competitors will adopt the minimum regulatory standard.

A second issue relates to the choice of type of rules. Black (1994) distinguishes different types of rules along three dimensions: precision (how much is prescribed and covered in the rule), simplicity (the degree to which the rule may be easily applied to concrete situations) and clarity. The trade-off is between precision and ease of enforcement, in that the more precise the rule the easier it is to enforce. On the other hand, the more precise are the rules the less flexibility is created within the overall regime.

A third issue is whether the degree of precision in rules has a positive or negative impact on compliance and the other components of the regime. For reasons already suggested, precision and detail may have a negative effect on compliance and compliance culture: if something is not explicitly disallowed it is presumed to be allowed. Conversely, a regime based more on broad principles than detailed and extensive rules has certain advantages: principles are easily understood and remembered, and they apply to all behaviour and are more likely to have a positive impact on overall compliance culture. It might also be the case (as suggested in Black, 1994) that principles are more likely to become board issues, with the board of financial firms adopting compliance with principles as a high-level policy issue, rather than a culture of 'leaving it to the compliance department'. As put by Black, 'it helps chief executives to see the moral wood for the technical trees'.

MONITORING AND SUPERVISION

Because of the nature of financial contracts between financial firms and their customers (potential principal–agent problems; the quality of a financial product cannot be ascertained at the point of purchase; the value of a product is determined by the behaviour of the supplier after it has been purchased and contracts committed to) continuous monitoring of the behaviour of financial firms is needed. The question is who is to undertake the necessary monitoring: customers, shareholders, rating agencies ...? In practice, there can be only a limited monitoring role for depositors owing to major information asymmetries which cannot easily be rectified, and because depositors face the less costly option of withdrawal of deposits. However, see Saunders and Wilson (1996) for empirical evidence on the role of informed depositors. The funding structure of a bank may also militate against effective monitoring in that, unlike the situation with non-financial companies, creditors tend to be large in number but with each having a small stake.

As most (especially retail) customers are not in practice able to undertake such monitoring, and in the presence of deposit insurance may have no incentive to do so, an important role of regulatory agencies is to monitor the behaviour of financial firms on behalf of consumers. In effect, consumers delegate the task of monitoring to a regulatory agency, and hence the agency can be viewed as supplying monitoring services to customers of financial firms. There are strong efficiency reasons for consumers to delegate monitoring and supervision to a specialist agency to act on their behalf as the transactions costs for the consumer are lowered by such delegation. However, this is not to argue that a regulatory agency should become a monopolist monitor and supervisor of financial firms.

When considering how the official sector conducts supervision, the potential beneficial impact it may have on the incentive structure of regulated firms needs to be considered. The form and intensity of supervision should differentiate between regulated institutions according to their relative risk and efficiency of internal control mechanisms, whether these relate to prudential or to conduct of business issues.

INCENTIVE STRUCTURES

A maintained theme is that the incentive structures and moral hazards faced by decision makers (bank owners and managers, lenders to banks, borrowers and regulators) are major parts of the regulatory regime. The overall theme is twofold: (a) there need to be appropriate internal incentives for management to behave in appropriate ways, and (b) the regulator has a role in ensuring internal incentives are compatible with the objectives of regulation. Overall, we need to know more about incentive structures within financial firms and whether, for instance, incentive structures align with compliance. Research is also needed into the way regulation affects positively and negatively incentives within regulated firms. We have already alluded to the possibility that detailed rules may have the negative effect of blunting compliance incentives.

Within the regulatory regime paradigm, a central role for regulation is to create appropriate incentives within regulated firms so that the incentives faced by decision makers are aligned with those of the objectives of regulation. At the same time, regulation must avoid the moral hazard danger of blunting the incentives of other agents (for example, rating agencies, depositors, shareholders and debt-holders) that have a disciplining role with banks. The position has been put well by Schinasi *et al.* (1999): 'Policy makers are therefore faced with the difficult challenge of balancing efforts to manage systemic risk against efforts to ensure that market participants bear the costs of imprudent risk taking and have incentives to behave prudently'. The authors argue that banks have complex incentive structures, including internal incentive structures (that is, incentives that motivate key decision makers involved with risk), corporate governance mechanisms (such as accountability to shareholders), the external market in corporate control, market disciplines which may affect the cost of capital and deposits, and accountability to bank supervisors. The presence of regulation and official supervision adds a particular dimension to the structure of incentives faced by bank decision makers. The key is to align incentives of the various stakeholders in the decision-making process. The alignment of incentive structures has three dimensions: between the objectives set by regulators and supervisors (systemic stability and consumer protection) and those of the bank; between the overall business objectives of the bank and those of actual decision makers in the management structure; and between managers and owners of banks. Conflicts can arise at each level, which is a major reason why the incentive structures with respect to decision making in banks are particularly complex.

Consideration needs to be given to the nature of incentive structures, and how they can be influenced by regulation. If incentive structures are hazardous, regulation will always face formidable obstacles. There are several dimensions to incentive structures within banks: the extent to which reward structures are based on the volume of business undertaken; the extent to which the risk characteristics of decisions are incorporated into the reward structures; the nature of the internal control systems within banks; internal monitoring of the decision making of loan officers; the nature of profit-sharing schemes and the extent to which decision makers also share in losses; and so on. High staff turnover, and the speed with which officers are moved with the bank, may also create incentives for excessive risk taking. A similar effect can arise through the herd behaviour that is common in banking.

It is clear that some incentive structures can lead to dysfunctional behavioural responses (Prendergast, 1993). This may often emerge when incentives within regulated firms relate to volume; that is, there is a clear bias towards writing business. Thus bank managers may be rewarded by the volume of loans made rather than their risk-adjusted profitability. Similarly, salespersons rewarded predominantly by commission have a clear bias towards writing business even though the products being sold may not always be appropriate for particular customers. Many cases of bank distress have been associated with inappropriate incentive structures creating a bias in favour of balance sheet growth, and with moral hazard created by anticipated lender-of-last-resort actions (Llewellyn, 2000). The personal pensions mis-selling episode can also be explained, in part at least, by the incentive structures faced by salespersons. Dale (1996) suggests that profit-related bonuses were an important feature in the Barings collapse.

Laws, regulations and supervisory actions provide incentives for regulated firms to adjust their actions and behaviour, and to control their own risks internally. As already noted, they can usefully be viewed as *incentive contracts*. Within this general framework, regulation involves a process of creating incentive-compatible contracts so that regulated firms have an incentive to behave in a way consistent with the objectives of systemic stability and investor protection. If incentive contracts are well designed they will induce appropriate behaviour by regulated firms. Conversely, if they are badly constructed and improperly designed, they may fail to reduce systemic risk (and other hazards regulation is designed to avoid) or have undesirable side-effects on the process of financial intermediation (such as imposing high costs). At centre stage is the issue of whether all parties have the right incentives to act in a way that satisfies the objectives of regulation.

There need to be appropriate internal incentives for owners and management of financial firms. Several procedures, processes and structures can, for instance, reinforce internal risk-control mechanisms. These include internal auditors, internal audit committees, procedures for reporting to senior management (and perhaps to the supervisors), and making a named board member of financial firms responsible for compliance and risk analysis and management systems. In some countries (such as New Zealand) the incentive for bank managers has been strengthened by a policy of increased personal liability for bank directors. In New Zealand, bank directors are made personally liable in cases involving disclosure of incomplete or erroneous information. The FSA has also recently proposed that individual directors and senior managers of financial firms should, under some circumstances, be made personally liable for compliance failures.

Supervisors can strengthen incentives by, for instance, relating the frequency and intensity of their supervision and inspection visits (and possibly rules) to the perceived adequacy of the internal risk-control procedures and compliance arrangements. In addition, regulators can create appropriate incentives by calibrating the external burden of regulation (number of inspection visits, allowable business and so on) to the quality of management and the efficiency of internal incentives.

With respect to prudential issues, capital requirements should be structured in such a way as to create incentives for the correct pricing of absolute and relative risk. The potential for regulation to create perverse incentives and moral hazard is well established. In this area, for instance, if differential capital requirements are set against different types of assets (for example, through applying differential risk weights) the rules should be based on actuarial calculations of relative risk. If risk weights are incorrectly specified, perverse incentives may be created for banks because the implied capital requirements are either more or less than justified by true relative risk calculations. A major critique of the current Basle capital requirements is that the risk weights bear little relation to the relative risk characteristics of different assets, and the loan book carries a uniform risk weight even though the risk characteristics of different loans within a bank's portfolio vary considerably. The current Bank for International Settlements (BIS) consultation paper addresses this issue.

The moral hazard associated with perceived safety net arrangements has been extensively analysed in the literature. For instance, three possible hazards are associated with deposit insurance: banks may be induced to take excessive risk as they are not required to pay the risk premium on insured deposits; there are particular incentives for excessive risk taking when a bank's capital ratio falls to a low level; and depositors may also be induced to seek high-risk banks by the one-way-option bet. Bhattacharya *et al.* (1998) consider various schemes to attenuate moral hazards associated with deposit insurance. These include cash reserve requirements, risk-sensitive capital requirements and deposit insurance premia, partial deposit insurance, bank closure policy and bank charter value.

Moral hazard can also arise in other forms of consumer compensation arrangements, such as the Investors' Compensation Scheme (ICS). Firstly, the knowledge of such a compensation facility may induce some consumers to take less care and may, under some circumstances, even induce consumers to gravitate to risky suppliers on the grounds of a one-way option: if the contract performs well the consumer keeps the gains, whereas if the firm becomes insolvent the consumer is compensated. Secondly, the costs of compensation are sometimes transferred to firms who are not part of the contract. For instance, if a financial adviser becomes insolvent and is unable to pay compensation, the financial industry as a whole is required to make payments to the ICS. The moral hazard is that behaviour may be adversely affected because to some extent risks can be passed on to others. Overall, the moral hazard is that, when safety net arrangements are in place, financial firms are sometimes able to pass on risks to others, and this may adversely affect their behaviour.

The overall theme here is twofold: (a) there need to be appropriate internal incentives for management to behave in appropriate ways, and (b) the regulator has a role in ensuring that internal incentives are compatible with the objectives of regulation. We need to know more about incentive structures within financial firms and whether, for instance, incentive structures align with compliance. Research is also needed into the way regulation affects positively and negatively on incentives within regulated firms. We have already alluded to the possibility that detailed rules may have the negative effect of blunting compliance incentives.

MARKET DISCIPLINE

The fourth component of the regulatory regime relates to the arrangements for market discipline on regulated firms. The central theme is that regulation can never be an alternative to market discipline. On the contrary, market discipline needs to be reinforced within the regime.

Monitoring is not only conducted by official agencies whose specialist task it is. In well-developed regimes, the market has incentives to monitor the behaviour of financial firms. The disciplines imposed by the market can be as powerful as any sanctions imposed by official agencies. The disciplining role of the markets (including the inter-bank market) was weak in the crisis countries of South East Asia in the 1990s. This was due predominantly to the lack of disclosure and transparency of banks, and the fact that little reliance could be placed on the quality of the accountancy data provided in bank accounts. In many cases standard accountancy and auditing procedures were not applied rigorously, and in some cases there was wilful misrepresentation of the financial position of banks and non-financial companies.

Overall, market disciplines can work effectively only on the basis of full and accurate disclosure and transparency. Good quality, timely and relevant information disclosure should be available to all market participants and regulators so that asset quality, creditworthiness and the condition of financial institutions can be adequately assessed.

Several parties have the potential to monitor the management of banks and other financial firms: owners, bank depositors and customers, rating agencies, official agencies (such as the central bank or other regulatory body) and other banks in the market. In practice, excessive emphasis has been given to official agencies. The danger is that a monopoly monitor is established, with all the problems normally associated with monopoly power. There may even be adverse incentive effects in that, given that regulatory agencies conduct monitoring and supervision on a delegated basis, the incentive for others to conduct monitoring may be weakened.

The role of all potential monitors (and notably the market) needs to be strengthened, and greater incentives are needed for other parties to monitor financial firms in parallel with official agencies. An advantage of having agents other than official supervisory bodies monitor financial firms is that it removes the inherent danger of having monitoring and supervision conducted by a monopolist with less than perfect and complete information, with the result that, inevitably, mistakes will be made. It has been noted that 'Broader approaches to bank supervision reach beyond the issues of defining capital and accounting standards, and envisage co-opting other market participants by giving them a greater stake in bank survival. This approach increases the likelihood that problems will be detected earlier ... [it involves] broadening the number of those who are directly concerned about keeping the banks safe and sound' (Caprio and Honahan, 1998).

Given the way in which the business of banking has evolved, and the nature of the market environment in which banks now operate, market discipline needs to be strengthened. The issue is not about market *versus* agency discipline, but the mix of all aspects of monitoring, supervision and discipline. In its recent consultation document on capital adequacy, the Basle Committee (1999a) has recognized that supervisors have a strong interest in facilitating effective market discipline as a lever to strengthen the safety and soundness of the banking system: 'market discipline has the potential to reinforce capital regulation and other supervisory efforts to promote safety and soundness in banks and financial systems. Market discipline imposes strong incentives on banks to conduct their business in a safe, sound and efficient manner'.

Some analysts (for example, Calomiris, 1997) are sceptical about the power of official supervisory agencies to identify the risk characteristics of banks compared with the power and incentives of markets. Along with others, Calomiris has advocated banks being required to issue a minimum amount of subordinated and uninsured debt as part of their capital base. Holders of subordinated debt have an incentive to monitor the risk taking of banks. Discipline would be applied by the market as its assessment of risk would be reflected in the risk premium in the price of traded debt. In particular, because of the nature of the debt contract, holders of a bank's subordinated debt capital do not share in the potential upside gain through the bank's risk taking, but stand to lose if the bank fails. They therefore have a particular incentive to monitor the bank's risk profile, compared with shareholders who, under some circumstances, have an incentive to support a high-risk profile; this is particularly the case when a 'gamble for resurrection' strategy becomes optimal for shareholders.

A scheme along these lines has been introduced in Argentina whereby holders of subordinated debt must be entities of substance which are independent of the bank's shareholders, and it requires issue of the debt in relatively lumpy amounts on a regular basis (ibid.). However, while there is a potentially powerful role for market discipline to operate through the pricing of subordinated debt, the interests of holders of such debt do not necessarily precisely coincide with those of depositors or the public interest more generally (Dewatripont and Tirole, 1994). It is not, therefore, a substitute for official monitoring. It is intended as an extension of the role of market monitoring. A further example could be the linking of deposit insurance premiums paid by banks to the implied risk of the bank as incorporated in subordinated debt yields or classifications of rating agencies.

The merit of increasing the role of market disciplines is that large, well-informed creditors (including other banks) have the resources, expertise, market knowledge and incentives to conduct monitoring and to impose market discipline. For instance, it has been argued that the hazardous state of BCCI was reflected in market prices and inter-bank interest rates long before the Bank of England closed the bank. Leaving aside the merits and drawbacks of particular mechanisms that might be proposed (and one such mechanism has been suggested above as an example), the overall assessment is that regulation needs to reinforce, not replace, market discipline. The regulatory regime should be structured so as to provide greater incentives than exist at present for markets to monitor banks and other financial firms.

In addition, there is considerable advantage in regulators, whenever possible, utilizing market data in their supervisory procedures. Evidence indicates that markets give signals about the credit standing of financial firms which, when combined with inside information gained by supervisory procedures, can increase the efficiency of the overall supervisory process. Flannery (1998) suggests that market information may improve two features of the overall process: (a) it permits regulators to identify developing problems more promptly, and (b) it provides regulators with the incentive and justification to take action more quickly once problems have been identified. He concludes that market information should be incorporated into the process of identifying and correcting problems.

If financial markets are able to assess a bank's market value as reflected in the market price, an asset-pricing model can in principle be used to infer the risk of insolvency that the market has assigned to each bank. Such a model has been applied to UK banks by Hall and Miles (1990). Similar analysis for countries which had recently liberalized their financial systems has been applied by Fischer and Gueyie (1995). On the other hand, there are clear limitations to such an approach (see Simons and Cross, 1991) and hence it would be hazardous to rely exclusively on it. For instance, it assumes that markets have sufficient data upon which to make accurate assessments of banks, and it equally assumes that markets are able efficiently to assess the available information and incorporate this into an efficient pricing of bank securities.

An additional route is to develop the role of rating agencies in the supervisory process. Rating agencies have considerable resources and expertise in monitoring banks and making assessments of risk. It could be made a requirement, as in Argentina, for all banks to have a rating which would be made public. In practice, most banks are in fact rated. Rating could also be extended to retail financial products with a league table of product performance. There could be considerable merit in establishing a rating agency (or rating function within a regulatory agency) to perform this function. The Consumers Association has frequently argued that, notwithstanding mandated disclosure requirements, the consumer often does not have access to relevant comparative data. It has argued that 'there is a clear requirement for comparative information to be available, perhaps in the form of league tables. In the same way, illustrations could be required to show industry averages as well as own charges' (Telford, 1998).

While market discipline is potentially powerful, it has its limitations. This means that, in practice, it is unlikely to be an effective complete alternative to the role of official regulatory and supervisory agencies. In the first place, markets are concerned with the private costs of a bank failure and reflect the risk of this in market prices. The social cost of bank failures, on the other hand, may exceed the private cost (Llewellyn, 1999) and hence the total cost of a bank failure may not be fully reflected in market prices. Second, in many countries, there are limits imposed on the extent to which the market in corporate control (the takeover market) is allowed to operate. In particular, there are often limits, if not bars, on the extent to which foreign institutions are able to take control of banks, even though they may offer a solution to under-capitalized institutions. Finally, the market is able efficiently to price bank securities and inter-bank loans only to the extent that relevant information is available. Disclosure requirements are, therefore, an integral part of the market disciplining process.

While there are clear limitations on the role of market discipline (discussed further in Lane, 1993) the global trend is appropriately in the direction of placing more emphasis on market data in the supervisory process. The theme being developed is not that market monitoring and discipline can effectively replace official supervision, but that it has a potentially powerful role which should be strengthened within the overall regulatory regime. In addition, Caprio (1997) argues that broadening the number of those who are directly concerned about the safety and soundness of banks reduces the extent to which insider political pressure can be brought to bear on bank regulation and supervision. In fact, the recent consultative document issued by the Basle Committee on Banking Supervision (Basle Committee, 1999a) incorporates the role of market discipline as one of the three pillars of a proposed new approach to banking supervision. The Committee emphasizes that its approach 'will encourage high disclosure standards and enhance the role of market participants in encouraging banks to hold adequate capital'.

As neither the market nor a regulatory agency is perfect, the obvious solution is to utilize both, with neither having a monopoly of wisdom and judgment. The conclusion is that more systematic research is needed into the predictive power of market data, and how market information can usefully be incorporated into the supervisory process both by regulators and the markets.

This section should not conclude without reference to competition. In the final analysis, effective competition is the major component of consumer protection and the assurance of good products at competitive prices. The purpose of regulation is, therefore, not to displace competitive pressures or market mechanisms, but to correct for market imperfections and failures. As there are clear consumer benefits and efficiency gains to be secured through competition, regulation should not be constructed in a way that impairs it. Regulation and competition need not be in conflict: on the contrary, when properly constructed they are complementary. It can also make competition more effective in the marketplace by, for instance, requiring the disclosure of relevant information that can be used by consumers in making informed choices. Regulation is ultimately designed to reinforce the efficiency of competition and market mechanisms rather than impede them. Providing regulation is properly constructed, it reinforces the efficiency of market mechanisms.

INTERVENTION

A key dimension in the regulatory regime is the issue of intervention by regulatory agencies either in the event of some form of compliance failure within a regulated firm or when financial distress occurs with banks. While not downgrading the significance of the former, in the interest of brevity we reserve discussion of this issue to the question of intervention in the event of bank distress. However, similar considerations are relevant for intervention in other areas, including conduct of business.

The concept of the regulatory regime also includes the arrangements for intervention in the event of bank distress and failures not the least because they have incentive and moral hazard effects which potentially influence future behaviour by banks and their customers. These arrangements also have important implications for the total cost of intervention (for example, initial forbearance often has the effect of raising the eventual cost of subsequent intervention) and the distribution of those costs between taxpayers and other agents. Different intervention arrangements also have implications for the future efficiency of the financial system in that, for instance, forbearance may have the effect of sustaining inefficient banks and excess capacity in the banking sector.

The issue focuses on when intervention is to be made. The experience of banking crises around the world (in both developed and developing countries) indicates that a well-defined strategy for responding to the possible insolvency of financial institutions is needed. A response strategy in the event of bank distress has several components: (a) being prepared to close insolvent financial institutions, (b) taking prompt corrective action to address financial problems before they reach critical proportions, (c) closing unviable institutions promptly, and vigorously monitoring weak and restructured institutions.

A key issue relates to rules versus discretion in the event of bank distress: the extent to which intervention should be circumscribed by clearly defined rules (so that intervention agencies have no discretion about whether, how and when to act) or whether there should always be discretion simply because relevant circumstances cannot be set out in advance. The obvious *prima facie* advantage of discretion is that it is impossible to foresee all future circumstances and conditions when a bank might become distressed and close to (or actually) being insolvent. It might be judged that it is not always the right policy to close a bank in such circumstances.

However, there are strong arguments against allowing such discretion and in favour of a rules approach to intervention. Firstly, the latter enhances the credibility of the intervention agency in that market participants, including banks, have a high degree of certainty that action will be taken. Secondly, the danger of discretion is that it increases the probability of forbearance which usually eventually leads to higher costs when intervention is finally made. Thirdly, and this is certainly relevant in some countries which have recently experienced banking distress, it removes the danger of undue political interference in the disciplining of banks and regulated firms. Experience in many countries indicates that supervisory authorities face substantial pressure to delay action and intervention. Fourthly, and related to the first argument, a rules approach to intervention is likely to have a beneficial impact on *ex ante* behaviour of financial firms. A rules-based approach, by removing any prospect that a hazardous bank might be treated leniently, has the advantage that it enhances the incentives for bank managers to manage their banks prudently so as to reduce the probability of insolvency (Glaessner and Mas, 1995). It also enhances the credibility of the regulator's threat to close institutions. Finally, it guards against the hazards associated with risk-averse regulators who themselves might be inclined not to take action for fear that it will be interpreted as a major regulatory failure, and the temptation to allow a firm to trade out of its difficulty. This amounts to the regulator also 'gambling for resurrection'. In this sense, a rules approach may be of assistance to the intervention agency as its hands are tied, and it is forced to do what it believes to be the right thing to do.

Put another way, time-inconsistency and credibility problems should be addressed through precommitments and graduated responses with the possibility of overrides. Many analysts have advocated various forms of predetermined intervention through a general policy of 'structured early intervention and resolution' (SEIR). There is a case for a graduated response approach since, for example, there is no magical capital ratio below which an institution is in danger and above which it is safe. Other things being equal, potential danger gradually increases as the capital ratio declines. This in itself suggests that there should be a graduated series of responses from the regulator as capital diminishes. No single dividing line should trigger action, but there should be a series of such trigger points with the effect of going through any one of them being relatively minor, but the cumulative effect being large. Goldstein and Turner (1996) argue that SEIR is designed to imitate the remedial action which private bond-holders would impose on banks in the absence of government insurance or guarantees. In this sense it is a mimic of market solutions to troubled banks. An example of the rules-based approach is to be found in the Prompt Corrective Action (PCA) rules in the USA. These specify graduated intervention by the regulators with predetermined responses triggered by capital thresholds. In fact, several countries have such rules of intervention (Basle Committee, 1999a).

The need to maintain the credibility of supervisory agencies creates a strong bias against forbearance. The overall conclusion is that there should be a clear bias (though not a bar) against forbearance when a bank is in difficulty. While there should be a strong presumption against forbearance, and that this is best secured through having clearly defined rules, there will always be exceptional circumstances when it might be warranted in the interests of systemic stability. However, when forbearance is exercised the regulatory agency should, in some way or another, be made accountable for its actions.

CORPORATE GOVERNANCE

In the final analysis, all aspects of the management of financial firms (including compliance) are corporate governance issues. This means that, if a financial firm behaves hazardously, this is, to some extent, a symptom of weak corporate governance. This may include, for instance, a hazardous corporate structure for the financial firm, lack of internal control systems, weak surveillance by (especially non-executive) directors, and ineffective internal audit arrangements. Corporate governance arrangements were evidently weak and underdeveloped in banks in many of the countries that have recently experienced bank distress.

There are several reasons why corporate governance arrangements operate differently with banks than with other types of firms. Firstly, banks are subject to regulation in the interests of systemic stability and consumer protection; this adds a new dimension to corporate governance arrangements. In part, regulation is a response to limitations in corporate governance mechanisms in banks. Secondly, banks are also subject to continuous supervision and monitoring by official agencies. This has two immediate implications for private corporate governance: shareholders and official agencies are to some extent duplicating monitoring activity, and the actions of official agencies may have an impact on the incentives faced by other monitors, such as shareholders and even depositors. However, official and market monitoring are not perfectly substitutable. Thirdly, banks have a fiduciary relationship with their customers (for example, they are holding the wealth of depositors) which is generally not the case with other types of firm. This creates additional principal–agent relationships (and potentially agency costs) with banks that generally do not exist with non-financial firms.

A fourth reason why corporate governance mechanisms are different in banks is that there is a systemic dimension to banks and, because in some circumstances (such as presence of externalities) the social cost of a bank failure may exceed the private costs, there is a systemic concern with the behaviour of banks that does not exist with other companies. Fifthly, banks are subject to safety net arrangements that are not available to other companies. This has implications for incentive structures faced by owners, managers, depositors and the market with respect to monitoring and control.

All of these considerations have an impact on the two general mechanisms for exercising discipline on the management of firms: internal corporate governance and the market in corporate control. It is also possible that restrictions imposed on the ownership of banks may reduce the disciplining power of markets.

While there are significant differences between banks and other firms, corporate governance issues in banks have received remarkably little attention. A key issue, and one noted by Flannery (1998), is that little is known about the way the two governance systems (regulation and private) interact with each other and, in particular, the extent to which they are complementary or offsetting.

A key issue in the management of financial firms is the extent to which corporate governance arrangements are suitable and efficient for the management and control of risks. The FSA has argued as follows: 'Senior management set the business strategy, regulatory climate, and ethical standards of the firm. ... Effective management of these activities will benefit firms and contribute to the delivery of the FSA's statutory objectives'. Corporate governance arrangements include issues of corporate structure, the power of shareholders to exercise accountability of managers, the transparency of corporate structures, the authority and power of directors, internal audit arrangements and lines of accountability of managers. In the final analysis, shareholders are the ultimate risk takers, and agency problems may induce managers to take more risks with the bank than the owners would wish. This in turn raises issues about what information shareholders have about the actions of the managers to which they delegate decision-making powers, the extent to which shareholders are represented on the board of directors of the bank and the extent to which shareholders have power to discipline managers.

Corporate governance arrangements need to provide for effective monitoring and supervision of the risk-taking profile of financial firms. These arrangements would provide for, *inter alia*, a management structure with clear lines of accountability; independent non-executive directors on the board; an independent audit committee; the four-eyes principle for important decisions involving the risk profile of the financial firm; a transparent ownership structure; internal structures that enable the risk profile of the firm to be clear, transparent and managed; and the creation and monitoring of risk analysis and management systems.

The Basle Committee has rightly argued that effective oversight by a bank's board of directors and senior management is critical. It argues that the board should approve overall policies of the bank and its internal systems. It argues in particular that 'lack of adequate corporate governance in banks seems to have been an important contributory factor in the Asian crisis. The boards of directors and management committees of the banks did not play the role they were expected to play' (Basle Committee, 1999b). According to the Committee, good corporate governance includes the following:

- establishing strategic objectives and a set of corporate values that are communicated throughout the banking organization;
- setting and enforcing clear lines of responsibility and accountability throughout the organization;
- ensuring that board members are qualified for their positions, have a clear understanding of their role in corporate governance and are not subject to undue influence from management or outside concerns;
- ensuring that there is appropriate oversight by senior management;
- effectively utilizing the work conducted by internal and external auditors;
- ensuring that compensation approaches are consistent with the bank's ethical values, objectives, strategy and control environment;
- conducting corporate governance in a transparent manner.

Some useful insights have been provided by Sinha (1998) who concludes, for instance, that, while the regulatory authorities approve the appointment of non-executive directors of banks, such directors are generally less effective in monitoring top management than is the case in manufacturing firms. Sinha has compared corporate governance arrangements in banks and manufacturing firms and finds that top management turnover in banks is less than in other firms, and that top management turnover seems not to be related to share price performance. Prowse (1997) also shows that accountability to shareholders and the effectiveness of board monitoring are lower in banks than in non-financial firms.

An interesting possibility to consider is the extent to which all this results from moral hazard associated with official regulation and supervision: a further negative trade-off within the regulatory regime. It could be that the assumption that regulatory authorities impose regulation and monitor the bank reduces the incentive for non-executive directors and shareholders to do so. The presumption may be that regulators have more information than do non-executive directors and shareholders, and that their own monitoring would only be wastefully duplicating the monitoring conducted by official supervisors. Further research is needed into the role of non-executive directors and institutional investors in the effectiveness of corporate governance mechanisms in banks.

There is a further dimension to this issue. A major market discipline on any firm comes from the market in corporate control where, in principle, alternative managements seek control of companies. It is reasonably well established that there is something of a trade-off between internal corporate governance mechanisms and the power of the market in corporate control (the takeover market). In general, corporate governance arrangements tend to be stronger when the market in corporate control operates weakly. Sinha (1998) argues that this trade-off does not apply to banks as corporate governance arrangements are weak and so is the discipline of the market in corporate control.

Financial regulators in the UK have made few public statements about the takeover market in the banking sector. In 1987 the Bank of England said that hostile takeovers to replace underperforming management were not to be encouraged. It is also evident that the Bank did not look favourably on bids for banks that put banks into play. Equally, and as in many countries, there was some resistance to foreign ownership of major UK banks. These public lines are now dated and it would be interesting to know whether the Bank or FSA have a view on the role of the market in corporate control in banking. This has obvious topicality in the context of the Bank of Scotland's (later, Royal Bank of Scotland's) bid for NatWest, and the market view at the time that this effectively put the bank into play.

DISCIPLINES ON THE REGULATOR

In the beginning of this paper four perspectives were offered, each of which reinforces the case for regulatory authorities being subject to strong disciplining and accountability measures: (1) there is an ever-present potential for overregulation as it may be both overdemanded and oversupplied, (2) regulatory agencies have considerable power over both consumers and regulated firms, (3) the regulator is supplying regulatory services as a monopolist, and (4) the regulator is not subject to the normal disciplines of the market in the supply of its services.

As well as conferring substantial powers, the Financial Services and Markets Bill in the UK also gives the FSA very substantial discretion in the way its powers can be used. In some respects, the way that this discretion is used will prove to be more significant than the powers the bill confers. This in turn emphasizes the importance of the disciplining and accountability mechanisms of the FSA, and of the FSA being open in the way it plans to develop its approach to regulation. The FSA has, in fact, been very open in describing its intended approach to regulation (see, for instance, its document 'Meeting Our Responsibilities' which is as open a discussion as any regulator has ever given about its approach).

Several accountability mechanisms have been put in place with respect to the FSA. Its objectives have been clearly defined in the bill. In addition, there is a formal legislative requirement for the FSA to use its resources in the most efficient way, and to make any regulatory burden proportionate to its benefits. The last-mentioned includes a requirement on the FSA to conduct cost–benefit analyses on its regulation. The bill also outlines a strong set of accountability mechanisms including the scope for judicial review, public reporting mechanisms to the Treasury, requirements for consultation, the creation of consumer and practitioner panels, independent review of its rules and decisions including that by the Office of Fair Trading (OFT), independent investigation of complaints against FSA and an independent appeals and enforcement procedure. A further disciplining mechanism is the requirement to conduct a cost–benefit study on major regulatory changes. All of this is to be welcomed.

CONTRACT REGULATION

We now return to the question of differentiation between regulated firms. A given degree of *regulatory intensity* does not in itself imply anything about the degree of prescription or detail. By 'regulatory intensity' is meant the standards set by the regulator, and the degree and extent of investor protection. The question arises as to whether this is to be achieved by detailed and formal rules or through the monitoring of an established set of principles. There is a trade-off between rules and discretion for a given degree of regulatory intensity.

Even within the regulation component of the regime a wide range of options is available, and in particular with respect to the degree of discretion exercised by the regulator. At the risk of oversimplification, two alternative approaches may be identified. At one end of the spectrum, the regulator lays down fairly precise regulatory requirements that are applied to all regulated firms. While there may be limited differentiations within the rules, the presumption is for a high degree of uniformity. At the other end of the spectrum is what might be termed *contract regulation*. Under this regime, the regulator sets a clear set of objectives and general principles. It is then for each regulated firm to demonstrate to the regulator how these objectives and principles are to be satisfied by its own chosen procedures.

A detailed and prescriptive rule book approach may add to compliance costs without commensurate benefit in terms of the objectives that regulation is designed to achieve. If the same objectives can be achieved by an alternative regime that is less costly for firms to operate (that is, the compliance costs are lower) there will be an advantage in reducing the dead-weight costs. It may, for instance, be possible to achieve the same objectives in a way that allows firms more scope to choose the manner in which they satisfy the regulator's requirements, and at the same time minimize their own compliance costs. This might be achieved through a regime of contract regulation.

Under this regime, the regulator sets a clear set of objectives and general principles. It is then for each regulated firm to demonstrate how these objectives and principles are to be satisfied by its own chosen procedures. In effect, the regulated firm chooses its own regulation but within the strict constraints imposed by the objectives and principles set by the regulator. Presumably, each firm would choose its own least-cost way of satisfying the regulator. Once the regulator has agreed with each firm how the objectives and principles are to be satisfied, a contract is established between the regulator and the regulated firm. The contract requires the firm to deliver on its agreed standards and procedures, and sanctions apply in the case of non-performance on the contract. If the firm does not deliver on the contract, sanctions apply in the normal way and the regulator has the option of withdrawing the choice from the regulated firm, which would then be required to accept a standard contract devised by the regulator.

The advantage of this general approach is that regulated firms are able to minimize their own costs of regulation by submitting to the regulator a plan that, while fully satisfying the requirements of the regulator, most suits its own particular circumstances and structure. As part of this paradigm, and in order to save costs in devising their own regime, regulated firms would always have the option of adopting an approach established by the regulator. In effect, what is involved is a regime of 'self-selecting regulatory contracts'.

An analogy can be drawn with regulation in other areas. For instance, pollution regulation (say with respect to factories not contaminating local rivers) is framed in terms of the ultimate objective related to the measurable quality of water. Regulation does not prescribe how the factory is to undertake its production processes in order to meet the objective. It is for each firm to choose its own least-cost way of satisfying water quality standards. Providing the standards are met, the regulator is indifferent about how the standards are achieved, or what the production processes are. This is in sharp contrast to most aspects of financial regulation.

Under a regime of contract regulation the role of the regulator is fivefold: defining the degree of regulatory intensity, establishing regulatory objectives, approving self-selected contracts, monitoring standards and the performance on agreed contracts, and disciplining infringements of contracts. A by-product advantage is that the regulator will learn more about optimum regulatory arrangements through the experience of the variety of contracts.

While there are clear limits to how far this regime could be taken in practice, in some areas the regulator could offer a menu of contracts to regulated firms requiring them to select for themselves. Many countries are moving towards a precommitment approach to regulation (Kupiec and O'Brien, 1997). In this approach, each bank agrees with the supervisory agency the models and procedures it will use to evaluate their risks, but are subject to penalties if they violate these procedures. There are several advantages to a precommitment strategy: it avoids the necessity of detailed and prescriptive regulation, it creates powerful incentives for bank decision makers (the choice of an excessive amount of capital imposes costs on the bank while choosing too low a level of capital risks the imposition of penalties) and it is flexible to the extent that it offers scope for each bank to choose a level of capital which is appropriate to its own particular circumstances. On the other hand, Estrella (1998) argues that the precise design of the penalty structure is likely to be complex.

SHIFTS WITHIN THE REGULATORY REGIME

Several shifts within the regulatory regime are recommended in order to maximize its overall effectiveness and efficiency. First, less emphasis is to be given to formal and detailed prescriptive rules dictating the behaviour of regulated firms. Second, a greater focus is to be given to incentive structures within regulated firms, and how regulation might have a beneficial impact on such structures. Third, market discipline and market monitoring of financial firms need to be strengthened within the overall regime. Fourth, there should be greater differentiation between regulated firms, different types of consumer and different types of financial business.

Fifth, less emphasis should be placed on detailed and prescriptive rules and more on internal risk analysis, management and control systems. In some areas, externally imposed regulation in the form of prescriptive and detailed rules is becoming increasingly inappropriate and ineffective. For instance, with respect to prudential issues, more reliance could be placed on institutions' own internal risk analysis, management and control systems. This relates not only to quantitative techniques such as value-at-risk (VaR) models, but also to the management 'culture' of those who handle models and supervise traders. There would be an advantage in shifting the emphasis towards regulatory agencies monitoring risk-control systems, and a recasting of the nature and functions of external regulation away from generalized rule setting towards establishing incentives and sanctions to reinforce such internal control systems. The recently issued consultative document by the Basel Committee on Banking Supervision (Basel Committee, 1999a) explicitly recognizes that a major role of the supervisory process is to monitor banks' own internal capital management processes and 'the setting of targets for capital that are commensurate with the bank's particular risk profile and control environment. This process would be subject to supervisory review and intervention, where appropriate'.

Finally, corporate governance mechanisms for financial firms need to be strengthened so that, for instance, owners play a greater role in the monitoring and control of regulated firms, and compliance issues are identified as the ultimate responsibility of a nominated main board director.

A maintained theme of this paper has been the central importance of incentive structures and the potential for regulation to affect them. The key is how to align incentive structures to reduce the conflict between the objectives of the firm and those of the regulator. It is not a question of replacing one mechanism with another, and it is not necessarily an argument for reducing the role of regulation. It amounts to a rebalancing within the regime. It is unfortunate that some public discussion of regulation poses false dichotomies rather than recognizing that the key issue is how the various mechanisms are to be combined. To make the case for regulation is not to undermine the central importance of market disciplines. Equally, to emphasize the role of incentives and market monitoring is not to argue that there is no role for regulation or supervision by an official agency.

In the final analysis, and as argued by Alfon (1997), the compliance culture within regulated firms is a crucial, if not overwhelming, determinant of the success of a regulatory strategy. The regulator, by its actions and the incentives it creates, can have a significant impact on culture. However, this also limits how far cost–benefit analysis (CBA) applied to specific regulatory measures can go in determining the ultimate value of regulation. This is because the main benefit may derive, not from the way regulatory measure X has an impact on benefit Y, but from the way regulation in total enhances consumer benefits through a more general impact on the culture of the industry.

The issue can be put in this way. Suppose we observe an improvement in consumer welfare derived through purchasing financial products. This could have been achieved through one of five routes: (1) because specific regulatory rules have successfully addressed specific problems (for example, disclosure requirements to increase transparency), (2) because consumers have become more aware and more conscious of some of the potential hazards when buying complex financial products, (3) consumers have become more sophisticated and have a greater understanding of the questions to ask, the comparisons to be made, and a greater understanding of financial issues, (4) because market conditions (such as competition) have improved, or (5) because of a general and diffused improvement in the culture of compliance and competence in the industry. However, it is only in case (1) that cost–benefit analysis can effectively be applied even though regulation may have contributed indirectly to each of the other four routes.

In the final analysis, the general culture and standards of the industry might be a more powerful route of consumer benefit than the impact of specific measures. And yet this will not be picked up through CBA. Put another way, the total impact of regulation may be greater than the sum of the measured parts. This is certainly not to argue against the application of CBA and other measures of effectiveness to regulatory measures: this is always desirable. However, the limitations need to be recognized.

ASSESSMENT

The concepts of *regulatory regime* and *regulatory strategy* have been introduced. Seven components of the regime have been identified: each is important but none alone is sufficient for the objectives of regulation to be achieved. They are complementary and not alternatives. Regulatory strategy is ultimately about optimizing the outcome of the overall regime, rather than any one of the components. Regulation in particular needs to consider that, if it is badly constructed or taken too far, there may be negative impacts on the other components, to the extent that the overall effect is diluted. It has also been suggested, however, that there may be positive relationships between the components and, for instance, that regulation can have a beneficial effect on incentive structures within financial firms.

Effective regulation and supervision of banks and financial institutions has the potential to make a significant contribution to the stability and robustness of a financial system, and to offer a degree of consumer protection. However, there are distinct limits to what regulation and supervision can achieve in practice. Although regulation is an important part of the regulatory regime, it is only a part and the other components are equally important. In the final analysis, there is no viable alternative to placing the main responsibility for risk management and general compliance on the shoulders of the management of financial institutions. Management must not be allowed to hide behind the cloak of regulation or pretend that, if regulation and supervisory arrangements are in place, this absolves them from their own responsibility. Nothing should ever be seen as taking away the responsibility of supervision of financial firms by shareholders, managers and the markets.

REFERENCES

Alfon, I. (1997), 'Cost-benefit Analysis and Compliance Culture', *Journal of Financial Regulation and Compliance*, 1(5).

Basel Committee (1999a), 'A New Capital Adequacy Framework', consultative paper, Basel Committee on Banking Supervision, Basel: BIS.

Basel Committee (1999b), 'Enhancing Corporate Governance for Banking Organisations', Basel Committee on Banking Supervision, Basel: BIS.

Benston, G. and G. Kaufman (1995), 'Is the Banking and Payments System Fragile?', *Journal of Financial Services Research*, September.

Bhattacharya, S., A. Boot and A.V. Thakor (1998), 'The Economics of Bank Regulation', *Journal of Money, Credit and Banking*, November, 745-70.

Billett, M., J. Garfinkel and E. O'Neal (1998), 'The Cost of Market versus Regulatory Discipline in Banking', *Journal of Financial Economics*, 333-58.

Black, J. (1994), 'Which Arrow? Rule Type and Regulatory Policy', *Public Law*, June.

Brealey, R. (1999), 'The Asian Crisis: Lessons for Crisis Management and Prevention', Bank of England *Quarterly Bulletin*, August, 285-96.

Briault, C. (1999), 'The Rationale of a Single Regulator', Occasional Paper no. 2, London: Financial Services Authority.

Calomiris, C. (1997), *The Postmodern Safety Net*, Washington, DC: American Enterprise Institute.

Caprio, G. (1997), 'Safe and Sound Banking in Developing Countries: We're Not in Kansas Anymore', Policy Research Paper no. 1739, Washington, DC: World Bank.

Corsetti, G., P. Pesenti and N. Rabini (1998), 'What Caused the Asia Currency and Financial Crisis?', Banca D'Italia, Temi di Discussione, December.

Dale, R. (1996), *Risk and Regulation in Global Securities Markets*, London: Wiley.

Dewatripont, M. and J. Tirole (1994), *The Prudential Regulation of Banks*, Cambridge, MA: MIT Press.

Estrella, A. (1998), 'Formulas or Supervision? Remarks on the Future of Regulatory Capital', *Economic Policy Review*, Federal Reserve Bank of New York, October.

Fischer, K. and J. Gueyie (1995), 'Financial Liberalisation and Bank Solvency', University of Laval, Quebec, August.

Flannery, M. (1998), 'Using Market Information in Prudential Bank Supervision: A Review of the US Empirical Evidence', *Journal of Money, Credit and Banking*, August, 273-305.

Glaessner, T. and I. Mas (1995), 'Incentives and the Resolution of Bank Distress', *World Bank Research Observer*, 10(1), February, 53-73.

Goldstein, M. and P. Turner (1996), 'Banking Crises in Emerging Economies', *BIS Economic Papers*, no. 46, Basle: BIS.

Goodhart, C., P. Hartmann, D.T. Llewellyn, L. Rojas-Suarez and S. Weisbrod (1998), *Financial Regulation: Why, How and Where Now?*, London: Routledge.

Hall, S. and D. Miles (1990), 'Monitoring Bank Risk: A Market Based Approach', Discussion Paper, Birkbeck College, London, April.

Kupiec, H. and J. O'Brien (1997), 'The Pre-commitment Approach: Using Incentives to Set Market Risk Capital Requirements', *Finance and Economics Discussion Series*, no. 14, Washington, DC: Federal Reserve Board, March.

Lane, T. (1993), 'Market Discipline', *IMF Staff Papers*, March, 55.

Lindgren, C.J., G. Garcia and M. Saal (1996), *Bank Soundness and Macroeconomic Policy*, Washington, DC: International Monetary Fund.

Llewellyn, D.T. (1999), 'The Economic Rationale of Financial Regulation', Occasional Paper no. 1, London: Financial Services Authority.

Llewellyn, D.T. (2000), 'Regulatory Lessons from Recent Banking Crises', De Nederlandsche Bank Discussion Paper, Amsterdam.

Prendergast, C. (1993), 'The Provision of Incentives in Firms', *Journal of Economic Literature*, March, 7-63.

Prowse, S. (1997), 'Corporate Control in Commercial Banks', *Journal of Financial Research*, 20, 509-27.

Saunders, A. and B. Wilson (1996), 'Contagious Bank Runs: Evidence from the 1929-1933 Period', *Journal of Financial Intermediation*, 5, 409-23.

Schinasi, G., B. Drees and W. Lee (1999), 'Managing Global Finance and Risk', *Finance and Development*, December.

Schwartz, A. (1995), 'Coping with Financial Fragility: A Global Perspective', *Journal of Financial Services Research*, September.

Simons, K. and S. Cross (1991), 'Do Capital Markets Predict Problems in Large Commercial Banks?', *New England Economic Review*, May, 51-6.

Simpson, D. (2000), 'Cost Benefit Analysis and Competition', in *Some Cost Benefit Issues in Financial Regulation*, London: Financial Services Authority.

Sinha, R. (1998), 'Corporate Governance in Financial Services Firms', Loughborough University Banking Centre Paper no. 121/98, Loughborough University.

Telford, R. (1998), 'The Consumers' Perspective', *Money Management*, 9 July

Wallman, S. (1999), 'Information Technology Revolution and its Impact on Regulation and Regulatory Structure', in R. Littan and A. Santomero (eds), *Brookings-Wharton Papers on Financial Services*, Washington: Brookings Institution Press.

CHAIRMAN'S COMMENTS
Howard Davies

David's paper is a very timely piece of work as far as we are concerned at the FSA, where we remain, as the saying goes, 'half pregnant' because we are now a single financial regulator *de facto*, in that we employ all the staff of the nine regulatory bodies that were merged into the FSA last year, around 2000 people in total, but we are not yet a single financial regulator because the Financial Services and Markets Bill still continues to wend its way through Parliament. It has taken the scenic route from the Treasury to Buckingham Palace because it was subject to an unusual innovative and, I think, quite successful pre-legislative scrutiny by a joint committee chaired by Lord Burns, former Permanent Secretary of the Treasury. It is also to be subject to another constitutional innovation in the form of the carry-over from one session to the next – something that was agreed, in the modernization of Parliament committee, as a mechanism which would be appropriate in future for particularly long and technical pieces of legislation. The committee restarts next week and we are not quite sure when the committee stage will end but it is hoped that it will be before the end of the year, and then it will go to the Lords.

In this lengthy legislative process which began with the publication of a draft Bill in July 1998, we are now quite well advanced. We are now in sight of the end of the road and we expect Royal Assent around Easter 2000, so we are thinking hard about the practical approach to regulation which we should take within the new regime. As the Bill has been going through Parliament, much of the public debate has been on enforcement issues, which are of course quite important to the firms and the individuals concerned in particularly contested cases. But enforcement represents less than 5 per cent of activity at the moment and I hope and expect that that will remain the case in the new regime. So what is far more important to firms and to their customers is how we set the regulatory balance between the various different things that we can do to the industry and how we operate from day to day. We set out some preliminary thoughts on the way in which we could make those judgments in a document called 'Meeting our Responsibilities' in August 1998.

David takes that, in some respects, as his starting point in discussing the way in which we should operate in future. Our paper was not as detailed as it might have been and our thinking has evolved quite a lot since we wrote it: in fact we are quite well advanced in preparing a paper which will describe how we propose to interpret our statutory objectives.[1] Another innovative element of the new legislation is that it begins with a set of four statutory objectives from the FSA, which are to maintain confidence in financial markets; to protect consumers, bearing in mind their own responsibilities; to promote consumer understanding of the financial system, which is a new objective for the regulator; and to help guard against financial crime: this too is new for a financial regulator because the previous legislation describes the tools you have but it does not in any other way describe what you are trying to achieve with those tools. So, if you look at the Banking Act, for example, you will be looking for any definition of what the Bank of England, then the banking supervisor, was trying to achieve. That is roughly the case with the Insurance Act as well – although that is slightly different, but still it is not purposive in its approach.

What we need to do now is to explain how we plan to interpret our objectives, how we plan to operate them within what the Bill also has, which is a set of principles of good regulation. We also plan to implement a risk-based approach to regulation, and furthermore we need to say what we will regard as success or failure in relation to the regulatory regime in the future. That is quite hard to determine, as is a performance management system for regulation. We have looked in vain around the world for examples of performance management for financial regulators. We aim to produce a paper along these lines in November, so David's paper, which covers many of the same issues, albeit from a slightly different angle, is in fact rather valuable to us at the moment in a practical way.

Note

1.   Since published as 'A New Regulator for the New Millennium', January 2000.

3. Competition Act assessments and economic efficiency

George Yarrow[1]

INTRODUCTION

The new Competition Act is a major landmark in UK public policy. Numerous documents dealing with the Act have been published already, and a considerable body of detailed information has been released by the Office of Fair Trading (OFT). I will not, therefore, dwell today on the general shape of the legislation, but simply take this as read. Instead I want to focus mostly on some issues of economic assessment raised by the policy shift embodied in the Act, giving one or two detailed illustrations of these issues along the way.

In respect of the restrictive practices aspects of the Act, it is frequently stated that the legislation marks a transition from a *form-based* to an *effects-based* approach to competition policy, in that the focus of Chapter I is on conduct that has, as its intention or effect, the prevention, restriction or distortion of competition. *Prima facie*, this might suggest a rather greater role for economic analysis than under the previous regime. It remains to be seen, however, whether such an expectation will be realized. It is quite possible, and perhaps even likely, that, in the event, enforcement will chiefly revolve around determining whether or not there is direct evidence of explicit coordination, for example from documentary sources or 'whistleblowers', and that economic analysis will play a secondary role, becoming more prominent only when exemption issues arise.

In relation to the Chapter II prohibition of abuse of dominance, the nominal shift in emphasis is arguably less great. The Monopolies and Mergers Commission (MMC) was required to assess business conduct against a public interest test, and this typically involved extensive economic assessments in which, at least since the early 1980s, effects on competition were a major factor.

Nevertheless, what I want to argue is that the shift from a focus on the effects of behaviour on the public interest to one which hinges on the effects on competition should, logically, induce a potentially radical shift in both the *role* and, more fundamentally, the *conceptual basis* of economic analysis, as it is applied to competition policy. Such a shift should, in turn, influence the way in which the question of legal certainty is addressed and resolved. I will argue further that these adjustments are necessary for the effective implementation of the Act, and that, if they are not made, there is a danger that the whole exercise could turn out to be counterproductive. Thus, while the Act provides opportunities for the development of more effective public policies, we should not be blind to the possibility that the Competition Act could, if inappropriately implemented, itself restrict economic progress. A high burden of responsibility will therefore fall upon the enforcement agencies.

THE OLD AND THE NEW

Both the Restrictive Trade Practices Act (RTPA) and the Fair Trading Act (FTA) were based around the notion that certain types of business conduct could be contrary to the public interest. The concept of the public interest was notoriously ill-defined, notwithstanding the guidelines in the FTA and the gateway provisions in the RTPA, which set out a range of factors to be taken into account. In their professional work, however, economists have usually tended to interpret the public interest largely in terms of effects on economic efficiency. On this approach, conduct might be judged contrary to the public interest if it gives rise to significant and avoidable losses of efficiency. Efficiency in this context is measured in terms of the gains from trade enjoyed by relevant market participants, expressed in monetary units and aggregated across all the relevant participants.

Given this perspective, the economic questions to be raised are: does the relevant company (or companies) possess market power and, if so, do any aspects of its (their) conduct give rise to avoidable reductions in the gains from trade available to market participants?[2] Two points about the approach should be noted immediately.

1. Some stress should be placed on the idea of *avoidable* losses. This is obvious, but not always recognized in more abstract economic analyses, which often use efficiency benchmarks from some imaginary, ideal world rather than from the world as it actually is (a tendency sometimes disparagingly referred to as 'Nirvana economics'). In practice, therefore, the resulting public interest approach to competition policy tends to be *remedies-driven*. Enforcement agencies are led to ask themselves: is there something that we can recommend that would improve the way in which this market works? And therein lies a danger: the approach can easily turn into a prescriptive form of state intervention, more akin to regulation or industrial policy than to antitrust policy.

2.   The resulting economic assessment is a form of cost–benefit analysis. In
     its pure form, it ignores the distribution of gains from trade among various
     market participants, and it therefore sits uneasily with the recent trend of
     public policy to focus on the interests of consumers. The analysis can,
     however, be adjusted to reflect changes in policy objectives by, for
     example, giving greater weight in the evaluation criterion to the gains
     from trade enjoyed by consumers relative to the gains from trade enjoyed
     by suppliers. This involves no substantive change in methodology,
     although it will, of course, lead to different outcomes.[3]

The new UK regime asks somewhat different questions: does the relevant
company (or companies) have market power and, if so, does any aspect of its
(their) conduct have the intention or effect of preventing, restricting or
distorting competition? Again there are some immediate points to be made
about this approach.

1.   Whereas it is clear, at least in principle, what is meant by efficiency (the
     total gains from trade enjoyed by market participants) and in what units it
     can be measured (monetary units), the position is less clear in relation to
     the notion of competition. For example, if it is prohibited to behave in a
     way that distorts competition, it might well be asked: what would
     undistorted competition look like in the specific circumstances of a
     particular case? (It should be obvious that this is not the sort of question
     that admits of a very easy answer.) Similarly, in what units is the degree
     of competition measured? Monetary units would appear to be inappro-
     priate, and no one has yet suggested an alternative such that an analyst
     could look at two industries and conclude, say, that the intensity of
     competition was 70 'comps' in the first and 80 'comps' in the second.
2.   Whereas it is not surprising to find that public policy is nominally
     interested in increasing the gains from trade of market participants, or in
     promoting the public interest (which policy maker would claim anything
     else?), it is less immediately obvious why policy should be so keen to
     promote greater competition. At bottom, competition means rivalry, and,
     at least to the man in the street, not all rivalry is a good thing.

The appropriate technical response to the second point is, of course, that
competition is not generally an end in itself,[4] but rather, in the right sorts of
circumstances, a means to other ends. The next questions that then occur are:

●   What are the relevant ends?
●   In what circumstances does competition contribute to those ends?
●   Why target, through public policy, the means rather than the ends?

The first two of these questions can be dealt with together. The fundamental theorem of welfare economics says that, in certain market conditions, 'perfect' competition leads to economic efficiency. Aspects of the required conditions include the absence of external effects (that is, uncompensated effects of trade on third parties, such as environmental spillovers) and cost and demand conditions that are consistent with very large numbers of sellers and buyers.

These conditions are rarely, if ever, fully satisfied, leading to two possible ways forward in dealing with economic reality. First, perfect competition can be treated as an approximation, in the expectation that, if the market conditions are close to those specified in the theorem, the outcomes will be close to efficient outcomes. Second, a different competitive benchmark can be specified, which takes account, for example, of the realities of likely cost conditions. Thus the theory of contestable markets (in which there is a complete absence of entry barriers) describes a form of competition that, subject to some further conditions that guarantee the existence of an equilibrium, realizes the maximum gains from trade in the relevant circumstances.

A defensible position to take, then, is that the reason for seeking to promote competition is that, in the right circumstances, it will lead to effficient outcomes in which maximum gains from trade are realized. This position also provides an answer to the question concerning the units in which competition is most appropriately measured (or, more accurately, assessed). Since efficiency is measured in currency units, the degree of competition can also be assessed in the same terms.

All these points can be summarized in the proposition that the aim of policy should be to promote *effective* competition, or at least to prohibit conduct that serves to prevent, restrict or distort effective competition. The adjective here does two things. First, it makes it clear that the competition referred to is a *teleological* concept, which is used with an end in mind, here assumed to be efficiency. Second, it can be used to filter out those circumstances in which competition would not, in fact, be the best way of promoting efficiency. Such competition could be deemed to be 'ineffective', even when it involves intense rivalry.

An Example

These arguments can be illustrated by a simple example, which also serves to bring out some other important points that are relevant to assessments of competition. Consider an industry in which firms compete first by developing and introducing new products to the market – the products might enjoy the benefits of patent protection – and then producing and marketing those products. For simplicity, suppose that, in the second stage, it is largely prices that drive consumer purchases. In this situation, competition takes place *in two dimensions*: product development and innovation, and pricing. Crucially, there is a trade-off between competition in the two dimensions. If price competition were very fierce – which, in this context, may be taken to mean that prices are forced down to close to the level of production and marketing costs, including a normal return on capital employed in those activities – the payoffs from successful product development and innovation would be relatively low. Given that these earlier activities are likely to be costly, and that the costs incurred will not be affected by later production volumes (they are fixed costs), the result will likely be muted innovation and limited competition to develop and introduce new products. On the other hand, if price competition is weaker, the returns from successful innovation may be higher, leading to more intense competitive activity in development and innovation.

Another way of thinking of this is to view fierce price competition as limiting or restricting the 'size of the market' for innovative activity: it reduces the potential revenues from innovative success, much in the way that, for more typical product markets, low levels of demand reduce the possible profits (producers' gains) from trading in a market. Small market size coupled with the existence of fixed costs will in turn tend to set limits on the degree of competition at the development and innovation stages.

The general points, then, are that competition is generally *multidimensional* – firms compete with one another in different ways – and that there exist trade-offs among those dimensions. Even in those cases where it may be relatively straightforward to assess the degree of competition in a particular dimension (for example, price competition), some aggregation procedure is therefore required in order to assess the competitive situation in its entirety.

Efficiency, or total gains from trade, provides the obvious measure to use for such a purpose. For given products in the market, weaker price competition reduces the gains from trade enjoyed by market participants. On the other hand, stronger competition in development and innovation will increase future gains from trade, via the introduction of more and better products to the market than would otherwise be available at any given moment. Fully effective competition could therefore be defined as the pattern of competition in each of the relevant dimensions at which the present value of total gains from trade is maximized. Movement away from this position could then be judged to be associated with one or other failure of competition. For example, the notion of distorted competition could be interpreted in terms of an inappropriate balance among the intensities with which competition takes place in its various dimensions.

This appears to resolve a number of difficult issues, but it should be clear that the approach described is just a variant of cost–benefit analysis. Indeed, abstracting from competition issues, similar reasoning is to be found in the simple *optimum patent life problem*, where the policy question concerns the duration of any intellectual property rights (IPRs) that might be granted.[5] Does this mean, therefore, that, in relation to the procedures used in economic assessments, the shift in the focus of policy, away from the public interest and towards the prevention, restriction and distortion of competition, is nothing more than a repackaging of existing approaches?

AN ALTERNATIVE PERSPECTIVE

It is possible that this will turn out to be the case. As already stated, the use of the efficiency criterion to evaluate and compare complex, multidimensional competition across different types of economic activity is logically coherent, and it can give more precise meaning to a number of terms that currently tend to be somewhat ill-defined (for example, effective competition, distortions of competition). The approach does, on the other hand, give rise to some uncomfortable implications and unanswered questions; in particular the following. If competition is to be evaluated, in the individual case, in terms of its anticipated effects on efficiency (gains from trade), what are we to make of legislation that introduces financial penalties when competition is, on this basis, judged to have been prevented, restricted or distorted? The implication is that the state will penalize firms for behaving in certain ways because their conduct is, according to the assessment made by the enforcement agency, *inefficient*. And while this may be a not unreasonable outcome in regulated industries – where, in setting price controls, regulators necessarily determine companies' incentive structures in some detail, including by explicitly or implicitly linking payoffs to efficiency performance – it would be much more suspect in the generality. In the limit it could, in effect, give rise to a widespread expansion of prescriptive regulation.

Secondly, repeating an earlier point, if economic efficiency (or some adjusted measure of gains from trade, weighted towards consumers) is the end, why target the means (competition)? Why not simply state that firms with an appreciable degree of market power should not act so as to cause avoidable reductions in aggregate benefits from trading in the market?

My own view is that the shift of focus towards 'competition' correctly (but at this stage only implicitly) recognizes that the links between competition and efficiency are somewhat more complex and difficult to handle than is implied by much of the economic analysis on the subject. If the Competition Act is to make the contribution to economic progress that its authors intend (and is to avoid the potential trap of having the unintended consequence of restricting economic progress), it is important that the underlying conceptual framework be clarified and debated. Once understood, this conceptual framework calls for adjustments, some of which are substantial, in the role of economic assessments in the implementation of competition policy.

Limitations of Cost-benefit Analysis

The first point to recognize is that, in general, it is extremely difficult in practice to derive precise estimates of the effects on gains from trade (efficiency) of the particular acts or conduct that are of interest. It may be possible to place approximate limits on the range of outcomes, and to render some opinion on the probabilities involved, but, if done honestly, considerable fuzziness/uncertainty will usually remain. And, notoriously, small changes of assumption can frequently lead to significantly different 'central estimates' of efficiency effects.

There are some difficult conceptual problems lying beneath the preceding observations, which, once exposed, indicate that (a) the observations are not just pieces of casual empiricism and (b) the difficulty cannot easily be remedied via the deployment of improved analytical techniques. These problems have to do with information. First, existing information relevant to the economic assessment will be decentralized: such information lies, in fragmented form, with a wide range of parties, including demand-side and supply-side market participants. It will therefore be necessary to gather and process relevant information, ready for analysis, but we know, not least from the history of state planning, that this type of information centralization can be highly ineffective. Problems include the sheer volume and complexity of the information required, and the distortions that occur in its transmission from one party to another, particularly when commercial interests are at stake. Competitive market economies leave information decentralized, and provide incentives whereby those holding it will benefit from its use. There is, therefore, an element of 'trying to push water up hill' in much cost-benefit analysis.[6]

More fundamentally, information conditions change over time. Even if the assessor could know everything that is known today, including who knows what, such knowledge will be out-of-date almost immediately. Discovery, learning and innovation are at the heart of competitive market processes, and the longer the time horizon the greater will tend to be the potential disparity between today's information conditions and tomorrow's.

In reality, then, determining the 'effectiveness' of competition via the cost-benefit route is an exercise that, except in some very simple cases, is difficult to carry out with any degree of confidence, and the difficulties are compounded further by resource (including time) constraints in enforcement agencies and the distortions caused by the frequent intrusion of interest group agendas (including political and bureaucratic agendas).

Rule-based Approaches

The only practical way forward in these circumstances is via the development and use of *rules of thumb* that can be applied in assessments (and which serve to economize on information). Such rules should not be rigid since, in particular cases, there may be sufficient evidence to indicate that their application would be inappropriate. Nevertheless, they can be used to establish presumptive findings, which would only be set aside if there were strong evidence that pointed clearly to a different conclusion. In the event that a rule is found to be inappropriate in a relatively wide range of cases, this can be taken as an indication that the rule itself may be inappropriate.

In this context, it can be noted that the Competition Act *does* signify a shift to a more presumptive approach, and it also provides, as does the EC legislation, for exceptions to the rules that will be adopted. Those who are advocates of legal certainty will see, in a rule-based approach, a more comfortable outcome than that associated with pure *rule of reason*. The adoption of a more rules-based approach to competition assessments leads on to a new set of challenging economic issues, however. The first and foremost of these concerns the criteria to be used in developing and changing the rules of thumb. What constitutes a good set of rules? How specific should the rules be? When should rules be changed?

More or less any set of rules, operated relatively rigidly and without substantial change, can satisfy the criterion of legal certainty, and the criterion therefore provides no basis for discriminating between the good and the bad. Further, overemphasis on legal certainty can serve to bias whatever set of rules is eventually chosen towards inflexibility, which is potentially damaging in markets that are subject to change and innovation.

Even with rule-based approaches, therefore, there is no escape from a consequentialist approach. The assessment rules themselves need constantly to be critically appraised on the basis of their possible consequences, and some notion of gains from trade (efficiency) is indispensable as an evaluation criterion. In this framework, economics has a twofold role: (a) assessing the appropriateness of the rules themselves, and (b) assessing particular cases where it appears that a straightforward application of the rules may give rise to wholly inappropriate conclusions. The first set of tasks relates to the *rule-making process* of the competition agencies, while the second is concerned with *application of existing rules.*

Particularly in relation to the first of these two roles, what is required is a conceptual framework that is somewhat different from that found in most of the economic textbooks. The rationale for rule-based approaches stems from the complex and ever-changing information conditions to be found in the marketplace, which is a feature of economic life that has been emphasized most strongly by the Austrian School. Just as the foundations of the cost–benefit approach lie in the neoclassical economics familiar to most undergraduates, so the intellectual pedigree of the kind of approach implicit in the Competition Act would appear to be largely Austrian.

Critical application of economic principles and careful sifting of evidence are common to all approaches, but whereas the neoclassical tradition has come to emphasize narrowly analytical, quantitative and largely static issues, the Austrian tradition places more weight on broader, more qualitative and, above all, dynamic and historical analysis. The Austrian perspective tends also to be less teleological, as is reflected by Hayek's view, set out in *The Road to Serfdom*, that 'it is more important to clear away the obstacles with which human folly has encumbered our path and to release the creative energy of individuals than to devise further machinery for "guiding" and "directing" them – to create conditions favourable for progress rather than to "plan progress"'.

Given the uncertain links between conduct (including rule making) today and consequences tomorrow, precise claims about the *magnitudes* of the economic effects of policy decisions should, on this view, be treated with considerable scepticism. Similarly, concepts such as *effective* competition are considered to be largely spurious if used, as they often are, in a way that implies that competitive conditions can be fine-tuned to yield readily predictable effects on efficiency. Indeed, even the notion of economic efficiency as an evaluation criterion can be questioned, as indicated by Hayek's preference for the term *progress*, a notional benchmark that was widely used by classical economists.

If there were only one message that I could communicate today, it would be this: since, for informational reasons, 'good' rules of competition cannot be deduced from a given performance criterion (such as economic efficiency) – and, if they could, they would arguably be redundant – they, too, are generated through a process of *discovery*. There is, therefore, a certain symmetry between the conduct of firms in the marketplace (discovering and acting on new information in the course of their business) and the rule-making aspects of the work of the competition authorities (developing and adapting the rules as new information is discovered and as market circumstances change). Discovery and innovation are processes not confined to production and trading activities.

Rule making is not, of course, the only activity of the competition authorities. There is also the matter of applying existing sets of rules, where more traditional economic assessments are likely to be more relevant, particularly in dealing with special cases. In practice, however, there is no completely clear-cut boundary between the two activities. Hayek, in his later work, placed considerable emphasis on the law-making powers of the judiciary, and a similar point applies in relation to the development of the rules of competition. When specific cases come to be decided, it may be found that the characteristics of those cases point to certain improvements that could be made in the rules themselves. That is, one of the ways in which new (and, it is hoped, better) rules are established is via decisions made in particular cases.

This dynamism in the rule-making process is well illustrated by the activities of sectoral regulators in relation to the specific sets of rules contained in licences and codes that govern conduct in liberalized network industries. Thus, for example, codes have been established as a result of requirements for close coordination in some dimensions of business behaviour in order to secure the effective operation of networks that are used by a relatively large number of different companies. The regulators have been afforded a major role not only in ensuring compliance with the rules/codes but also in the processes by which the rules/codes are changed.

CRITICAL ANALYSIS OF THE RULES USED IN ECONOMIC ASSESSMENTS

Having suggested, on general grounds, that evaluation of the rules used in assessing competition is an important task for economic analysis, let me give a more concrete example of how this might be done. The example also serves to illustrate how things can be got wrong (that is, how inappropriate rules might be adopted) and how economic evaluations can contribute to the discovery and adoption of alternatives that better contribute to economic progress.

The particular assessment rules of interest concern the determination of whether or not a particular company is dominant for the purposes of the Chapter II prohibition of the Competition Act. They are as follows:

1. Define a relevant market using the hypothetical monopolist test (that is for a group of products including those supplied by the allegedly dominant firm, ask whether a price increase of either 5 per cent or 10 per cent, from the competitive price level, can profitably be sustained for a nontransitory period). The market is defined as the narrowest set of products for which this test is passed.
2. Calculate the market share of the firm in question.
3. If the market share is 40 per cent or above, conclude that there is a presumption that the firm is dominant.[7]

Let me consider this procedure in reverse order, starting with stage 3.

The Concentration Doctrine

The concluding stage of these rules has its intellectual basis in the concentration doctrine, which holds that the market power of a company is greater the higher is its market share, and that the degree of competition in a market is inversely related to market concentration. Conversely, market shares and concentration indices can be used as indicators of market power.

Like all propositions in economics, the relationships cited are contingent on certain assumptions about other economic factors. The problem is not that the claimed relationships between the variables are false, but rather that they will not always hold; and if they fail to hold in a significant number of cases, the value of the rule is called into doubt.

Consider, for example, a market in which concentration is observed to be falling. Can we safely infer from this observation that, say, price competition is intensifying? The answer is clearly no. It is quite possible that price competition is actually softening and that what is happening is that new companies are entering the market in order to enjoy some of the benefits of the higher prices. Far from being a welcome sign, the falling concentration may be an indicator of cartelization. Assuming that entry barriers are modest, the final equilibrium may be characterized by high prices, high unit costs associated with excess capacity, modest profitability and low concentration.

Reversing these arguments, it follows immediately that increasing concentration in a market is not necessarily a sign of monopolization and of increasing market power. In the absence of further information, increasing concentration could equally well be the result of intensifying price competition, perhaps due to the breakdown of some previous, collusive equilibrium.

Consider now a second example. In this case the concentration doctrine actually holds – there is a positive relationship between market share and market power – but the interpretation of any observed data is clouded by capacity constraints (inelastic supply) and the degree of elasticity in demand. Suppose that a number of firms supply a homogeneous product at a constant long-run unit cost (the same for all) and that demand is linear (that is, a given price reduction always gives rise to the same increase in quantity demanded). The aggregate capacity in the market is assumed to be equal to the level of demand (Q^*) at the competitive price (equal to the constant long-run unit cost), but each firm's capacity is fixed for some period, say of a year of more. Let the elasticity of demand at the competitive price be η.

Consider a company, A, that controls some fraction θ of the total capacity. That is, θ is its share of total capacity in the market and θQ^* is the company's maximum production. Figure 3.1 shows the firm's residual demand curve, BD, on the assumption that all other companies price competitively (residual demand is taken to be the total market demand at a given price less the output

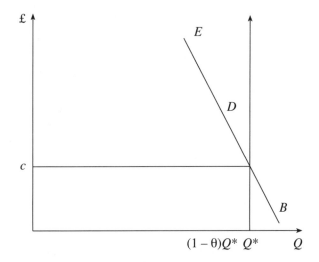

Figure 3.1   Residual demand with capacity constraints

of all other firms at that price).[8] At the competitive price the level of demand
is Q^*, but other firms only have capacity to supply a volume of $(1-\theta)Q^*$. If A
sets price equal to long-run unit/marginal cost, it will sell θQ^* units, but, if it
increases price, its demand will fall as it moves up the line *BD*. Beyond *D*, it
will price itself out of the market (all demand will be met by its rivals).

   Assuming that firm A sets price and output to maximize profit, it is
straightforward to find an expression for the price it will set in terms of the
demand, cost and share-of-capacity parameters. From this, it is also possible
to derive an expression for the share of capacity that the firm would need to
have in order to be able to raise price to 10 per cent above the competitive
level:

$$\theta = 0.2\eta$$

Thus, if the elasticity of demand were equal to 2 at the competitive price, a
share of capacity of 0.4 (40 per cent) would be required to achieve the 10 per
cent price hike. On the other hand, if the demand elasticity were 0.2, the share
of capacity required to be able to affect price in this way would be only 4 per
cent. In terms of output, the required market share is even lower, since, given
that demand is assumed to be linear, the output of the 'residual monopolist'
will be only half of its capacity. That is, in the inelastic demand case, *a firm
that was observed to have only a 2 per cent share of output would be able to
increase price to 10 per cent above the competitive level.*[9]

What this shows is that, even in circumstances where the concentration doctrine is valid, it is inappropriate to rely on market share indicators alone. Any general rule should also take account of estimates of demand and supply elasticities. For example, a test of dominance that relies on a market share benchmark of, say, 40 per cent may be satisfactory for some values of the elasticities, but it will give a completely misleading indication of market power for other values of these elasticities. Put another way, a general rule, applied to all markets, is simply too economical with the *actualité*. A minimally satisfactory adjustment would be to vary the market share benchmark according to the relevant demand and supply elasticities, with the benchmark level set at (possibly substantially) higher levels when elasticities are high and at (possibly substantially) lower levels when elasticities are lower.

Market Definition

The calculation of the market share of a company requires that there be some prior definition of the relevant market, and the first of the set of rules listed above sets out a procedure for doing this. Is it a good procedure? As with rule 3, the answer is, unfortunately, in the negative.

A simple way of seeing this is to consider a group of products that are good substitutes for one another but much weaker substitutes for all products outside the group. This is a well-defined market in the normal economic sense and, although the substitutability relationships among products are usually much more complicated than this in practice, the aim here is to show that the hypothetical monopolist test can fail even in the simplest of cases.

Specifically, assume that there are three companies A, B, C supplying the well-defined market, and that the interest is in whether or not A is dominant. The test is started with A. Can A profitably increase the price of its products by 5–10 per cent above the competitive level for a non-transitory period? If the answer is yes, the market is defined as the products of A, which is an incorrect conclusion (by assumption, the market comprises the products of all three companies). If the answer is no, the next step is to add the products of one of the other firms, say B, and repeat the question, on the assumption that a single firm controls the products of both A and B. If the answer to the price hike question is now yes, then the market is defined as the products of A and B, which again is incorrect. Only if the answer is no at this second stage is it likely that the correct conclusion will be reached, effectively by accident. The following points can be noted:

1. If the market is defined incorrectly, the market share will be incorrectly measured, rendering its interpretation even more problematic. For example, if the actual market shares are equal and, in the event, the market

is defined as the products of A and B, the measured market share of A will be 50 per cent. This might lead to a presumption that A is dominant, even though it might have no ability to raise prices to any significant degree.

2. If the market definition procedure can lead to false conclusions in the way described, the rule is not only inappropriate but is also likely to lead to uncertain outcomes. Even the very weak requirement of legal certainty may not be met.

3. The procedure conflates the concepts of 'the market' and 'market power'. To ask whether a firm can raise prices above the competitive level (against given assumptions) is to ask whether it has market power, *not* whether its products comprise a market of their own.

The second observation here suggests an alternative assessment rule: an undertaking might be said to be dominant, for the purposes of competition law, if it is judged to have the ability profitably to raise prices by some designated percentage compared with the competitive level for a non-transitory period.[10] This might further be refined by linking the level and duration of the price hike to the degree of harm suffered by consumers as a result of such pricing behaviour.

The hypothetical monopolist test was first adopted by the Department of Justice in the USA in the context of merger cases. Economic thinking has since moved on from that position (if indeed it was ever there in the first place) and the translation into mergers policy of the alternative assessment rule suggested above leads to what is sometimes, rather grandly, called the *doctrine of unilateral effects*. This simply says that analysis should move directly to consideration of the anticipated effects of a proposed merger by, for example, assessing whether, as a result of amalgamation, it would be profitable for the resulting undertaking significantly to raise prices above competitive levels.

Further Comments

The above discussion is intended to indicate how economic analysis can be used (a) to evaluate the rules of thumb that will necessarily come to be used in Competition Act assessments and (b) to suggest better alternatives. The analysis at this point, however, is still static in character, and does not get to grips with the informational problems that give rise to a policy focus on competition rather than on efficiency.

This is a major task for the future, but I believe it is possible to see, at least in outline, the type of question that should be built into Competition Act assessment procedures and rules. Since the motor of economic progress is innovation – in processes, products, management, marketing, trading, market rules and so on – a key question is whether, as a result of the exercise of market power, innovation in any of the relevant dimensions of inter-firm rivalry is likely to be significantly retarded. Are, for example, the returns of a firm that has something new and valuable to offer being significantly diminished by the conduct of incumbents with dominant positions?

As a minimum, this would help shift the focus of attention somewhat, away from static market 'failures' (inefficiencies) and towards the factors that are important for dynamic competition.[11] For, in very many cases, the best remedies for market failures come from the market itself, rather than from state intervention. Existing inefficiencies (unrealized, feasible gains from trade) represent profit opportunities for those who can do better. They are therefore an aspect of the structure of incentives that are inherent in market processes. What matters, therefore, is not so much whether the exercise of market power is causing inefficiencies today, but rather whether it is preventing or restricting the timely discovery and adoption of innovations that could be expected to increase the future gains from trade.

CONCLUSIONS

The shift in emphasis marked by the Competition Act, away from rule-of-reason, case-by-case analysis of monopolies and the form-based approach of the RTPA, and towards consideration of effects on competition, makes a good deal of sense. It reflects an acknowledgement of the realities and significance of decentralized information, discovery and innovation in the marketplace. These factors have always been important, but their significance can only have been increased by the nature, scale and scope of technological advance over the past two decades.

Given this, it is desirable that there should be some accompanying shift in the contribution of economic assessments to competition policy. More attention needs to be given to critical evaluation of the rules and procedures that are an integral feature of the revised policy framework, and of the rule-generation or rule-making process itself. What is most important is whether certain types of conduct serve to restrict market innovations (broadly defined to include trading, marketing, management and so on, as well as production methods and products) and hence to restrict economic progress. Short-term market failures are, for the most part, best remedied by market innovations, and the point that it is *persistent* monopoly, not *temporary* monopoly, that is the source of potential problems for public policy (and indeed for good management) dates back at least as far as The Wealth of Nations.

None of this implies that more narrowly based analysis of the consequences of particular types of conduct in specific economic circumstances should disappear. There will always be special cases that require more extensive evaluation than is the norm and, at least for the moment, mergers policy may continue to operate under the old regime. Detailed, in-depth assessments are also potentially of importance in evaluating the efficacy of the rules of thumb and procedures that are used to economize on information in the generality of cases. If it is discovered that an existing set of rules is leading to unsatisfactory outcomes in a significant number of cases, the efficacy of at least some of those rules may be called into question.

While welcoming the Competition Act, it is necessary also to recognize that the opportunities it affords can be used foolishly as well as wisely. Poor rules and an inflexible rule-making process may in some (but not all) circumstances provide legal certainty, but they may also restrict economic progress. That would be an ironic outcome – a policy designed to remove obstacles to economic progress would itself become such an obstacle – but, if only because the policy process itself is monopolistic in its nature, it is an outcome whose possibility cannot easily be discounted. Appeals procedures and open, vigorous debate will help, but it is crucial that the competition authorities themselves recognize the importance of adaptation and innovation in conducting their own activities.

My final message is in two parts. To economists I would say that we need to focus more on market and policy dynamics, more on the rules of competition and their broad-brush consequences for economic progress, and somewhat less on static analysis of market failures. To lawyers the plea is to recognize that some sets of rules are better than others, that it is appropriate that the rules themselves should change over time, and that the overzealous pursuit of legal certainty, without due regard to relevant trade-offs, can itself have adverse effects on competition.

NOTES

1. This was originally planned as a joint paper with Michael Beesley, and parts of it are based on a series of lively discussions we had, usually chaired by Eileen Marshall, in the period before his untimely death deprived the UK academic and public policy communities of one of their outstanding thinkers, still in full flow. The final product is, inevitably, the poorer for his absence.
2. In answering the first part of the question there are the usual questions of appreciability. Market power, in the strict sense of an undertaking being able to influence market prices, is very common, and competition policy tends only to be interested in the resulting consequences in circumstances where the level of market power exceeds some threshold, usually only vaguely defined.
3. Applying differential weights to different interest groups does, however, reintroduce uncertainties surrounding the interpretation of the public interest. In effect, the competition authority is afforded considerable discretion on the matter in circumstances where small shifts in distributional weights can have substantial effects on outcomes/decisions. Consequentially, uncertainty concerning outcomes/decisions is also increased.

4. Although competition can be a 'good' in that it is sometimes enjoyable, sport being one of the most obvious examples. Thus the greater the degree of rivalry between two football clubs, the greater will tend to be the demand to watch a match between them.

5. More sophisticated IPR analyses take explicit account of competition issues, and also deal with other dimensions of IPRs, such as the 'breadth' of the protection (that is, precisely how similar an alternative product has to be before it is judged to violate the IPR).

6. There is also an incentives issue to consider. Faced with limited information, participants in markets will have incentives to find and use information, since their gains from trade will depend, in very direct ways, upon their success in these activities. In contrast, rewards for public officials are much less dependent upon their effectiveness in acquiring, processing and acting on information.

7. In practice, this presumption is subject to rebuttal, but, for the procedural rules to have any substance, a significant burden of proof can be assumed to be placed on the company.

8. It is implicitly assumed that, if A prices above the competitive level, it is the more highly valued demands that are successful in obtaining supplies from the competing companies. One case in which this is a reasonable assumption is when there is a secondary market in the product. Alternatively, the residual demand curve might reflect 'price following' by other companies.

9. This type of problem has arisen in the gas industry, where shippers are able to purchase capacity rights to enter gas at beach terminals whose capacity is, in the short-to-medium term, strictly limited. A traditional competition law approach might seek to address the issue by promoting deconcentration, but, as the analysis shows, concentration might have to be reduced to a very low level indeed to mitigate market power. The solution adopted has been to introduce a new 'rule', in the form of use-it-or-lose-it provisions. This means that capacity held by a company that is not utilized by that company must be made available for others to use. It is easy to see that this 'rule innovation' resolves the underutilization problem in an effective way.

10. Note that this could lead to a conclusion that there are two or more (individually) dominant firms in a market. While it might be objected that such a conclusion would offend against the commonsense meaning of dominance, it is surely much less of an offence to contemplate the possibility of several 'masters' than of the several 'single suppliers' allowed under FTA scale monopoly and complex monopoly situations.

11. The approach could also bring competition policy closer to law in relation to IPRs.

CHAIRMAN'S COMMENTS
John S. Bridgeman

Introduction

Thank you, George, for, as ever, a thought-provoking lecture. You have raised several themes which will be of interest to all of us here – whether regulators or businesses, economists or philosophers! Now I do hope you will forgive me for not addressing all of your themes in the exact order in which you raised them.

The Old and New Regimes

You highlighted some differences between 'the old and the new' competition legislation. By introducing prohibitions of certain types of activity, the 'new' legislation is immediately quite different from most of the existing regime. With the exception of the Resale Prices Act, existing UK competition legislation is not based on prohibitions.

At the moment, particular agreements, practices or courses of conduct which are detrimental to competition must first be investigated and found to be against the public interest by the Restrictive Practices Court or the Competition Commission.

This applies both to hard-core price fixing, like the ready-mix concrete cartel discovered in 1988 and to what was referred to as 'deplorable' predatory pricing in the case of Darlington Buses in 1995. Under a prohibition regime such behaviour, of course, is unlawful from the outset. This, I would hope, will act as a strong deterrent to those businesses contemplating anti-competitive agreements or conduct. This is an important departure from the old regime and should not be understated.

I do acknowledge that the new regime confers on me some strong powers, at least by UK standards. I make no apologies for that. Strong powers are necessary to combat the types of anti-competitive activity that have been allowed to continue largely unchecked as a result of the inadequacies of our existing laws. They are equally, or perhaps more, important in deterring firms from engaging in such activities at all. It is much better for UK consumers and the wider economy if vigorous competition can be preserved from the outset. I firmly believe that much of the value of the strong powers in our new regime lies in their deterrent effect.

One of the most effective deterrents in the new regime is the power to levy substantial financial penalties on firms found breaching the prohibitions. I would suggest to you that such a power provides a strong deterrent to firms from engaging in such behaviour in the first place. I intend also to encourage 'whistleblowers' through an immunity regime. The effectiveness of this approach is most clearly demonstrated in the USA, where 'whistleblowing' leads to the prosecution of a significant number of cartels.

Rules versus Assessment

Let me turn to your discussion of rules versus assessment, which I found very interesting. Assessment of competition policy cannot be based upon a set of rigid rules. As economists know, it is not possible to draw up an exhaustive list of agreements or types of behaviour that are always and everywhere anti-competitive. This means that in most, if not all, cases a competition assessment will be required. I am required by the Act to produce guidelines describing how I will carry out a competition assessment. Within a wider series, I have so far produced guidelines on *Market Definition*, *Assessment of Market Power* and *Assessment of Individual Agreements and Conduct*. These have been widely circulated and generally well received. While the OFT cannot and should not offer absolute certainty based on rigid rules, we have tried to provide the best possible guidance as to how the competition legislation will be interpreted.

This leads me on to 'discovery and innovation'. I agree with you wholeheartedly that competition authorities can learn and can innovate. Our guidelines are intended to be 'living' documents. We shall update them regularly to take on board our experience of the new legislation. Of course, you all have a role to play too. We have found the comments that we have received on our guidelines most useful. I hope we shall continue to hear your views. I should also like to encourage the academics among you to focus more of your research on policy issues. Let us know what you think are the strengths and weaknesses of our approach. Please let us know, too, how you think our procedures and analysis might be improved.

I am determined the office shall always be willing to learn. All our case officers are currently undergoing an extensive period of training in law, economics and financial analysis. This will increase further the professionalism of my staff. The economists and lawyers in the audience tonight might also be pleased to see that I have recently increased significantly the number of staff with economic and legal backgrounds.

Moreover, as relative latecomers in the Europe-wide movement towards prohibition-based competition law, we have had the advantage of being able to study international practice in some detail, incorporating approaches that have proved successful and disregarding those that have not worked so well. We are trying to produce a modern regime which is best suited to the needs of the UK. I should say that there are certain areas where, for good reason, we have decided not to tread our own path. I refer, of course, to the effect of section 60 of the Competition Act 1998 that is designed to ensure consistency with the operation of the EC competition regime. Lord Simon of Highbury has described section 60 as a central plank in achieving certainty for business.[1] Section 60 provides the new Competition Act with a ready-made history through 35 years or so of Community law. This body of law will provide businesses with a clear indication of how the new UK legislation is likely to affect them.

Guidelines and Innovation

George, you have made much play of the need to adopt a dynamic rather than static approach to analysing competition issues. I can endorse this view wholeheartedly. Throughout my guidelines I have made clear that any competition assessment will include a time dimension. For instance, I have made clear that I would not normally be concerned by periods of transient high prices and that excessive prices may be considered to be an abuse only if they have persisted in the absence of continuing successful innovation and/or without stimulating successful new entry or a significant loss of market share.

As you have indicated, it is the persistence of abuse that is the key to economic competition analysis under a Chapter II investigation. Indeed, this is the approach I have always taken to analysing competition issues in innovative markets such as pay-TV.

Over the years, the Office of Fair Trading has learnt from analysing a great number of different sectors and a wide range of market conditions. Not all markets face rapidly changing demand or cost conditions. Experience and theory both suggest that, when there are only a few undertakings in such *static* markets, cartels may be more likely to arise. I cannot remind you often enough that I shall be taking the firmest possible stance against cartels which I believe to be one of the most serious infringements caught under the new Competition Act.

I would also encourage you all not to believe mistakenly that I will use some mechanistic approach to analysing cases based solely on market share thresholds and market definition. Market definition is only one step in the process of assessing a competition case. I will also clearly have to assess whether, for instance, there are barriers to entry, what is the nature of counter-vailing buyer power and what is the possibility of supply-side substitution.

Conclusion

In sum, I welcome George's exhortation that competition authorities must continually learn and be prepared to adapt policy from time to time to promote the interests of economic progress. This is just what we are trying to do and how I would try in turn to sell the new Competition Act to you tonight. I am sure it is going to mean a change for the better.

Note

1.   Hansard, House of Lords, 25 November 1997, column 961.

4. NETA and transmission

Ralph Turvey

INTRODUCTION

The Review of Electricity Trading Arrangements (RETA) has now produced some proposals known as the New Electricity Trading Arrangements (NETA). The aim is to introduce the new arrangements towards the end of 2000 and to introduce new arrangements for transmission pricing subsequently.

Economic efficiency requires, among many other things, that transmission losses and constraints are taken into account in the daily operation of the system and that transmission losses and transmission capacity costs are taken into account in investment decisions concerning transmission reinforcement, the location of new generation and the location of new loads. We want trading arrangements that will provide incentives:

- to consumers and generators, who should pay higher transmission charges and/or pay more or receive less for energy in locations where marginal losses are high or transmission constraint costs are high;
- to the National Grid Company (NGC) that reward it for operating in such a way as to minimize the cost of generation to meet the load plus losses and satisfy constraints.

In what follows I first explain how the new electricity trading arrangements in their initial, interim form will deal with transmission losses and transmission capacity costs. Then I proceed to the main issue of how better locational incentives might be introduced thereafter. The opportunity for this is given by the Office of Gas and Electricity Markets' (OFGEM's) forthcoming review of NGC's price control. OFGEM's consultative document of July 1999, on the New Trading Arrangements, included a brief provisional and tentative discussion of these matters, making it clear that there was still a lot of thinking to be done. Subsequently, in December, OFGEM produced a document, *NGC System Operator Incentives, Transmission Access and Losses under NETA*. In this paper, written before the publication of that document, and amended only marginally since, I examine the issues discussed in its chapters 8 and 9. As will become apparent, the problems are much easier to foresee than to solve.

In order to concentrate upon the problems of reflecting transmission losses and constraints in some form of locational pricing, I shall ignore some of the many other issues which make the introduction of new trading arrangements so complicated but nevertheless fascinating.

NETA

Bilateral Contracts

Under the new trading arrangements, generators, acting as suppliers, will make contracts with consumers and they will also make contracts with other suppliers who make contracts with consumers. There may also be inter-mediaries who contract with both generators and suppliers. Generators will self-commit and dispatch except insofar as they are called upon to provide increments or decrements under the balancing mechanism or insofar as they provide ancillary services[1] under contract to the system operator, NGC.

Long- and medium-term bilateral contracts between generators and suppliers will relate to large blocks and slices of energy. They will not specify the locations of generation or of delivery since, in many cases, the parties will contract on a portfolio basis.

Power exchange transactions will relate to individual half-hours, though the exchange may also mediate forward and futures transactions. They will not specify locations.

Balancing

There will always be residual energy flows that were not contracted for. Generators' actual outputs can be slightly different from what they had expected, while users often take a little more or a little less energy than was forecast even a short time before. These imbalances – differences between physical positions and contractual positions – will be dealt with by the balancing mechanism, in which NGC buys and sells energy, that is, accepts offers to increase generation or decrease demand and bids to decrease generation or increase demand at specified locations. The submission of these offers and bids will be voluntary.

Balancing mechanism purchases and sales will also be required for two other sets of reasons: (a) to ensure that transmission constraints are observed and system stability is preserved, and (b) to deal with variations of production and demand within each half-hour or to reconfigure plant to provide frequency response, voltage support or reserve. How within-half-hour variations will be dealt with is a complex problem, but it can be ignored in the present context.

Offers accepted will be paid as offered and bids accepted will pay as bid.[2] The balancing mechanism for each half-hour will open at what is called gate closure – three and a half hours before the start of that half-hour – and run until the end of the half-hour. Bids and offers will initially have to be submitted to the system operator by gate closure.

Participants in the electricity market will have to report their contract positions to NGC ahead of time, stating MWh to be generated and to be delivered in each half-hour, without any breakdown by location and without stating prices. But they will also have to provide initial physical notifications the day before, to allow NGC to make provisional plans for its balancing actions. They will later provide final physical notifications, at least three and a half hours in advance. These physical notifications will forecast half-hourly expected generation for each genset and half-hourly offtake for each exit point of the grid. Thus they will specify the location of generation and the grid supply zone of offtake. Except for this locational detail, final notifications will mirror the reported contract positions, *unless* participants choose to risk relying upon the balancing mechanism to take part of their output or provide some of their offtake.

These locational physical notifications will serve two functions: (a) enabling NGC to identify transmission constraints, and (b) providing the baselines for balancing mechanism offers and bids which will naturally also be location-specific. Imbalances will be computed separately for production and for consumption, as the differences between producers' aggregate contracted and metered deliveries into the grid and, for consumption, as differences between contracted and actual offtakes from it, after allowing for any accepted balancing mechanism bids or offers.

Taking all their bilateral transactions together, participants are likely to attempt to secure *ex ante* balance before gate closure. In other words, they will seek to match their contract positions (allowing for possible participation in the balancing mechanism) and their anticipated physical positions. The incentive to do this will be that, at settlement, a production participant's nationwide sum of excess deliveries will be paid the weighted average cost of accepted bids, while a consumption participant's nationwide sum of excess offtakes will pay the weighted average cost of accepted offers which will normally be higher; *mutatis mutandis* with shortfalls.

Besides charging and paying participants who are out of balance, the settlement process will settle accepted balancing mechanism offers and bids, and calculate the system operator's costs of balancing the system. Thus NGC's balancing mechanism role will be as follows:

- the resolution both of any *ex ante* imbalances which participants opt for and of the inevitable *ex post* imbalances that will arise;
- the resolution of transmission constraints, by accepting offers in import-constrained zones and bids in export-constrained zones;
- load following within the half-hour. NGC will contract for balancing services such as reserve, frequency control and voltage support. These contracts, along with its purchases and sales in the balancing mechanism, will enable it to balance the system on a second-by-second basis.

Cash-out Prices for Imbalances

For every half-hour, settlement will compute two weighted average prices per MWh. One averages the prices paid to participants for accepted offers to provide output increments or offtake reductions. This average price will be charged for imbalances of contracted over actual generation or of actual over contracted offtake. Similarly, the weighted average price received from participants for accepted bids for output decrements or offtake increments will be paid on actual in excess of contracted generation or for shortfall of offtake from contracted offtake.[3]

It is expected that the weighted average of offer prices will be considerably higher than the weighted average of bid prices. Thus the cash-out price charged for generation shortfalls or offtake excesses is expected to be higher than what generators will get for excess generation or suppliers will get for offtake shortfalls. The higher price should discourage participants from planning to buy from the balancing mechanism, while the lower price should discourage the idea of selling to it. Thus nearly all participants are expected to try to balance their contracted purchase or planned production with their contracted sale or planned consumption. They can seek to adjust their net contract positions to do this up to three and a half hours before gate closure by trading on the screen-based power exchange. To the extent that they do this, imbalances will only reflect unforeseen plant outages or misforecast demands.

It does not follow that, in these circumstances, balancing mechanism transactions will be unimportant and the differences between the two cash-out prices will be small. For half-hours when transmission constraints are binding, NGC will have to accept high-priced offers to produce more or consume less in import-constrained zones and accept low-priced bids to reduce generation or increase offtake in export-constrained zones. Also a scatter of bids and offers from flexible generators may frequently have to be accepted to provide reserve or ancillary services or to accommodate minute-to-minute variations in demand or unplanned plant outages.

Several hundred large suppliers and consumers whose offtake is flexible will presumably choose to provide offers and bids to the balancing mechanism, as will, presumably, most of the 200 or so gensets. Whether smaller players will do so will depend upon the costs – dedicated information technology (IT) links will be necessary – and upon the possibility of agents acting for them.

Costs

As under the present pool system, uniform average transmission loss factors will be applied to all participants on the demand side but not to generators. For each half-hour in which a participant is a net importer from the grid, its offtake will be scaled up by a transmission loss multiplier to allocate to it a share of the total transmission losses of that half-hour. These scaled-up offtakes will be used in calculating imbalances, so net importers will want to contract to buy energy to cover their expected loss allocations.

This system will, in the first stage of NETA, simply spread out the cost of losses among all customers, which is what is done at present. (However, with the future in mind, the balancing and settlements system is to have the capability both to scale generation as well as demand for losses and to apply different loss factors to different entry and exit points of the transmission system.)

NGC will bear all balancing mechanism costs remaining after payment and receipt of energy imbalance cash-out prices. This means that they will bear the cost of redispatching to satisfy transmission constraints, together with the cost of ancillary services procured under contracts with generators. These costs, and the cost of running settlements, will be 'smeared', that is, spread out over all grid users, as at present, as one component of transmission use of system charges. A Transmission Services Incentive Scheme may continue to provide NGC with an incentive to minimize them.

Weaknesses of the Interim Arrangements

The interim system that I have just described has admitted weaknesses where locational matters are concerned. Four important desiderata for subsequent developments can be listed, as follows.

1. Efficient dispatch would take account of marginal transmission losses. (Marginal losses at peak range from 6 per cent to minus 5 per cent.[4]) Note that optimizing dispatch in a way which takes account of losses is *not* the same as minimizing the aggregate cost of losses; what matters, for any given constellation of loads, is minimizing the cost of generation to

provide the sum of load plus losses, subject, of course, to security constraints.

Efficient dispatch would result in locational price differences between nodes or, more approximately between zones, which would reflect differences in marginal transmission losses. Locational energy price differences which appear regular and persistent would help to provide one part of the appropriate incentives for the location of new generation and new loads.

2. Appropriate incentives for the location of new generation and new loads require a locational pattern of prices and marginal costs which reflects *either* the long-run marginal costs of transmission capability reinforcement *or* the short-run costs of transmission congestion.

3. Incentives are required to induce NGC to time outages of the transmission system for maintenance so as to minimize the sum of generation costs and NGC maintenance costs. This is not the same as minimizing maintenance costs regarded in isolation.

4. There should be *either* an incentive to NGC to initiate and undertake transmission reinforcement when, and only when, the cost is likely to be outweighed by the gains to generators and consumers, *or* coalitions of transmission users should be able to require, pay for and obtain property rights in reinforcements from which they would benefit.

This fourth requirement is the most difficult to achieve.

Locational Price Differences

A fully optimized centralized dispatch would not suffer the first two of these weaknesses. It would produce marginal costs and prices that differed between nodes or zones – all of the time to reflect differences in marginal losses, and some of the time, because of transmission constraints. A single marginal price for each half-hour at each location reflecting the marginal cost of energy would be ideal.

Under NETA as it is proposed to be initially introduced, there will be no locational prices. For each half-hour only two cash-out prices will result and contract prices will not vary according to location. Furthermore, instead of NGC making a centralized dispatch, it will only provide centralized dispatch *amendment* – by accepting balancing mechanism bids and offers. Providing that it is incentivized to minimize system costs, the result should be approximately the same as would be provided by a central dispatch that ignored locational differences in marginal losses.[5] Thus, if bids and offers for increments and decrements from final physical notifications were consistent with the bids and offers that would have been provided to a centralized dispatcher, cost-minimizing *changes* from final physical notifications would result in the same pattern of generation and consumption as would a cost-minimizing zero-base dispatch.

I now consider how to avoid, or at least reduce, the weaknesses which I have just described as a feature of the initial interim implementation of NETA. I consider losses first, then constraints.

The Treatment of Losses

Marginal losses depend upon the whole constellation of line flows in a meshed system. A power flow analysis can compute marginal losses *ex post* and they can be computed *ex ante* for typical load flow situations. The excess over 1MWh of the incremental or decremental generation at any specified node required to provide 1MWh more or less offtake at a specified offtake node will differ between each pair of nodes and will depend upon all other flows in the system. However, the resulting n^2-n marginal loss factors between n nodes (or their averages for n zones) can be simplified into $n-1$ marginal loss factors for flows to and $n-1$ marginal loss factors from some central node (or zone), so that the marginal loss factor applicable to a contract relating to any particular pair of nodes (or zones) could be computed by combining two of these. Note that some marginal loss factors are negative.

NGC could achieve optimized balancing under NETA *if* its balancing mechanism acceptances of bids and offers took account of marginal transmission losses. This would mean that offers to increase generation or decrease demand in one part of the country at prices exceeding the price of bids to decrease generation or increase demand in another part would be accepted whenever the difference was more than covered by the marginal loss between them. Fairly stable patterns of locational differences at different times could be expected to emerge. But whether or not NGC achieves such optimized balancing through the balancing mechanism, what is required is that participants should take account of marginal losses in their contracts and self-dispatch. Two alternative ways of ensuring this are as follows:

1. each participant would be required to provide the energy necessary to meet the losses from its contracted flows;
2. NGC would purchase the energy to meet losses and charge participants appropriately for its cost.

In either case the participants would take the expected cost of losses into account when agreeing contract prices, thus reflecting anticipations of locational loss differences in the prices agreed in forward and short-term contracts. These would have to be locationally specific.

Participants provide losses
This can be achieved by scaling up offtakes, and/or scaling down injections proportionately to losses when calculating imbalances, so that one or both of the parties to a contract have to provide or pay for their losses. This is the alternative favoured by OFGEM (whose December consultation paper has a footnote reference to this section of my paper).

Under NETA, scaling up all offtakes uniformly to make them equal in aggregate to contracted injections when calculating imbalances *ex post* for each half-hour is proposed only as an interim measure. The proposed settlement system will allow scaling factors that vary between nodes and could be applied to injections as well as to offtakes. The idea was originally that their average value would still reflect average losses *ex post* in each half-hour, so that differences between them would understate differences in marginal loss factors by about half, marginal losses being about twice average losses. Nevertheless, such locational differentiation would produce a significant improvement in the cost reflectivity of prices. It was proposed for application to pool prices under the existing system, but so far has been prevented by impending litigation.

The scaling factors could presumably be computed either *ex post*, as part of the settlement process, or *ex ante*, with their relative values reflecting regular locational and time of day and year variations in marginal losses as estimated by NGC. With *ex ante* promulgation of the scaling factors, contracts and final physical notifications could take account of losses. With *ex post* calculation, considerable uncertainty about the size and cost of imbalances might be introduced. This raises the obvious question of whether financial instruments allowing participants to hedge against this uncertainty could be developed. I am unable to answer this question.

NGC provides and charges for losses
Under this alternative, imbalances would continue to be computed as differences between contracted injections and metered offtakes without applying any scaling factor for losses. To cover these, NGC would (other things being equal) have to be a net buyer of energy in the balancing mechanism, as in the interim stage of NETA. The cost of this, being part of the net cost of all its balancing mechanism trades, would enter into its allowed revenue. The difference would be that it would receive part of that allowed revenue through a locationally differentiated component of its use of system KWh charges. This would reflect *ex ante* estimated regular locational and time of day and year variations in the value of marginal losses. Generators would pay charges reflecting the value of marginal losses to a central node; suppliers would pay charges reflecting the

value of marginal losses from that node. These charges would be negative in some cases.

How would marginal loss factors be translated into charges? Presumably, this would be done by using cash-out prices in some way. The problem of deciding how to use cash-out prices to determine charges also arises with the second of the three approaches to dealing with transmission constraints described below, so discussion of the matter is postponed.

Marginal and average losses
If participants provided their own losses and if loss charges entered into use of system charges, marginal losses could be fully reflected rather than being scaled down to make their average value equal average losses. The result would be to yield a surplus to NGC reflecting the excess of marginal over average losses.[6] This is highly desirable for two reasons.

1. It avoids attenuating the incentive to participants to take full account of marginal losses.
2. It would reduce the amount of *other* charges required to provide NGC with its allowed revenue. These other charges, which have to cover all other NGC capital and operating costs, have to be spread over all MWh and MW, creating variable charges. Since most of these other costs do not vary with MWh or MW, these charges would constitute marginal costs to participants that do not reflect marginal costs to the system. So the smaller they are, the better.

The Treatment of Constraints

The nature of the problem
Security standards require that the transmission system should be configured and generation should be scheduled so that no interruption to electricity supply from the grid would result from credible transmission circuit outages[7]. The result is that certain zones can be delimited such that power flows across the boundaries separating them must be constrained not to exceed the aggregate capability of the cross-boundary circuits. This is the simplest case. There are also occasions where tighter constraints exist because of stability and voltage issues. In these cases, the thermal capability of the interconnection does not matter.[8]

The significance of these boundary capabilities is twofold, short term and long term.

Short term in some half-hours it may be necessary to reduce generation or increase offtake on the export side of the boundary and to do the opposite on the import side in order to ensure that the cross-boundary flows do not exceed the boundary capability. The consequence is an increase in total generation running costs and marginal cost differences between zones at times when the unconstrained cost-minimizing load flow would exceed capability. So the problem is to minimize the extra costs and decide who bears them.

Long term   new generation on the export side and load growth on the import side of a boundary may threaten greater and more frequent overloading of the cross-boundary capability. The result is that there is a choice between accepting a greater cost increase and larger differences in marginal cost in more half-hours of the year, and investing in transmission reinforcement to increase capability. The problem is how to influence the location of new generation and loads and to decide on reinforcement investment and how participants should pay for it.

Initially, under the New Electricity Trading Arrangements, NGC will undertake balancing mechanism transactions so as to reduce cross-boundary flows to the levels of capabilities. An alternative, for subsequent implementation, would be to make the market work in such a way that participants have an incentive to balance their contractual positions so that the cross-boundary flows, in aggregate, do not exceed capabilities. Physical transmission rights, discussed below, might achieve this. (So, too, could centralized dispatching with nodal pricing, but OFGEM's preference is for fewer centralized mechanisms and more market mechanisms.)

In the long term, the aim is to provide messages and incentives for the location of generation and consumption and of transmission investment. Many transmission constraints are irrelevant in this context; they reflect temporary or short-term transmission limitations that result from temporary or short-term planned and unplanned outages of lines and of generation units. Dealing with them is a short-term problem. The investment incentives and disincentives that are provided to generators, suppliers and their consumers should reflect only the costs imposed by those constraints which are *long term*, resulting from the configuration and capability of the transmission system. Such major constraints are certain to be enduring, for it would never be economical so to expand transmission capacity that they all disappeared.

There are three alternative possible zonal approaches to these problems: (a) to charge transmission users an approximation to the long-run marginal cost of system reinforcement, (b) to charge them short-run marginal transmission congestion costs, or (c) to create physical transmission rights and have users pay for the costs of adding to them.

Long-run marginal cost (LRMC) pricing

The transmission use of system charges are annual charges levied on suppliers' triad demands and on generators' registered capacities. They are partly made up of what NGC calls 'Investment Cost Related Prices'. These are defined in terms of injections and offtakes from the grid at peak, not in terms of transfers across constraints, which are what is relevant. They are calculated within a simple transport model, which uses the following data:

- the annuitized gross asset value plus maintenance cost of lines, cables and substations per MWkm of its system;
- next year's forecast peak demand at each grid supply point;
- the registered capacity of each generating plant linked to its system;
- the distances along existing routes between these nodes.

The model is employed to minimize the cost of the sum of (peak flow times distance times cost per MWkm) for all routes. Instead of merit order operation it is assumed that input from each generator is its capacity scaled down by a uniform factor to make total generation equal the sum of peak demands at grid supply points. The resulting dual for each node is the marginal cost of an increase of 1MW in its net input or output. Nodes are grouped and average values calculated for each of 16 generation zones and 12 demand zones.

This simple transport model of an imaginary system ignores physical laws relating to flows in electrical networks. It neglects security considerations. It assumes that transmission reinforcement investments are not lumpy. It assumes that they involve line construction, whereas much reinforcement in practice involves the installation of quadrature boosters and reconductoring and reprofiling circuits to increase their ratings.[9] Furthermore, it does not yield results for cross-constraint boundary flows. Its one advantage is that it uses no confidential data, so that generators and large users can see how the charges are computed.

Some of these defects might be overcome by a new approach to the calculation of long-run marginal transmission costs to be charged to transmission users. These marginal costs, being forecasts, should be estimated probabilistically. The estimates could be made by examining the boundary transfers and capabilities that would occur under alternative scenarios (NGC calls them 'backgrounds') concerning generation developments and load growth and costing the necessary reinforcements for each case.[10] Thus, instead of relating to entry to and exit from the grid at peak, it would estimate costs of increased flows across zone boundaries, providing a better reflection of locational cost differences. Since such estimates would use confidential data, only the methodology could be made public, so OFGEM would have to check the acceptability of the data and assumptions employed.[11]

Short-run marginal congestion charges

Under this alternative, a charge equal to the price difference across an enduring constraint – between an import and an export-constrained zone – in each half-hour would be levied on the whole of the flow across the constraint. Each participant with a flow across the constraint would pay a transmission congestion charge equal to its allocated share of the total constrained flow multiplied by the difference between prices on either side of the constraint.

The resulting annual revenue might be of the order of £200–400m., since the cost of constraining on and off has been running at £20–40m., involving some 10 per cent of what the unconstrained cross-constraint flows would have been. This revenue could be paid to participants who owned financial transmission rights, as in PJM. If the rights were transferable, they could provide participants with hedges against zone price differences. But in the context of the New Electricity Trading Arrangements it would appear more appropriate for them to be kept by NGC. They would then replace that part of its transmission use of system charges which are currently based on 'Investment Cost Related Prices', so transmission users would pay short-run marginal costs for transmission use rather than some approximation of long-run marginal costs.

Because, with such congestion charges, tighter constraints would mean a larger revenue, this approach would appear to provide NGC with a disincentive to invest in transmission reinforcement. However, OFGEM's price control could deal with this; tighter congestion constraints would not increase NGC's total allowed revenue. NGC's price-controlled charges would be set to recover the difference between its overall revenue requirements and the congestion charge revenue.

Is such a system feasible? It would require a measure of each participant's share in each cross-constraint flow, so all notifications would have to be aggregated separately for each zone of injection and zone of delivery. It would also require a unique price in each zone to be used for calculating the differences, somehow computed from the prices of the balancing bids and offers which the system operator accepts for each zone. These zones would be delineated as zones regularly separated by transmission constraints. The half-hourly average prices for each zone would then provide a locational price pattern roughly resembling that which would result from centralized dispatch.

Differences across constraints in cash-out prices will necessarily be established, since participants will be paid for those of their offers and will pay for those of their bids which have to be accepted by NGC in order to achieve the necessary reductions in total contracted flows across the constraints. The price differences used to compute the charges would have to be computed from accepted offer and bid prices in a way which was acceptable to participants. Furthermore, the working of the charges would have to be such as to allow the development of financial instruments that facilitated hedging against any uncertainties about the incidence of charges and their magnitude.

These uncertainties would be fewer if a small number of zones were delimited for a whole year at a time than if less enduring constraints were allowed to define zones over shorter periods – albeit with an obligation upon NGC to declare them ahead of time. Even so, major difficulties would still arise in establishing the price differences used to fix the charges.

1. In each half-hour there would be *two* cash-out prices in each zone, a weighted average bid and a weighted average offer price, not a single one.
2. These locationally specific prices would not represent *marginal* bid and offer costs, being *averages* for each half-hour over all each zone's accepted bids and offers.
3. The accepted bids and offers would reflect, not only the cost of between-zone energy balancing, but also costs arising from reconfiguring plant (a) to resolve within-zone transmission constraints, (b) to provide ancillary services (for example, part-loading generation so that it can furnish frequency response), (c) to provide reserve and (d) to address within-half-hour imbalances and other short-term effects.
4. Prices would have to be imputed for half-hours when either no bids or no offers were accepted within a zone. Since imputation would be required less frequently with fewer, larger zones, there is another argument for distinguishing only a small number of zones, in consequence providing less locational detail.[12]

Because of these difficulties I am sceptical about whether locationally specific prices could be used to compute transmission congestion charges which would provide appropriate marginal cost signals and incentives. Would, for example, a simple average of the two cash-out prices within a zone provide a good approximation to what would be appropriate? Could the difference between cash-out offer prices in the import-constrained zone and cash-out bid prices in the export-constrained zone be used? (If the former are to be high enough to discourage suppliers in the import-constrained zone from planning net purchases from the balancing mechanism, while the latter are to be low enough to make it unprofitable for generators to sell through the balancing mechanism, would not the difference be excessive?) Would some average of marginal prices in each zone make sense, if it were clear how these could be defined and ascertained? (It might seem odd to use average price for imbalance cash-outs but marginal prices between zones.)

Physical transmission rights

A market solution, which is favoured by OFGEM, would avoid both the problem of estimating long-run marginal costs and the difficulty of determining appropriate price differences from accepted bids and offers.

The key to such an approach is that locational price and marginal cost differences stemming from transmission constraints create valuable transmission rights. A flow across a binding transmission constraint will be from a lower to a higher price zone and will thus provide a cost saving or a revenue to whoever has the right to transmit across that constraint. The cost saving or revenue equals the flow across the constraint multiplied by the marginal cost or price difference. If that right to transmit is a physical right, its owners can exercise that right to earn that revenue themselves. They could also sell part of the right to other participants who would then earn some of that revenue.

This alternative would allow the value of transmission rights to be established by a direct market process, not by using half-hourly offer and bid price data for each zone. Enduring transmission constraints would form the boundaries of zones, and transmission rights for flows across these boundaries would be established and allocated between participants. Temporary constraints due to generator and transmission outages would still have to be dealt with in the balancing mechanism, with their cost borne by NGC and spread out over all participants. The purpose of a system of valuable transmission rights is to allow competition to produce economic efficiency under normal enduring conditions, not to accommodate every transitory change.

In such a system, as I see it, participants would have to aggregate their reported contracts and notifications by zone of generation and of delivery instead of nationwide. Zonal cash-out prices would then be paid or received by each participant at settlement for any differences between (a) imbalances computed separately for each zone and (b) the amount of transmission rights in or out of each zone. If, to give a simple example, a generator in an upper zone contracted to sell the whole of its output to a supplier in a lower zone, it would have to own correspondingly large transmission rights both from the upper to the middle zone and from the middle to the lower zone.

The sum of the rights across each zone-defining constraint would be fixed so as to equal the capability of that constraint as determined *ex ante* by NGC. The features of such a scheme might include the following.

- The rights would be tradeable on the power exchange in the same way as energy. They would acquire a positive value for half-hours when a constraint was expected to be binding, reflecting the difference in market prices negotiated in bilateral deals: lower in the export-constrained zone than in the import-constrained zone. Markets in the different zones would thus be partially separated at times when transmission constraints were binding.

- A generator in an import-constrained zone wishing to move energy in the opposite direction (selling to a supplier in an export-constrained zone) would sell an equal and opposite incremental constrained flow right. If his reverse flow then fell short of the amount of this, he would be subject to an imbalance cash-out charge for underdelivery.

- The capability of a permanent constraint, and hence total available rights across it, would have to be revised following new investment in generation or transmission or major load developments.

- Errors in determining the rights would be dealt with through the balancing mechanism.

- Initially, rights could either be sold by auction or they could be grandfathered to existing market participants. Since the rights would provide a hedge against zonal price differentials, grandfathering would have the advantage of indemnifying the losers from the introduction of zonal pricing.

- Transmission reinforcement investments, adding to the volume of rights, would be paid for by those participants acquiring the additional rights.[13] Thus the investments would have to be agreed by negotiations between participants and NGC. Investment paid for by participants would, of course, not add to NGC's regulatory capital value and so would not increase its allowed revenue.

There would be a problem of dominant market participants securing excessive profits in import-constrained zones by strategic behaviour, but that problem is not unique to this approach. With it a dominant generator on the import side of a constraint could obtain high prices in bilateral agreements; in its absence he would quote high prices to the balancing mechanism for increments.

There is a danger that this system could allow dominance in transmission rights as well. Thus a dominant owner with generation in an import zone might be tempted to restrict import in order to raise the prices at which he could sell energy there, or a dominant owner might wish to keep some of his transmission rights unused in order to raise the value of the rest. But if transmission rights owners were obliged to offer the rights they were not planning to use on the power exchange, and if none of them were to acquire rights in excess of a prescribed fraction of the total, a sharp-eyed regulator should be in a position to rule out anti-competitive practices.

Defining the zones

Both of the last two approaches that I have considered require the division of England and Wales into zones bounded by transmission constraints. Such zones are in fact delimited daily by NGC. An example, showing 11 system boundaries for a certain set of assumed peak demand conditions, is provided in Figure A7 of NGC's *1999 Seven Year Statement.*

The trouble is that transmission constraints and hence the number of zones and their boundaries vary through time because of loop flow.[14] It is a fundamental physical fact that, in a meshed system, the flows along any transmission line at any time depend upon all flows in the system at that time. Thus transmission capability between any two zones is *not* just a function of the engineering rating of the lines interconnecting them.

It is true that, given locationally specific initial physical notifications received by NGC on the preceding day, a load flow analysis could allow zonal boundaries to be announced a day or two in advance (as happens in Norway). However, this would not do. Both with financial and with physical transmission rights it would be necessary to define them firmly for a much longer period. This means that either scheme would have to be limited to *enduring* transmission constraints, that is, those not caused by transmission and generation outages and which are binding over sufficiently many half-hours in the year to make the idea of established transmission rights worth bothering about.

Three zones could perhaps be delineated without difficulty, bounded by North to Midlands and Midlands to South boundaries. The transfer capability across even these boundaries can vary according to the pattern of generation and loads within these zones, not to mention planned transmission maintenance, so it is not certain that they could be defined and quantified so as to establish three sets of acceptable transmission rights.

A more detailed delineation of zones might prove even more difficult. Their boundaries would presumably have to be such that only one or a single set of boundaries separated any two zones. If flows between two zones could pass through alternative boundaries, the loop flow phenomenon would make any firm advance determination of their capabilities impossible. A relevant load flow analysis could not be conducted until after the locational pattern of loads and generation had been notified, a day or some hours before gate closure.

Furthermore, boundaries could not cross any grid supply point group zones, since settlement entails aggregation of all offtakes within them for suppliers of non-half-hourly metered consumers. Hence, if the introduction of transmission rights were feasible, it could only provide a very broad-brush treatment of locational differences.

CONCLUSIONS

I have approached these problems from a belief that reflection in prices of constraints and locational differences in marginal losses is desirable. NGC use of system charges which do not reflect marginal costs should thus be minimized, subject to NGC recovering its allowed revenue.

My only firm conclusion is that finding the best way to do this under the New Electricity Trading Arrangements will be very difficult! My other main conclusions are more tentative. They can be summarized as follows.

1. **Consistency with the RETA approach.** The most market-oriented approaches would be (a) for participants to own, and trade in, physical transmission rights and (b) to contract to provide their own (marginal) losses. The feasibility of determining *ex ante* marginal loss factors for the latter purpose is accepted.
2. **Long-run marginal costs.** NGC's 'Investment Cost Related Prices', used to determine its transmission use of system charges, could perhaps be replaced by proper long-run marginal cost estimates, though these would relate to cross-constraint flows rather than to peak grid entry and exit flows.
3. **Establishment of zones.** It is uncertain whether enough constraint-delimited zones could be defined with their boundary capabilities sufficiently firmly quantified for physical transmission rights both to be tradeable and to produce the desirable degree of locational market price differences. The same uncertainty would aflict the delimitation of zones necessary to introduce the alternative of short-run congestion charges.
4. **Locational prices.** (a) For NGC to base a MWh component of use of system charges on locationally differentiated marginal loss factors would require the invention of some acceptable way either of estimating single *ex ante* half-hourly prices or of computing them *ex post*. (b) Single half-hourly prices would also be required, zone by zone, for charging short-run marginal congestion costs. It is not clear how they could best be related to the two cash-out prices.

Summary of Alternatives

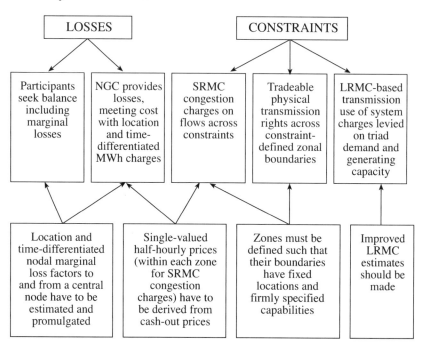

Figure 4.1

NOTES

1. Frequency control, reserve generation, reactive energy, black start capability.
2. They may be accepted out of price order because of differences in dynamic characteristics of gensets. It will not be possible to attribute individual bid and offer acceptances to constraint alleviation, balancing or other reasons.
3. NGC has expressed serious reservations about determining cash-out prices as weighted averages of accepted bids and offers. It has put forward some alternative proposals. If these are accepted, and if they were applied on a zonal basis, they might form a better basis both for settling for imbalances and for dealing with marginal losses and with transmission congestion.
4. Although average losses at time of peak are only about 2.5 per cent, marginal losses can be large. 100MW of new generation in the north would meet only 94MW of national demand averaged over the system at time of winter peak; 100MW of new generation in the south coast would meet 105MW. See NGC, *1999 Seven Year Statement*, Table 6.4.
5. SuperGoal adds losses to demands.
6. With participants providing their own marginal losses, NGC would, other things being equal, accept enough bids to reduce generation and/or increase consumption by the excess of marginal over average losses, thus obtaining revenue.
7. The list of contingencies considered depends upon forecast weather conditions.
8. Capability is defined as the power flow that can be transferred without infringing limits on

system voltage level, without voltage collapse and without overloading any of the circuits that would remain following credible circuit outages. This thermal limit is usually less than the sum of the ratings of the remaining circuits, since one of them usually reaches its rating limit before the others. Ratings vary seasonally.

9. For further discussion, see Ralph Turvey and Brian Cory (1997), 'Inefficiencies in electricity pricing in England and Wales', *Utilities Policy*, 6(4), 283–292.

10. Probabilistic winter peak transfers across the 11 system boundaries separating the 16 generation use of system tariff zones have in fact been estimated and are presented in outline in Chapter 7 of NGC's *1999 Seven Year Statement*, where future reinforcements not yet planned which would prove necessary under some of the scenarios are listed in Table B8.

11. Generators and large consumers might object to this confidentiality, but would have to lump it – they are not in the habit of making public their own projections and cost estimates!

12. It has been suggested that, in the absence of a cash-out price and, therefore, in the probable absence of a constraint on one boundary, the cash-out price could be imputed as the cash-out price across that boundary.

13. They would also have to buy rights across any other constraints which would be tightened or created elsewhere as a result of the reinforcement.

14. Its consequences have been stressed, for example, in an important series of papers by Professor Bill Hogan: ksgwww.harvard.edu./people/whogan

CHAIRMAN'S COMMENTS

Eileen Marshall

Introduction

I would like to start my comments by thanking Ralph for a very constructive and timely contribution to the debate about future electricity trading arrangements.

Trading Arrangements include Energy Balancing and Transmission Issues

Ralph quite rightly points out that in network industries such as electricity it is important to consider in any review of trading arrangements both the arrangements for energy balancing, that is, the efficient balancing of overall supply and demand in real time; and the arrangements for transmission access and pricing, taking into account electrical losses and the likelihood of capacity constraints at different places on the network and at different times.

When we started a review of gas trading arrangements in spring 1997, we began with the gas balancing regime and then turned our attention to the network capacity regime. The new gas balancing system and the first phase of the new capacity regime were introduced on 1 October 1999. Further changes are to come.

Similarly, the review of electricity trading arrangements, which began in autumn 1997, has concentrated first on the energy balancing arrangements, which need to accompany the greater contractual freedom which is at the heart of the proposed pool reforms. But now we are addressing, too, the transmission issues, a move that just about all respondents to our recent proposals document supported.

NETA Governance

Many of the points raised by Ralph in his paper have been recognized for some time, but it has proved difficult to obtain change. It is important to emphasize that the new electricity trading arrangements that we expect to be introduced in autumn 2000 will mark an important development. But it is not a once-and-for-all change. The arrangements will continue to develop thereafter. One of the important features of NETA is governance reform, to facilitate subsequent modification. Post-NETA, further development should be easier.

Overall Efficiency Issues

Ralph is right to emphasize not only the importance of transmission arrangements, but also the requirement to promote overall efficiency, including giving appropriate signals to the location of generation. He is also correct in emphasizing the importance of establishing incentives that link short-term and longer-term decisions, including the interactions between trading arrangements and the price controls.

All of these are being actively addressed by OFGEM in electricity as in gas, although, as I mentioned earlier, the process in electricity is currently lagging behind gas reforms which are dealing with similar issues.

OFGEM also recognizes the opportunities for exploitation of market power arising from transmission constraints. We believe that the new Competition Act and the proposed new market abuse licence condition for generators will help considerably here.

Transmission Losses

On transmission losses, Ralph argues for greater cost reflectivity. We agree. The questions are when, how and to what degree?

Ralph notes that zonal or nodal charging of loss factors can be reduced to charges to and charges from some central node or zone. This is very much in line with present OFGEM thinking. We see energy trading taking place at some central balancing point (or central hub) – in gas the National Balancing Point (NBP) and the transmission regime dealing with locational adjustments around that central energy market.

Ralph points out that if NGC, as system operator, purchases losses and charges them out on a marginal basis, there will be a significant revenue yield to NGC. If this method of dealing with losses was implemented, the surplus revenue could help to reduce the other system-related shared charges. However, Ralph also considers the possibility of requiring participants to contract to provide their own losses. This is very much in line with NETA principles and is certainly something that needs to be considered further.

Transmission Constraints

In considering the treatment of transmission constraints, Ralph sets out three possible approaches: (a) approximation to long-run marginal cost, (b) short-run marginal cost, or (c) creation of physical transmission rights and charging users costs for adding to them. This last approach, though not identical, is closest to OFGEM thinking and consistent with the new arrangements in gas.

However, Ralph says that firm capacity rights would need to be defined well in advance, and that therefore the scheme would have to be linked to enduring constraints, providing thereby only a very broad-brush treatment of locational differences. 'Transitory' constraints would then presumably still be resolved by the buying and selling of electricity at different locations via the balancing mechanism. We think it is possible to be more ambitious by defining capacity rights with different durations and characteristics. Some of the rights can be defined and sold well in advance. Others could be created and sold much closer to real time (for example, a day ahead).

The quantity and definition of rights can therefore be varied to reflect short-term constraints, around a 'base' of long-term rights. The new entry capacity regime in gas has primary capacity auctions being supplemented by Transco selling extra capacity very short term or buying back capacity which it has sold firm and cannot deliver. The accompanying incentive scheme helps to ensure that Transco maximizes the amount of physical capacity available on the day.

I think a somewhat similar regime could be developed for electricity. This would build on Ralph's concept of simple firm long-term rights covering enduring constraints, but develop it more fully.

Conclusion

In sum, then, I find Ralph's paper timely and thought-provoking, both in terms of its general concepts and in relation to the detail. It will be very interesting to know what the rest of the audience thinks.

5. The future of European communications regulation: an assessment of the European Commission's 1999 communications review

Martin Cave and Luigi Prosperetti[1]

INTRODUCTION

In November 1999, the European Commission published its *1999 Communications Review* (EC, 1999a), proposing a legislative framework to come into effect from 2003. The review comes 15 years after the first step forward in liberalization in the field of equipment and ten after the first concerning services. It is published amid growing concerns in the USA about the effectiveness of the new policy framework set up there by the 1996 Telecommunications Act. It thus has the benefit of perspective in time and space. It was released by a newly formed Commission, and thus provides a good occasion to set forth a strong policy statement.

Because the review proposes a legislative framework which will not take effect until 2003, it has to adopt a medium-to-long-term perspective, a hard task in an industry as dynamic as telecommunications. One of its major challenges is to combine a vision of the future with some policy specifics. As we argue below, it has not yet wholly succeeded in this respect.

The review sets out three major policy objectives: to promote an open and competitive European market for communications services and equipment; to benefit the European citizen; and to consolidate the internal market in a converging environment. It is hard to disagree with these general aims. The problem is what consequences to draw from them.

In our view, in order to benefit the European citizen, Europe needs to make up quickly its gap in Internet penetration and e-commerce development *vis-à-vis* the USA. In order to do that, an open and competitive European communication market is essential, but this cannot be fostered without solving the institutional shortcomings which have marred several areas of EU policy throughout the 1990s, and have repeatedly given rise to enforcement problems.

Consolidation of the internal market is increasingly entailing cross-border mergers and acquisitions. In this regard, we should not forget that two major telecom carriers (and many major broadcasters) are still publicly owned in Europe. We thus regard an increasing reliance upon competition law (both within member states and on the part of the Commission) as an essential step to achieve the policy objectives set out in the review. This point is made in the review, but its implications are not drawn out as clearly as they should be. The review also promises some welcome adjustments to the existing framework, together with some measures that, although mentioned in a subdued tone, are likely to have a major impact.

The paper is organized as follows. The next two sections give an account, respectively, of the current regulatory framework and of the review's proposals, some of which are examined in more detail in the fourth section. The fifth and sixth sections are devoted to institutional change and issues of enforcement, while the seventh section concludes.

THE STRATEGY OF DEREGULATION AND LIBERALIZATION OF TELECOMMUNICATIONS[2]

The background against which the review has been conducted is one in which the 15 member states have liberalized entry into telecommunications at different dates and in which existing European legislation has been implemented in a rather patchy way. While the UK and some of the Nordic countries liberalized fully in the early 1990s, a large tranche of countries followed suit in early 1998, while three countries still have to liberalize. There have been persistent delays in the transposition of EU directives into national legislation, and national regulatory agencies have addressed the task of allowing competition to flourish with different degrees of speed and rigour. The five pillars of the liberalized regime are as follows.

Licensing

There should be no limitations on operators' ability to enter infrastructure or service markets, save where there are inevitable limitations based upon, for example, spectrum scarcity. The key elements necessary to the successful attainment of this objective are the speed with which licence applications are processed, the criteria applied and the cost of the licence. One of the allegations levied against some national regulatory authorities (NRAs) is that they require unnecessary quantities of information of a technical and financial kind: this has the effect of making the licensing process needlessly expensive and protracted. There are also clear advantages to be had in one-stop shopping for licences in the EU.

Interconnection

The terms on which entrants interconnect with the incumbent's network are fundamentally important to the success of their business plans. The language of 'cost orientation' in the Interconnection Directive leaves NRAs with considerable discretion in setting charges. The facility (until 2000) of incorporating an access deficit contribution also acted as a hindrance to entrants where it was applied. Although long-run incremental cost has been widely accepted as a suitable basis for setting interconnection charges, lack of the relevant cost data has hampered the process of providing proper price signals for firms making make-or-buy decisions. The Commission has attempted to make up this deficiency by the use of benchmarks designed to bring interconnection rates throughout the EU down to the levels prevailing in the countries with the lowest rates.

We also note below the related issue of local loop unbundling, which is a form of access not covered by the Interconnection Directive.

Retail Price Control

Regulating retail prices has been relegated to a secondary position in member states where effective wholesale markets have permitted high levels of retail competition. Unbalanced tariffs remain, however, a major obstacle to the development of competition in all market segments.

Universal Service Obligations

The regime here has been relatively successful. NRAs have generally taken consistent decisions in setting the level of the obligation and have adopted, where the task has been undertaken, a consistent methodology for estimating their costs. Universal service funds have been set up in only two member states. In the remainder, the burden rests with the incumbent operator, or is borne by that operator's profitable customers.

Control of Anti-competitive Prices

Entrants remain vulnerable to conduct by the incumbent which undermines their ability to win business in the markets which they are attacking. In addition to setting excessive interconnection charges, incumbents can pursue pricing and related strategies which have the effect of eliminating or weakening competition. These cover the range of potentially anti-competitive pricing available to a dominant firm, including predation, price squeezes, bundling practices and a variety of forms of price discrimination. This conduct creates difficult problems for NRAs, since practices typically have to be examined on a case-by-case basis in the light of the overall level of competition existing in each market.

All these regulatory instruments are needed in the course of the transition from a telecommunications monopoly to a more competitive situation. Existing EU legislation creates a broadly satisfactory framework for doing so. The crucial questions are: does the regime work in practice, and what more is needed from the review?

A BRIEF SUMMARY OF THE REVIEW

The review is a complex document, in which broad policy statements are intertwined with technical discussion. We provide here a summary of the major points from a broad perspective which stresses strategy rather than detail.

The review starts out by stating that the existing legislative framework was originally designed to create a competitive market. A new framework is now needed to manage new, dynamic markets, where competition is growing. Hence *ex ante* regulation of dominant market players should continue, but be progressively reduced as competition develops. New markets should be subject to a light regulatory touch.

The new regulatory framework should be built upon five principles: regulation should be based upon clearly defined policy objectives, should be kept to a minimum to achieve those objectives and should enhance legal certainty. It should also aim towards technical neutrality and – once put in place at the global, European or national level – be enforced at the lowest possible level, in obedience to the principle of subsidiarity.

The new proposals will be enshrined in a framework directive, and will be enacted through a broad set of instruments, including directives on licensing, access and interconnection, universal service and privacy and data protection, but relying more than in the past upon 'soft' regulatory means, such as recommendations, guidelines and so on. This framework directive will look much like a European Telecommunications Act. It will specify policy objectives to be pursued by each member country using its methods of choice, and consolidate the powers and responsibility of the NRAs, including possibilities for judicial review and obligations to avoid arrangements that are contrary to Community competition law. Specific legislation should introduce 'sunset clauses' to NRA-introduced obligations, as objectives are gradually met. NRAs should be prevented from placing new obligations on market players.

Greater reliance than in the past will be placed upon the competition rules of the Treaty of Amsterdam. The Commission will increase its surveillance of the communication sector, although, before taking action, it will consider whether NRAs have powers to deal with the matter effectively. The review stresses that such a difficulty may arise with reference to 'cross-border elements'. NRAs should, however, always rule in accordance with EC competition law. If they do not, governments will be liable to pay damages under article 86 of the Treaty.

The review proceeds to mention a number of specific issues, where new directions are outlined and consultation is sought. In the field of *access*, it is proposed to employ general, rather than specific, authorizations, both for telecommunications and for broadcasting, reserving specific authorization to cases where scarce resources (for example, spectrum) are to be allocated. Authorizations should be tradeable. A transition to Europe-wide licences is envisaged. The fact that the allocation of rights of way in member states is chiefly in the hands of local authorities, which may have an interest in restraining entry, is mentioned, although no specific remedy is discussed.

Some interesting innovations are outlined with reference to *interconnection*. The Commission shows an increasing inclination towards mandating local loop unbundling (LLU), though with the usual disclaimer that it should not create disincentives to investment.

The Commission is aware of the fact that the *rebalancing of tariffs* is at best incomplete in several countries, but does not address the prospect that unbalanced tariffs may encourage inefficient entry in the long-distance market. A stronger emphasis upon rebalancing, with abatement of monthly rentals for particular groups in the interest of universal service, is a better solution.

Leased lines seem largely to escape the Commission's attention, but this may actually be a false impression. The ineffectiveness of the directives relating to them seems implicitly to be recognized, but much hope is pinned upon a subsequent recommendation, which we discuss below.

The Commission plans to do little about the way the member countries allocate *spectrum*: 'beauty contests' and auctions are likely to coexist for a while. Significantly, secondary trading of spectrum should be explored with a view to making it legal (an overdue reform) but not mandatory.

The definition of the scope of *universal service* (US) at the EU level is discussed (see below). The financing of US obligations has so far turned out not to be too problematic. Only two countries have created a US fund. It may, however, become a more general problem in the future, as the market share of the incumbent falls below a certain threshold, and will be kept under review. The Commission recommends consideration of 'pay or play' schemes.

All in all, the *Internet* is to remain free from regulatory intervention. Providers will not need authorizations. If and when voice-over Internet services will qualify as voice telephony services, they will require a general authorization.

The review contains a wealth of other specific issues, some of which (such as numbering) will not be discussed here, while others are considered further below.

PARTICULAR ISSUES

Controlling Market Power

One of the novel but questionable features of the current regime is its use of the concept of 'significant market power' (SMP). If an operator is considered to be in such a position, it is subject to a number of duties, ranging from obligations to supply to cost-based pricing.

A telecommunications operator is deemed to possess SMP if its market share on a relevant market is above 25 per cent. Market share is strictly neither a necessary nor a sufficient condition, as national regulatory authorities can issue or withhold the SMP designation below or above the 25 per cent threshold, taking into account an operator's 'ability to influence market conditions, its turnover relative to the size of the market, its control of the means of access to end-users, its access to final resources and its experience in providing products and services in the market' (EC, 1997, article 4.3).

The SMP label implies different obligations in the four relevant markets identified by the directive: Public Switched Telephone Network (PSTN) services, leased lines services, mobile services supplied to consumers, and the national market for interconnection. For PSTN and leased lines services, the SMP provision is of limited relevance, as they are subject to a number of obligations with respect to access, non-discrimination, cost orientation and accounting separation, which derive from other articles of the directive.

Mobile service operators are also subject to obligations in the area of access and non-discrimination in the sale of final services to consumers, quite independently of their market power, by other articles of the directive. The SMP designation does, however, restrict an operator's ability to design bespoke packages for large customers.

Both fixed-line and mobile operators operate in the 'national market for interconnection'. Again, the incumbent fixed-line operators are subject to the full set of obligations (including cost orientation of interconnection charges) by other provisions of the directive. Cost orientation for mobile operators providing interconnection, however, is not provided for elsewhere in the directive: this is where the real 'bite' of SMP as a regulatory concept lies.

As these are all relevant questions, *to be solved in each member country by the relevant NRA*, one cannot avoid the suspicion that the 'domestic interconnection market' has been intentionally defined in a hazy way, so as to give NRAs substantial leeway in the use of SMP labels for mobile operators. So far, Finland, Sweden, Austria, France and Italy have chosen to apply the SMP label to their incumbent mobile operators (EC, 2000). The UK, after an extensive Monopolies and Merger Commission investigation, decided to go for immediate price cuts plus price-cap regulation under its domestic telecommunications legislation. (OFTEL was also able to determine that BT Cellnet and Vodafone have 'market influence' under a condition of their UK licences, and this finding triggers certain obligations: OFTEL, 2000.) The issue is under review in several other member countries, but there are no signs of a widespread application: *none* of the very large national operators in France, Germany or Italy has so far been labelled as having a SMP in the 'domestic market for interconnection': they therefore enjoy rather profitable termination charges.

The SMP case is an interesting instance of a short cut providing the NRAs with a potentially lethal device, leading to the discovery that nobody really wants to use it. As elsewhere, reliance upon the national level in telecom regulation is a source of asymmetries within the European market.

What the review does is keep the notion of SMP, but in a different form. It proposes that the traditional competition notion of dominance – the ability to act independently of one's customers or competitors – should be the trigger for more rigorous obligations, such a cost orientation and non-discrimination. At the same time, SMP should cut adrift from the four relevant markets previously stipulated. Instead, the standard method of defining markets adopted for competition purposes in the EU and other jurisdictions would replace it. A finding of significant market power by the NRA would entail an obligation to negotiate with firms requesting access to the network and an obligation to be transparent. One implication of the new arrangements is that the finding of SMP for mobile operators would have much less impact on them, assuming they were not in a dominant position, because they would not in future be subject to the requirement not to discriminate.

The inevitable question this new approach raises is whether the concept of SMP has outlived its usefulness. When it was introduced, it was widely regarded as a blunt instrument principally designed to restrict the power of dominant incumbents, probably to be in place for a limited time period. This view was consistent with the prior specification of 'relevant markets'. The abandonment of this method of market definition in favour of a more standard approach, which can accommodate technological change, suggests that SMP is intended to be a more durable feature of this regulatory scene. The best case for it can probably be made in terms of one or both of the following arguments. The communications sector is characterized by a large number of gateways or bottlenecks, which accord their owners a degree of temporary market power which can be used to the considerable disadvantage of consumers; giving the NRA an *ex ante* regulatory instrument in the form of the restrictions associated with the finding of SMP can alleviate this problem. Alternatively (or additionally), communication markets might be widely characterized by abuses of joint dominance, because barriers to entry associated with economies of scale or regulatory constraints (such as a limited availability of the spectrum) will not constrain. On balance, we find neither of these arguments wholly persuasive and have significant doubts about whether SMP is necessary or useful, except in particular contexts.

Universal Service

One of the worries about the review was that, in a fit of enthusiasm for new technology, the Commission might recommend an extension of Universal Service Obligations to include broadband access. This would have serious adverse effects on competition. The logic underlying the USO is that the majority cross-subsidize a fairly small minority, within the context of the funding regime which is transparent and competitively neutral. However, if the proportions are amended, even to the extent that a majority have to cross-subsidize a sizeable minority, then any funding regime is likely to be tested to destruction. The principal victims of this process would be entrants, whose financial position is inevitably more precarious than that of the historic operator. This is recognized in the proposition that, before being assimilated into a USO, a service's spontaneous take-up rate should be very high, say 70–80 per cent.

Discussion of the USO issue within the Commission must have been fairly intense. The signs are, however, that there is no intention to do anything more with the scope of universal service than to keep it under review. A radical extension would not only imperil competition but also redistribute income regressively, as new services would take time to 'cascade down' the income distribution.

A further issue addressed in the review is that of affordability, which currently is not defined in quantitative terms at EU level. We would regard the definition as falling within the scope of member states, and hence wonder how the Commission will in practice be able to achieve its proposed objective of setting out clear pricing principles at a European level.

Access and Interconnection

The communications sector is distinguished by the numerous highly complex ways in which firms need access to one another's facilities in order to provide services. The traditional issue of interconnection terms and conditions (for example, call termination) has given way to the much broader issue of access. The list of actual and potential areas for dispute over access given in the review comprises the following:

- access for new entrants to the local loop of incumbent network operators (local loop unbundling);
- access to mobile network infrastructures;
- access to intelligent network functionality of fixed and mobile networks;
- access to broadband networks;
- access to submarine cables;
- access to satellite systems;
- access for content providers to cable TV networks or satellite systems;
- access for Internet service providers to cable TV networks;
- access to set-top box facilities, notably conditional access systems, application programme interfaces (APIs) and electronic programme guides (EPGs);
- access to broadcasters' networks for interactive applications.

In most of these cases the seeker after access wants to achieve a direct relationship with the access provider's customers. This is inevitably more adversarial than the use by operators of one another's networks to complete call delivery, which characterizes traditional interconnection of telecommunications systems.

The review proposes to embody in framework legislation a set of principles for dealing with access, rather than issue a set of specific measures relating to particular cases. One approach would be simply to rely upon competition law. In each case the regulator or competition authority would have to consider whether the conditions for the European equivalent of the essential facilities doctrine apply. In many cases, as a result of convergence, there is a technological substitute for the asset in question. The key issue for the regulator or court to resolve thus becomes whether the alternative is commercially rather than technically feasible. Timing is crucial in almost all cases, particularly in relation to local infrastructure. If the notion of a time-limited essential facility had adequate support, reliance on competition law would be a more reliable option. Given the lack of cases in European courts, and the delays involved in developing precedents, there may well be a case for adopting a regulatory approach *pro tempore*, in parallel with the competition law approach. (It is noteworthy that some regulators have already adopted this time-dependent tactic in relation to local loop unbundling. A good example is provided by the regime introduced by OPTA, the Dutch regulator, for setting prices for the unbundled local loop which rise over time.)

Particular difficulties arise where the access involves a proprietary standard, as exemplified by the set-top box. In several member states, regulatory authorities have intervened to ensure interoperability of equipment. For example, the Italian Parliament has passed legislation which requires that digital programmes with conditional access must be receivable on a single apparatus. It is an open question whether competition law, despite its flexibility, is speedy enough to deal with such cases.

What general principles might govern a regulatory access framework? The Commission's preferred approach is to rely as far as possible upon commercial negotiations. Access providers with significant market power would have an obligation to negotiate (see Table 5.1). Finally, the regulator could be called in *in extremis* by either party. The degree of regulatory intervention should be inversely proportionate to the level of competition.

The key point is, of course, that negotiations take place in the shadow of some expectation of how the regulator or competition authority will act. In the case of call termination, which is regarded at the local level as a durable bottleneck, the review favours a long-run average incremental cost (LRAIC) pricing basis, proxied in the interim by benchmarking.

Table 5.1   Treatment of market power

	Dominant position	Significant market power	Other
Nature of obligation	Provide interconnection and access	Negotiate interconnection and access	Negotiate interconnection
Pricing	Cost orientation	Commercial negotiation	Commercial negotiation
NRA role	*Ex ante* price regulation	Reserve power to intervene	Dispute resolution

Source: EC (1999a, p.29).

This leaves open the question of markets which might be viewed as potentially competitive, such as call origination. The Commission's thinking here seems to be that some kind of 'retail minus' pricing rule would be appropriate, to the extent that – in the manner of the efficient component pricing rule – it would encourage efficient 'make or buy' decisions, given any imbalance in the tariff. The outcome thus depends upon how competition is assessed, which itself hinges upon market definition. But whereas a variety of alternatives may exist for originating a voice call, Internet access in many member states may only be available via the historic operator. Consigning this to a retail minus rule would have adverse effects.

This discussion makes it clear that the Commission has no magic bullet for slaying the access pricing devils. Correctly, it recommends a case-by-case approach. Wrongly (in our view), it invokes the SMP notion for the apparently limited purpose of imposing an obligation to negotiate. Inevitably, it puts the whole issue back to NRAs of varying levels of competence and different degrees of enthusiasm for competition.

INSTITUTIONS

The legal notion of subsidiarity sits at the core of the European regulatory problem. The concept can be stated very simply and traced back to a rule expounded by mediaeval philosophers (Occam's razor): let an issue be dealt with at the lowest possible level within an organization. Obviously, within the context of a Union of 15 countries (and expanding), subsidiarity is a very complex issue, and may lend itself to instrumental use to protect national vested interests.

The text of the Treaty of Amsterdam, however, is clear, and should limit any instrumental use of the concept: article 3B states that 'the Community shall take action, in accordance with the principle of subsidiarity, only if and insofar as the objectives of the proposed actions cannot be sufficiently achieved by the member states and can therefore, by reason of the scale or effects of the proposed action, be better achieved by the Community'.

The article can be given a straightforward economic interpretation,[3] by stating two necessary conditions for Community action in areas that do not fall in its exclusive competence: (a) the existence of scale effects in some areas, creating a situation in which the individual action by a member state would be inadequate, in that it would entail excessive costs or provide reduced benefits; and (b) the existence of relevant effects that go beyond the frontier of that particular country and affect other member countries or the Union as a whole.

In the case of telecommunications, point (a) probably applies in many cases. Instances where point (b) could be very relevant abound in the information industries. Nonetheless, subsidiarity has been very often invoked whenever the Commission has tried to take away regulatory powers from member countries. Hence neither (a) nor (b) was deemed to entail relevant effects: this is the basic reason why NRAs have far greater powers than any European-level body in telecom regulation.

Could this be changed by the creation of a European-level regulatory authority (ERA)? This is a recurring theme in the European debate. It officially surfaced for the first time in the early 1990s, as concern was growing among operators and Brussels officials about the slowness with which member countries were implementing the first Open Network Provision (ONP) Directives. The Commission concluded that any such body would require an amendment to the European Treaty (a very cumbersome process, involving not only approval by national governments, but, in several countries, even a referendum).

The issue is now surfacing again, where it is argued that heterogeneous local rules favour local incumbents and slow the pace of liberalization; deregulation is easier if regulation is centralized; moreover, Internet growth is making the very concept of 'local' obsolete. While it is easy to agree with this analysis, it should be pointed out that institutional considerations are of paramount importance here: unless an ERA could take substantial powers away from the NRAs (and this may not happen unless the European Treaty is modified), the regulatory framework in Europe could actually become more complex, with a growing risk of conflict among different bodies.

If an effective ERA cannot be envisaged in practice, one could take a Darwinistic stance, by stating that competition in the telecommunications market takes place among firms *and* among regulatory systems. This is, however, hardly an option for a European would-be Union, fragmented in 15 different countries: we believe that an increased reliance upon competition law could provide a solution to the European regulatory problem.

Unsurprisingly, the Commission has avoided proposals for a major centralization, which are unlikely to command support among the member states. It proposes instead the creation of a High Level Communications Group (HLCG) composed of the Commission and NRAs, to succeed the current High Level Regulators Group. This group would work with European-level bodies such as standards organizations and industry representative groups. It would concentrate on 'assisting the Commission in maximising uniform application of national measures adopted under the regulatory framework laid down in community legislation' (EC, 1999, p.52). This would include the following:

- agreeing NRA positions on the detailed application of legislation, thus facilitating pan-European services;

- assisting in the development of EU guidelines on market definitions with respect to obligations relating to connection and access;
- endorsing codes of practice associated with community legislation;
- resolving cross-border disputes between consumers and operators;
- identifying the need for Commission measures, such as recommendations or decisions, to address specific issues.

There would in addition be a Communications Committee (COCOM), which would replace the ONP and licensing committees and advise the Commission on draft measures. In addition, COCOM would vote on draft measures of a binding nature relating to infrastructure and associated services.

This sounds much like business as usual. Relations between NRAs and the Commission are almost bound to contain an element of conflict. In some cases, the Commission is spurring on reluctant NRAs to make a reality of liberalization. Others are more inclined to regard the Commission as being, in some respects at least, an interfering nuisance. The latter kind of tension is probably both inevitable and healthy.

ENFORCEMENT

Unfortunately, it is by no means clear that these developments are capable of improving the appalling record of some member states in implementing directives. The 'Services' directive was implemented years late in Spain, Italy, Denmark and the Netherlands, and the European Court of Justice has recently issued rulings against a number of countries including Greece for their failure to implement the 1992 ONP Directive on Leased Lines.

Indeed, leased lines are a flagrant demonstration of the problems of enforcement. There are specific directives covering them, which have liberalized their provision since July 1996, and imposed an obligation to supply at cost-oriented prices upon SMP operators (that is, all European incumbents). It is remarkable that these pieces of 'hard' legislation have been flatly ignored by most member countries. As recently pointed out by the Commission, the average rental cost of a 300km, 2Mbit/s circuit within an EU country was at end-1998 about four times its US equivalent; this price difference went up to 15 times when EU cross-border circuits were considered. On 64kbit/s lines, at the end of 1999, prices in France and the UK were more than twice as high as in Germany, and three times as high as in Italy. On higher capacity lines, price dispersion was smaller within the Union, but comparisons with the USA are still highly unfavour-able.

The impact on European competitiveness of such large price differentials hardly needs to be stressed in the Internet age: short-distance leased lines represent a relevant bottleneck for the supply of cheap connectivity and data services. Nonetheless, NRAs, which under the Interconnection Directive had an obligation to intervene, have turned a blind eye on the whole issue until very recently, and so has the Commission.

In such a disheartening landscape, the *1999 Review* takes the view that some further benchmarking should solve the problem, and in a recommendation (EC, 1999b) published immediately after the review, it follows the path already taken with regard to interconnection prices: charges are examined across EU member states, and the three lowest are taken to calculate a 'price ceiling' (the Commission is too embarrassed to call this average a 'best practice' price). NRAs are recommended (this is a recommendation, after all) to require full justification from incumbents if current charges exceed the calculated ceiling.

Such an approach can obviously be questioned upon general grounds, as the resulting ceiling is an average of what are almost certainly excessive prices (though less excessive than elsewhere). It is of course true that the recommendation is carefully crafted, so that such a short-cut is presented as a temporary device, to be employed only until cost data for an efficient operator will be gathered. This task may, however, take some time – if the recommendation is followed by NRAs – leased lines prices will be regulated for quite a while with reference to the price ceiling set by the Commission. It is an open question whether such regulatory decisions could be successfully challenged in court.

Secondly, there must be doubt about the effectiveness of a 'soft' measure (a recommendation) where 'hard' law (a directive) has failed. True, such an expedient device has already worked once with interconnection charges, and competition among NRAs has made the higher rates drop. There are signs, however, of a regression towards the mean of charges set on the basis of a benchmark. While it is impossible not to sympathize with the Commission's enforcement problems, their solution may lie in a different direction.

A regulatory system is only as effective as it is enforceable, and a blind faith in the willingness of member states to fulfil their duties under the Treaty of Amsterdam is at worst misplaced, and at best optimistic. The compliance mechanisms at Community level are weak: a fine can only be imposed by the European Court of Justice after the Commission has brought infringement proceedings against the offending country twice, and this takes years. Aggrieved 'entrants' may be able to rely on non-implemented directives against operators where the operator is classified as an 'emanation of the state', although damages are not necessarily available where these are not recognized under national law. Finally, the possibility for operators to obtain damages from a member state through its failure to respect its treaty obligations does exist, but the conditions under which this may be possible are unclear, and require clarification from the European Court of Justice. Unless a way forward can be found here, the objectives set out in the review may only be achieved patchily.

AN OVERALL EVALUATION

On balance, we do not think that the review goes far enough as far as access is concerned. We also think that the remedies it proposes do not make full use of the powers available to the Commission under competition law.

A coherent access policy should seek to accelerate broadband development across Europe. Current trends here are positive, but slow: new entrants deploy high-capacity connections to large customers, but small and medium-sized firms are not being connected fast enough. The Commission seems to be more preoccupied with opening existing infrastructures than encouraging the construction of new ones. Thus entry is vigorous, but prices are not dropping as fast as they could. Local loop unbundling (LLU) will accelerate present trends, but will hardly bring about a fast upgrading of existing capacity.

The provision of incentives to build new infrastructures is far more important outside than inside the UK, given the clear choice in favour of a facilities-based competition exercised there at the beginning of the 1990s. Generally speaking, the EU regulatory framework does not promote this option. Would a pervasive LLU approach provide the necessary incentives in Europe for massive broadband investment, both by the incumbents and by the newcomers? It might not do so if it is perceived by all sides as a permanent feature, and cable TV operators see the ghost of LLU in their futures. In that case, we could end up having modern networks for large firms and old networks (with some xDSL patches) for the other users. This is no way to compete in the information society.

A related issue concerns rate rebalancing. As we know, this has been at best an uneven process across Europe. By and large, though, the rate structure is still quite far from the cost structure. Line rentals are too cheap, while long distance is too expensive. New entrants get access to incumbents' networks at cost-related interconnection charges, and then exploit arbitrage opportunities between those charges and the unbalanced long-distance tariffs. This is all right as an asymmetrical, pro-entry provision, but it cannot go on for long, as it gives incorrect investment incentives to all relevant parties.

These issues are not tackled at all in the review, but in our view, no coherent European policy for the information society can be developed without a clear long-term option which favours the construction of new, broadband networks. Mandatory LLU might be implemented in some countries in a way which hindered investment and technological upgrading.

Quite apart from such general issues, the remedies envisaged by the Commission to deal with the already existing access issues seem to rely too much upon a regulatory framework which has clearly shown several shortcomings, and too little upon a full deployment of its powers under competition law: this is all the more surprising to us, as a major step in this direction has actually already been taken by the Commission, in the Access Notice published by the Competition Directorate at the beginning of 1998. This Notice set out a very relevant principle: the market for telecommunications is, in general, the Union as a whole. Hence Commission antitrust powers should fully apply to what had hitherto been considered as purely national markets.

Until 1998, the Competition Directorate's activities in telecommunications had concentrated upon the vetting of agreements, joint ventures and mergers under articles 81 and 82 of the EC Treaty. Only one case – in 1997, against Deutsche Telekom – was concerned with the abuse of dominant position. Under (new) article 86, very few cases were reported to the Commission, mainly based on discriminatory actions by the administration of a member country against new entrants. In two cases, a formal action was taken against the government; in others corrective measures were proposed by the member states to remedy the distortions.

With the beginning of 'full competition' in Europe, and the liberalization of alternative infrastructures from 1998, the Competition Directorate has stepped up its action on telecommunications issues. It has started monitoring implementation of liberalization and harmonization directives, as well as issuing policy notices on topics related to telecommunications (access, voice-over Internet, separation of cable and telecommunications activities). On the basis of such monitoring, the Commission has opened several infringement proceedings against member states who failed to comply adequately with the directives. It conducted a survey in 1998 on the fixed-to-mobile termination charges, pushing operators and NRAs to act on the matter. It has recently begun a similar enquiry in the cost of leased lines.

The most far-reaching action by the Directorate, however, was the release, in March 1998, of its 'Notice on the application of the competition rules to access agreements in the telecommunications sector'. The definition of 'access' chosen is very broad, and it includes, not only interconnection, but access to any facility necessary to provide service to end-users. Thus the Commission's powers of intervention in *purely national* access and abuse of dominance issues are clearly established for the first time in this notice: articles 81 and 82 can be directly applied even if the companies involved operate within the same member country.

Although the Commission is politically correct about subsidiarity, stating in the notice that ONP-related procedures (basically the NRAs) should resolve access problems in the first place at a decentralized, national level, with a further possibility of a proceeding at Community level in certain circumstances, it also makes it clear that the NRAs must ensure that actions taken by them are consistent with EC competition law.

If the application of the principles set forth in the notice are consistent, and they stand up in court, and also if the Directorate has enough staff to handle a growing telecommunications-related workload, the construction of a 'coherent legal and regulatory framework for the Information Society in Europe' – a primary goal set forth by the Bangemann Report in 1994, but always found to be elusive – would take a decisive step forward.

This combination of national application of limited *ex ante* regulatory rules, with an *ex post* vetting based upon the application of *European* competition law within *national* markets, would also provide a flexible framework for the very large number of issues that the development of broadband, multi-media services and convergence will generate in the near future.

Thus a stronger reliance upon the Commission's competition powers *within* national communication markets seems a very good thing. This view is not fully shared by the review, which pays some lip service to 'a broader reliance upon competition law', but actually, as noted above, foresees a more complex and interactive regulatory structure which, arguably, would give NRAs more weight in Brussels.

In summary, achievement of a competitive communications market involves a delicate combination of telecommunications and competition law. The opposite dangers are of excessively intrusive (or, alternatively, ineffective) regulation through the former, and belated *ex post* intervention via the latter. Like us, the review is looking for a trajectory somewhere in the middle, with some flexibility to take account of variable progress in the member states. Our inclination is to place more reliance than does the review on competition law.

NOTES

1. The authors are grateful for help and advice to Michaela Cimatoribus and Cinzia della Torre.
2. The focus of this section is on telecommunications rather than the broader topic of convergence which the review addresses.
3. For a fuller discussion, see Cave and Crowther (1996).

REFERENCES

Cave, M. and P. Crowther (1996), 'Determining the level of regulation in EU telecommunications; a preliminary assessment', *Telecommunications Policy*, 20(10), 725–38.

EC (1997), 'Directive 97/33/EC of 30 June 1997 on Interconnection in Telecommunications with regard to ensuring universal service and interoperability through application of the principles of ONP'.

EC (1999a), 'Towards a New Framework for Electronic Communications Infrastructure and Associated Services', *The 1999 Communications Review*.

EC (1999b), 'Leased Line Interconnection Pricing', *Commission Recommendation on Leased Line Interconnection Pricing in a Liberalised Telecommunications Market*.

EC (2000), 'Notification of organisations with significant market power', 1 January, available at: http://www.ispo.cec.be/.

OFTEL (2000), 'Draft decision and statement on the Director General's intention to determine that Vodafone and BT Cellnet have Market Influence in Condition 56 of their respective licences'.

CHAIRMAN'S COMMENTS
David Edmonds

Martin, thank you for your thoughtful and provocative lecture which gives me a degree of satisfaction, as OFTEL has been heavily involved in leading a working group of European regulators which has been feeding its views into the Directorate-General Information Society. My fellow regulators agreed in London at a meeting last year that OFTEL would lead a working group where we would try and enunciate principles for regulators to feed directly into the EU. I hope that, through the interventions that we in OFTEL make, and through the regulators' group, we have been influential in developing some of the principles that you said have been incorporated. I do not think the paper as drafted gives the UK too many problems because I think it is consistent with the way in which we have been operating and the way in which we are going to operate. I think the approach of a better focused regulation to meet the needs of a changing market is absolutely right.

I would like to comment on a couple of things. I am not sure, but did you use the word 'consumer' at all in your presentation this evening? My role is to be changed to give me a primary duty to protect the consumer. There is significant underemphasis on the role of the consumer as the proper object of regulation in the draft as currently emerging.

You did talk about access to networks, which is important, and I think access to third parties will continue to be crucial. There probably needs to be greater emphasis on how bottleneck control is actually implemented and its regulatory implications. I think the split of responsibility between national regulators is something to do with that. Quite often the need to balance the short-term interest of consumers through regulation, and in the long term through emerging competition, does get overlooked, and again I think the document could say more about that.

Martin talked about universal service. I do not know how many of this audience have either read or heard the remarkable lecture that Peter Mandelson gave to a European group not long before he came back to government. There are a couple of really thoughtful pages about the whole issue of social exclusion where he talked about the kids in the tower blocks in his constituency having been further socially excluded, and I paraphrase, because of the impossibility of their being able to afford, in those kinds of homes, access to broadband going beyond cheap or ordinary Internet access. I genuinely believe that, in the UK in 18 months to two years' time, for everybody in this audience, there will be an affordable link to the home either through ADSL or through a cable modem. I am prepared to bet that most of us can afford it. I think Peter Mandelson has raised, very interestingly, the implications for the UK of extending universal access to broadband. This is touched on in the document, as Martin says, but not discussed.

Maybe it is too early to have the debate. I happen to think that over the next three years, as broadband connectivity does come on-stream, a major issue of public policy will be who pays if it is to be extended to those unable to afford it. The universal fund has not been necessary across Europe, but it could be if the obligation is extended to broadband, because the sums would be so enormous. There are major issues there, which I think the review has ducked.

I think the endorsement of the national regulatory agency as the best mechanism for regulation is again quite interesting. It does not fully take on the board what the national regulatory authority should cover. I suspect in the UK we now have only a relatively short time left, perhaps, three or four years, to continue with the split regulation we have at the moment. I think that convergence between telecoms and broadcasting is becoming a reality and means that regulation of these sectors split between two or three different agencies is outmoded. I think that reform is needed and once the government is very clear about what its own objectives are, it is very likely to look more seriously at that reform than it has done hitherto. We might be looking at a step change rather than gradual change, though not in this Parliament. That has implications for the kind of committee structure that is being proposed in the EU draft review. We already have the group of national telecoms regulators which comprises 16 or 17 countries and which meets every six months. We also meet from time to time with the European Commission at the high-level regulators' group. The last meeting of that was in Helsinki, the week before last. They are very interesting occasions. I vividly remember that, during one of them, when I was talking about the Independent Regulators' Group, I tried to make a joke which was translated into four different languages, to the effect that the Independent Regulators' Group is, in effect, a cartel of regulators. Afterwards a gentleman from the Competition Directorate came up and said, 'If you have evidence of a cartel, you must give it to me!'

So, the possibility of these committees taking a more central role in EU regulation is interesting. I think it will be useful. The Regulators' Group is starting to get its act together and formalization of the process is important.

The final remarks I would like to make are about your questions as to whether in the UK we do move to a situation whereby we focus on competition law. OFTEL is going to produce in the next three or four weeks, for the first time in its existence, a clear strategic statement as to how we believe we should regulate and what we believe we should be regulating. You will see in that document an absolutely clear commitment on our part that we are going to move to the greater reliance on competition law and less reliance on sectoral regulation and the use of licence conditions. Hopefully, it will lead to fundamental reviews of licences consistent with what is being proposed in

Europe. We can promote more competition through the use of licence conditions where that is necessary, but we are fully aware that regulation is not costless and we think that competition, where feasible, is the best protector of the interest of the consumer. That does mean better-informed consumers, so back to my remark about consumers.

Last Thursday night at the Café Royal I was giving an after-dinner speech, on mobile telephony. I took as my theme the shambles there was last Christmas when 1.75 million pre-paid phones were sold in three months. At Christmas 1999, apparently 3.5 million mobile phones are going to be sold in two months. I thought I made a fairly innocent series of remarks, such as that I have written to the chief executives of the four mobile companies asking them to make sure (a) that they have enough people to man the telephone lines, (b) that people could top up their cards, (c) that the phones worked in the first place, and (d) could they please ensure that OFTEL was not swamped with complaints, as it was last year. I quoted Hans Snook, the chief executive of one of the mobile companies, saying, broadly, that consumers were being ripped off and misled by the industry because of the lack of adequate pricing information. And I said it was the role of the regulator as we moved into this new area of reliance on competition to ensure that the consumer was protected: what we call 'competition plus' in our strategy. The 'plus' bit means helping the consumer in a rather proactive way to have sufficient information to make an adequate choice. A large section of the audience from the mobile companies booed and shouted. So, clearly, we still have some persuading to do.

So Competition Act instead of existing legislation, yes, and more reliance on the Competition Act, certainly. Finally, I would like to say again that we have nothing to fear from the European review, certainly as it now stands. I think we have influenced it reasonably significantly. I think the consultation period will be an important part of policy development because other governments may take a different view from the Commission. It is very important for the industry to come back because the EU does listen very hard to the industry as well as to regulators and academics.

6. Railway franchising: is it sufficient? On-rail competition in the privatized passenger rail industry

Ian Jones[1]

INTRODUCTION

This paper examines the role of on-rail competition in the provision of passenger rail services, an important area of unfinished business in the development of public policy towards the privatized and restructured railway industry in the UK. The uncertainties surrounding the issue were first highlighted by the delay on the part of the rail regulator in implementing stage 2 of the 'Moderation of Competition' regime, a key element of the policy framework. Originally scheduled to occur in March 1999, it was subsequently delayed until September 1999 by the previous regulator, John Swift, QC; the new regulator, Tom Winsor, has not so far pronounced on the matter. Further development of policy must now await the outcome of the recently announced decision to renegotiate passenger rail franchises.

The background to the discussion is the increasingly persuasive evidence, briefly reviewed in the next section, that significant parts of the passenger railway face a more prosperous future than seemed likely even when the Railways Act 1993 was passed. Continuing pressure on the public finances might dictate that any continuing improvement in financial performance beyond the end of the current generation of franchises would flow mainly into further reductions in the overall level of external support to the passenger railway. Under this scenario, surpluses earned from the profitable core will be used to cross-subsidize the 'social railway', operating mainly on former regional railways parts of the network. However, transport policy considerations, emphasizing the need for efficient use of the rail infrastructure and for encouraging the transfer of traffic from an increasingly congested road system, may dictate that some or even the majority of potential monopoly rents are 'returned' to consumers.

One way of doing this would be to retain or possibly strengthen existing restrictions on on-rail competition but to alter the basis of franchise bidding.

Instead of franchises being awarded to the bidder offering the maximum financial return, subject to constraints on prices and outputs, a Chadwick auction approach could be used. The franchising agency[2] would declare *ex ante* the level of 'rent' it sought for a franchise and the franchise would be awarded to the bidder offering the lowest level of fares or the 'best' combination of fares and service levels. Recent pronouncements from the franchising authority appear to envisage a process of renegotiating franchises around deals that utilize a less steeply declining subsidy bill to 'purchase' commitments from franchisees to fund increased investment in rolling stock and infrastructure (the latter via increased track access payments to Railtrack).

A quite different approach would be to relax or even remove current restraints on on-rail competition over the more profitable parts of the network, enabling actual competition or the threat of it to reduce franchisee profitability directly and secure benefits for consumers in the form of lower fares or increased levels of service.

The paper traces the development of policy towards on-rail competition to date and attempts to throw some light on how policy should develop in future by examining evidence on market outcomes since privatization.

THE PASSENGER RAIL SECTOR: CURRENT PERFORMANCE AND PROSPECTS

In the corresponding lecture in last year's series,[3] Stephen Glaister made some tentative projections of the long-run market prospects for the passenger rail industry, based on an analysis of Family Expenditure Survey (FES) data on current patterns of rail use by household composition, combined with long-term projections of changes in household composition. His analysis indicated that, given current expenditure propensities, the effects of an increased number of households would be substantially offset by an increase in the proportion of households in categories who (currently) make relatively little use of rail, such as pensioner households. Glaister went on to suggest that, while growth in real incomes would generate increased demand for rail travel (an elasticity of demand with respect to GDP of 0.7 was estimated over a very long run of data), other factors, such as an increasing proportion of households living in lower density locations, and continuing increases in the relative price of rail travel, would tend to depress demand growth. Putting some numbers to these effects to assist comparison with other forecasts, we can say that, if rail fares remained constant in real terms, and GDP grew at 2.5 per cent per annum on average, demand for rail travel might increase by a little over 1 per cent per annum, implying a growth in traffic of around a quarter over a 15-year period.

Although derived quite differently, such a projection would be consistent with the picture of market prospects indicated by industry planning documents originally developed by British Rail business planners, but still widely used in the privatized train operating companies (TOCs).[4] These suggest that demand, especially on London-based InterCity routes, is highly sensitive to variations in GDP. However, this effect coexists with a negative time trend, which varies inversely in magnitude with the size of the GDP elasticity (Table 6.1).

The inclusion of both a positive GDP parameter and a negative time trend was intended to capture the effects of increasing economic activity in stimulating demand for all types of transport, but also in causing growth in car ownership, which reduces the demand for public transport.

Table 6.1   Passenger Demand Forecasting Handbook (PDFH) recommended parameter values

	GDP elasticity	Time trend (% per year)
London-based InterCity	1.5	−2.5
Non-London interurban	1.5	−2.0
Non-London urban, commuting	0.5	−1.0
Non-London urban, non-commuting	1.0	−1.5
South east London-based, commuting*	0.5	−
South east London-based, non-commuting	1.0-1.5	−2.0
South east non-London-based	1.0-1.5	−2.0

Note: * The PDFH states that forecasts of central London employment (rather than GDP) should be used. The GDP elasticity shown may be used, however, for sensitivity testing.

Given constant real fares and a growth of 2.5 per cent per annum in GDP, the combined effect of the GDP and time trend parameters is to predict a growth of a little over 1 per cent per annum in former InterCity markets. A broadly similar result is obtained for other service groupings.

The PDFH parameters are mainly based on research into the demand for rail travel undertaken in the 1980s. Econometric analyses of the market for passenger rail services carried out in the past year to two years suggest that the net effect of growth in economic activity on the demand for rail travel may have become significantly more favourable in the 1990s than in the two previous decades, especially in markets served by former InterCity services. Using data on ticket sales and revenue drawn from the same database accessed in earlier research, both AEA Technology and NERA have each concluded that there is no longer evidence of a negative time trend operating independently of a positive economic activity effect. The results of the more recent studies suggest that the demand on London-based InterCity routes might increase by 50–70 per cent over a 15-year period (equivalent to a 2.5 to

3.6 per cent annual growth) if real fares remained unchanged. This markedly more bullish picture of market prospects is echoed in recent remarks by well-informed industry sources.

Factors exogenous to the rail industry which help to explain the change in outlook are (a) a slowdown in the growth of private car ownership, (b) a significant real increase in fuel costs for motorists, and (c) a deterioration in the quality of service on some parts of the road network. Table 6.2 shows the key data on private car stock, real petrol prices and traffic for the years 1980, 1990 and either 1997 or 1998.

Table 6.2   Annual percentage changes in car stock, petrol prices and traffic, 1980-97/8

	Car stock (private cars)	Real petrol prices		Vehicle kilometres in private cars and taxis
		4-star	Unleaded	
1980–90	+2.96	–1.16	NA	+5.5
1990–97/8	+1.53	+2.94	+2.58	+1.3

Note: Data are taken from Transport Statistics, 1999.

This picture emerging from Table 6.2 is one of quite radical change between the 1980s and the 1990s in the market environment for rail services:

- although car ownership has continued to grow, the rate of growth has slowed very markedly;
- real petrol prices, which declined steadily in the 1980s, have increased at rather more than 2.5 per cent annually in the 1990s, as a result of the petrol duty escalator, introduced by the previous Conservative Government and retained by the present administration;
- although the level of private vehicle traffic continues to increase, the rate of increase has slowed markedly.

An important final part of the jigsaw, which may contribute to the slowdown in traffic growth recorded in Table 6.2, is the quality of service on the road network. Unfortunately, there appear to be no directly relevant official published data that would throw light on this factor, apart from data on traffic speeds in the Greater London area, which are regularly monitored. However, the behaviour of the Automobile Association's so-called 'Gridlock Index', which records the frequency and extent of major traffic incidents, whatever the cause, may offer some clues to the effects in recent years of heavier traffic volumes on a road network where cuts in public investment in

Regulating utilities

roads have slowed the growth of capacity. As shown in Figure 6.1, the index has shown a steady upward trend since it was first produced in 1996.

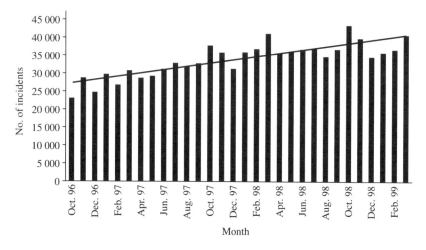

Figure 6.1   Number of incidents per month

Commenting on his tentative projections, Stephen Glaister rightly emphasized the limited degree of interdependence between the demand for private car and rail use, so that rail can never offer a realistic alternative for the great majority of trips by car. However, because the volume of travel by private car is so very much greater than by rail (approximately 15 times), it is equally true that only a relatively small diversion of demand from road to rail might result in a quite disproportionate increase in demand for rail.

We conclude that, even if the recent rapid growth in traffic and revenue experienced on substantial parts of the rail network moderates somewhat in the longer term,[5] future policy on the development of the passenger railway will need to address the issues arising from an increasingly prosperous industry. Determining the role of on-rail competition as an instrument for transferring the benefits of increased prosperity to users is one such issue.

THE EVOLUTION OF POLICY TOWARDS ON-RAIL COMPETITION

Background

A recent paper by Welsby and Nichols (1999) provides an authoritative account of the early stages of public policy development in relation to railway restructuring and privatization. The authors make clear that, while the July 1992 White Paper (Department of Transport, 1992) setting out the government's strategic vision of the restructured industry anticipated the transfer of passenger train operations to the private sector through a franchising process, there was no detail on how precisely franchising would operate, or whether the new structure could accommodate competition in as well as for the market. The subsequent Railways Bill, introduced shortly after the White Paper, indicated that franchised passenger operators would compete with open-access operators on the basis of non-discriminatory track access charges set by a publicly owned infrastructure manager. The industry regulator was given a duty to promote such competition.

Further important details on the *modus operandi* of the new industry structure were added in February 1993, with the publication of the government's proposals for the track access regime (Department of Transport, 1993). These confirmed that the infrastructure would be operated by a public sector agency, Railtrack, which would allocate access to the network on a non-discriminatory basis, as required by European legislation. However, the government's proposals went far beyond the relatively limited scope of access liberalization contained in EC Directive 91/440, whose provisions were restricted to access rights for international services. Two types of access agreements for passenger services were envisaged:

- franchised passenger services access agreements, for packages of train paths defined by the franchising director, who would negotiate a package price directly with Railtrack to be reflected in the franchise bids. The franchisee would subsequently enter a track access agreement with Railtrack covering the provision by Railtrack of the train paths in return for payment of track access fees by the franchisee;
- open-access agreements. Although open-access competition would need to be moderated to the extent necessary to ensure the successful launch of the first generation franchises, 'subject to these constraints and the oversight of the regulator', operators of non-franchised services would be able to negotiate terms with Railtrack for 'open-access' train paths. Open-access charges would generally cover avoidable costs; any contributions to common costs would reflect ability to pay.

The statement marked the first official recognition of the inherent tension between the objectives of encouraging on-rail competition and containing or reducing public subsidy to passenger rail operations. Subsequent developments in public policy, which we now trace, have sought to reduce the tension primarily by limiting the scope both for new entry and for price competition.

Restricting Entry

Following the passage of the Railways Act in 1993, responsibility for moderating new entrant competition passed to the rail regulator, through the criteria applied by the regulator in approving track access contracts. A series of consultative documents and policy statements on the issue have appeared, beginning with a consultation paper published in July 1994 (Office of the Rail Regulator, 1994a) and a policy statement published the following December (Office of the Rail Regulator, 1994b).

The need to restrict entry
Taking the approach to the track access regime set out in the government's proposals as its starting point, the July 1994 consultative document noted that a regime of negotiated charges for open-access operations would encourage the more efficient use of the network and maximize financial contributions to fixed and common infrastructure costs, 'both highly desirable objectives'. However, the approach 'sat uneasily' with the franchising process, and with the regulator's duty to take account of the franchise director's financial position in approving track access contracts.

Stronger competition from open-access operators would, it was argued, produce uncertainty among potential bidders for franchises, especially with the industry still at an early stage of a process of fundamental restructuring, making it difficult to predict the extent of unrestricted competition. Also, given the highly peaked nature of demand, all types of passenger operations on the busier sections of the network are characterized by widely differing levels of contribution (over short-run variable costs of train operation and track wear and tear) to fixed and common costs. Under such conditions, incumbents would be vulnerable to 'cherry-picking' competition from new entrants, restricting incumbents' ability to cross-subsidize between commercial and social services. Both factors meant that the external subsidy bill would tend to increase the fewer were the restrictions on open-access competition.

The regulator concluded that, given the potential for increased competition on routes where there were overlapping franchises, and the uncertainty of the effects of unrestricted competition, it was necessary for competition between passenger train operators to be substantially restricted. Nevertheless, on-rail competition, or the threat of it, would create beneficial pressures on train operators both to reduce their costs and to become more innovative. Any protection from competition for incumbents should therefore be the minimum required to enable franchises to be sold successfully, and should be time-limited, with provision for increasing exposure to competition over the lifetime of the initial franchises.

These early statements of regulatory policy may have reflected a concern that the threat of new entry would constrain incumbents' incentives to restrict output (by reducing train miles) to improve profitability. Although it was recognized that each franchisee would be required to offer a contractually guaranteed minimum level of service, known as the Passenger Service Requirement (PSR), in return for public subsidy support, it was perhaps unclear precisely how far below existing output levels the PSR would lie.

In his December 1995 statement on the criteria and procedures to be used in approving moderation of competition proposals (Office of the Rail Regulator, 1995), the regulator described PSRs as a 'key element of the policy context' for moderating competition, representing an important mechanism for protecting consumers' interests in the absence of on-rail competition. In retrospect, it appears that this recognition marked the beginning of the subsequent shift in regulatory policy which we discuss below (see 'Recent Policy Development').

Mechanisms for moderating competition
The regulator examined two possible pricing mechanisms for moderating competition: equalized access charging and access deficit charging. Under equalized access charging, track access charges for both franchised and open-access operators would be set equal to Railtrack's average total costs. However, given the structure of rail infrastructure costs, the resulting charges would greatly exceed short- or long-run marginal costs, pricing off open-access traffic which would have contributed to fixed and common costs. At the same time, such a regime would offer little protection to franchised operators on busier parts of the network against cherry-picking entry, based on limited service provision during peak periods, when average net revenues per train were far higher than average infrastructure costs.[6]

The rationale for an access deficit charges approach is that, in the absence of open-access competition, the total subsidy to the rail network may be contained through internal cross-subsidy within a monopoly service provider. By reducing the capacity for internal cross-subsidy, open-access competition, or the threat of it, would therefore tend to increase the total subsidy requirement. An access deficit charging mechanism, possibly based on licence condition 19 of the British Telecom (BT) licence, would contain the risk to the subsidy budget by requiring open-access operators to compensate the franchisee for the reduced capacity for cross-subsidy resulting from competition.

This approach would clearly discourage the efficient use of the network by open-access operators, by pricing off some services where incremental revenues exceeded incremental costs. It would also encounter what the regulator described as 'severe problems of practicability', in measuring the incidence and extent of cross-subsidy in rail markets and quantifying the effects of possible open-access services on incumbent revenues.

Not surprisingly, both pricing options were rejected by the regulator, in favour of an administered approach, under which new entry would be restricted through contractual control over Railtrack's ability to sell access rights additional to the rights contained in the franchise track access agreements. It was envisaged that the regime for mandatory competition would be applied in two stages.

During stage 1, covering the early post-franchise period to March 1999, competitive entry on any substantial flow, generally defined as a point-to-point flow generating 0.2 per cent or more of franchisee revenue, could occur only with the approval of the franchisee. All such nominated flows would normally be approved by the regulator and included in a schedule to the franchisee's track access agreement with Railtrack. The regulator would also consider requests for nominations of additional flows not served by an existing franchisee if competitive services on the flow threatened the franchisee's core markets. On the other hand, so-called 'through flows', where an operator did not provide a direct service between two stations comprising the flow, would normally be open to competition, in order to encourage the provision of direct services, where such services had not previously been provided.

After March 1999, it was expected that there would be some relaxation in the restrictions on developing competitive services both for open-access operators and for existing franchisees outside their franchise service areas. Incumbent franchisees would nominate flows, again subject to the same materiality constraint applied in stage 1, but competition would be permitted to develop up to a threshold (usually 20 per cent) of the revenue arising from the set of nominated flows. Any flows not nominated would be open to competition. This approach would, the regulator hoped, encourage operators 'to make realistic nominations of contestable markets. If they nominate too few, they risk leaving potentially profitable markets exposed with no protection. If they nominate too many, they will have a larger contestable revenue pool which would allow more genuinely contestable markets to be opened to competition before the threshold is triggered'.[7]

As informed commentators have noted (O'Donnell, 1997) this framework offers the potential for strategic game playing by incumbents, the preferred strategy with respect to flow nomination depending on the characteristics of the markets served by the franchisee, and the extent of existing competition with overlapping franchises.

According to the December 1994 policy statement, the second stage of the moderation of competition regime would terminate automatically on 31 March 2002, following a regulatory review of on-rail competition in 2001, to be held in parallel with the review of access charges. However, the statement indicated that any changes in the regime following the review were unlikely to be radical in nature.

Restricting Price Competition

The potential for price competition in situations where franchise territories overlap is significantly curtailed by the provisions of the Ticketing and Settlement Agreement (TSA), one of several arrangements with other TOCs and third parties in which passenger franchisees are obliged to participate as a condition of their licences (Office of Passenger Rail Franchising, 1996).

The TSA covers fares setting, fares distribution, ticket interavailability and related matters. It is intended both to generate commercial benefits to operators by enabling them to offer network-wide products (such as student railcards) and to preserve 'network benefits' for consumers, such as the use of tickets on more than one operator's services, even if the facility may not be commercially attractive.

The TSA conditions most directly inhibiting price competition cover the provision on multi-operator flows of interavailable fares and operators' ability to create dedicated (that is, non-interavailable) fare types. The constraints differ as between lead operators, normally the franchisee with the largest share of fare revenue on the flow, and other operators. *Lead operators* set the price of a fully interavailable fare for use on any train serving the flow. The lead operator may also propose more restricted interavailable fares, such as off-peak or saver tickets, but these can only be made interavailable with the agreement of other operators. Unlike similar agreements in the deregulated bus industry, the relevant terms of the TSA have been exempted from legislation on anti-competitive practices. Lead operators' rights to create dedicated fare types are circumscribed to prevent the interavailable fare being marginalized through the creation of close substitute dedicated products. The lead operator is therefore only able to create certain narrowly defined types of dedicated fare, such as first class fares or advance purchase train specific tickets. *Non-lead operators* are obliged to accept interavailable fares, but may create their own competitive dedicated fares.

The constraints on the lead operator clearly restrict the possibility of price competition. However, it can be argued that they are, on balance, pro-competitive, by protecting minority operators and entrants from the kind of vigorous incumbent responses observed in other deregulated transport markets.

The franchising director may lift the interavailability restriction on certain flows if he considers that the benefits of interavailability will be outweighed by the potential benefits of price competition and service diversity if the requirement is lifted. To date, however, compulsory interavailability has only been lifted on certain flows on services operating between London and Gatwick airport, where Gatwick Express, Connex South Central and Thameslink operate a wide range of services in close competition.

Recent Policy Development

Restricting entry

Consistent with the timetable for moving from the first to the second stage of the moderation of competition regime set out in the December 1994 policy statement, the rail regulator issued a consultative document in September 1997 (Office of the Rail Regulator, 1997a) reviewing options for the develop-ment of on-rail competition. This was duly followed by a policy statement in March 1998 (Office of the Rail Regulator, 1998a), confirming the regulator's intention to implement stage 2 of moderation of competition in September 1999, rather than in April 1999, as originally planned.

Both documents emphasized the importance of encouraging both cooperation and competition to promote the use of the network for the greatest benefit of passengers. This aim was also stressed in a statement on regulatory objectives for passenger and station operators published in June 1997 (Office of the Rail Regulator, 1997b).

As well as the potentially adverse effects on the future level of subsidy to the passenger rail industry identified in earlier documents, the regulator's recent pronouncements have identified other possible public interest detriments from more extensive on-rail competition.

- Despite capacity constraints in some parts of the network, relaxing restrictions on market entry might lead to 'rail wars' similar to those observed in the bus industry, and characterized by predatory service timetabling or erosion of network benefits. Competitive outcomes of this kind appeared to generate little benefit to consumers. Any relaxation of entry restrictions would therefore be contingent on sponsors of new services being able to demonstrate clear consumer benefits.
- Increased on-rail competition could result in the more widespread marketing of dedicated tickets, and the resulting increase in the costs and complexity of ticket retailing could discourage demand. Other network benefits might also be at risk of more widespread use of dedicated tickets. For example, an incumbent franchisee would have less of an incentive to assist a competitor selling dedicated tickets and whose service failed, although it was accepted that this problem might be addressed through appropriate contractual mechanisms.
- Some franchisees also argued that a lead operator could be disadvantaged when competing against new services by the TSA constraints on introduction of dedicated tickets, and that PSR conditions might restrict incumbents' ability to adjust output in response to new entry (although the relative fixity of incumbent output could itself act as a deterrent to entry by reducing the possibility of accommodation).

Despite these possible detriments, the regulator concluded that, on balance, there was a case for relaxing the blanket restrictions on entry introduced to facilitate franchising, in order to encourage the development of potentially beneficial new services. Because the granting of any new access rights was subject to regulatory approval, the regulator expressed confidence that the introduction of additional on-rail competition could be managed so as to ensure that the cost to the subsidy budget was tightly contained.

However, this would require a mechanism for evaluating new service proposals case-by-case to ensure that they generated real consumer benefits and were not primarily abstractive. To this end, it was envisaged that the regulator would apply a social cost–benefit framework, similar to that promulgated by the franchising authority (Office of Passenger Rail Franchising, 1997) to evaluate new service proposals (Office of the Rail Regulator, 1998b). The evaluation process would also involve consultations with local authorities and other parties. Finally, the regulator argued that, although the incentives for anti-competitive conduct and erosion of network benefits would certainly be stronger the fewer were the constraints on market entry, such actions would be efficiently inhibited by the combination of licence conditions and competition legislation.

These recent pronouncements mark a clear shift in the stance of regulatory policy towards on-rail competition. In the earlier statements there is a presumption that open-access competition was a desirable long-term policy objective, to be moderated only as a temporary measure to ensure the success of franchising. By contrast, the 1998 policy statement puts the onus on potential new entrants to demonstrate that the services will be in the interests of passengers and taxpayers, and there is a far stronger recognition of the potential detriments of competition. A similar shift is evident in recent government policy statements, such as the response (Department of Environment, Transport and the Regions (DETR), 1998a) to a Parliamentary Select Committee report on railway regulation.

The government's response also indicated that it would bring forward legislation to establish a Strategic Rail Authority (SRA) to replace the Office of Passenger Rail Franchising and take over the residual duties of the British Railways Board. The authority would be responsible for the strategic development of the rail network, including freight operations, and would set the longer-term policy framework for on-rail competition, ensuring continuing safeguards against erosion of a properly integrated rail network. The legislation would also alter the regulator's duties, so that he would be required to promote competition only where there was benefit to passengers. The regulator would be required to take account both of the SRA's policy aims and of its assessment of the overall benefits of individual service proposals in implementing the moderation of competition policy.

Price competition

Tighter constraints on fare setting by passenger franchisees were anticipated in a transport policy White Paper published in July 1998 (Department of Environment, Transport and the Regions, 1998b). The White Paper claimed that the privatized passenger rail industry had failed to develop 'a clear, understandable national fare structure. Although train operators have introduced some new and innovative fares, this had led to a multiplicity of different and rapidly changing fares for similar services with, in some cases, complex and varied conditions, for example, in relation to advanced booking'. Such an outcome, of course, parallels developments in the liberalized intra-European air transport market, in which context increased product differentiation would generally be regarded as benign. It has also been accompanied by the exceptional growth in traffic noted in the second section of this paper, although the White Paper understandably did not draw attention to this.

The White Paper went on to suggest that, 'when opportunities arise for renegotiating the franchises, the SRA, guided by Ministers, will ensure that arrangements are made so that train operators structure and market their fares to offer value for money for their customers and to reflect the fact that the railway is a national network which needs to be marketed accordingly and in a way which encourages people to switch from car to train'.

The new policy stance thus emphasizes intermodal competition rather than on-rail competition, and anticipates a more interventionist role in fare selling for the SRA (and ministers).

Renegotiating franchises

Recent government policy on the passenger railway has sought to respond to sharply differing market stimuli. On the one hand, there is continuing public disquiet at the service quality performance of many franchisees (and Railtrack) and the apparently modest financial penalties incurred through poor performance. On the other, demand for rail travel and real revenues from passenger operations continue to grow strongly. The prospect of continuing strong growth in demand in turn raises the issue of whether the current industry structure offers appropriate incentives to invest to meet future growth in demand.

An initiative launched by the then Minister for Transport, Dr John Reid, at the so-called 'Railway Summit' held in February 1999, addressed both concerns. Dr Reid announced that the SRA would welcome proposals for extending a limited number of the initial franchise contracts to secure benefits for consumers, franchisees and the government. In return for longer franchises, he suggested that franchisees would be willing to accept more demanding contractual terms on service quality performance, and to offer enhanced programmes of investment in rolling stock.

The scope of this initiative has subsequently been greatly extended in pronouncements by the chairman of the shadow SRA, Sir Alistair Morton. Sir Alistair has indicated that his authority will seek to renegotiate all of the initial franchises, with priority given to renegotiation of franchises with less than five years to run. The new franchise contracts would be of 10–20 years' duration, in order to create strong franchise units with incentives to develop new services and to commit to greater investment in rolling stock and infrastructure. Indeed, the new initiative is, in Sir Alistair's words, all about 'investment, investment, investment'.

Although neither Dr Reid nor Sir Alistair Morton's statements allude to on-rail competition, it can be plausibly argued that they represent a further step away from the vision of open-access competition espoused by the previous administration. Protection for consumers against abuse of the market power enjoyed by incumbent franchisees is to be secured primarily by tightening franchise contracts, rather than through actual or potential on-rail competition. Even more important, the very strong emphasis on investment in the recent statements tends to march with a preference for 'orderly markets', and greater exclusivity, rather than the rough and tumble of more extensive and vigorous on-rail competition.

ON-RAIL COMPETITION AND ITS EFFECTS

Competitive Entry

The track access agreements between the franchised TOCs and Railtrack negotiated and approved under the first stage of the 'Moderation of Competition' regime precluded competitive entry on over 4000 point-to-point flows. The policy had the intended effect of leaving little scope for developing new services, other than those planned by BR's business units prior to privatization, for which provision was made in the relevant track access agreements inherited by franchisees, and which were therefore anticipated in the franchise bids. Apart from new services of this kind, a very small number of new competitive services have been developed by operators combining existing track access rights to run extended through services. Because of the very small revenue potential there has been virtually no entry on non-nominated flows.

As anticipated, far fewer flows, around 2900, have been nominated and approved under the second phase of moderation of competition. Early indications are that the new regime would enable more 'innovatory' services to be offered, such as Anglia's proposed Ipswich–Basingstoke service. Anglia has also sought informal guidance from the regulator on opening a

Waterloo–Southampton service in direct competition with South West Trains (SWT), one of the franchisees least exposed to on-rail competition. SWT, in turn, has responded to this threat by seeking, and obtaining, additional access rights to run more frequent services to Southampton and Portsmouth from Waterloo.

Whether or not the second stage of moderation of competition is implemented, a major section of the network will be exempt from its provisions as a result of the regulator's approving new track access arrangements for the upgraded West Coast Main Line. Under the so-called PUG2 agreement with Railtrack, Virgin Trains has gained rights to operate faster and more frequent services when the upgrading is completed early in the new millennium, and will be protected from new entrant competition on core London flows until 2012. The agreement also provides for revenue sharing between Virgin and Railtrack.

The Effects of On-rail Competition in Theory[8]

With new entrant competition curtailed by the restrictions on new entry, competitive provision of rail services has been largely confined to situations where franchise territories overlap.

Although a glance at the franchise map suggests rather widespread overlap of territories, in reality, the scope for on-rail competition in the privatized passenger rail industry has been restricted by the characteristics of the existing British Rail profit centres used as the basis for the new franchise units, which were highly differentiated according to the type of markets served. InterCity businesses, such as the Midland Main Line, generally provided high-speed medium- or long-distance services linking London with major urban centres outside the south-east region. The principal exceptions were the Gatwick Express operation, offering high-frequency non-stop services between central London and Gatwick airport, and the InterCity Cross-Country services, operating mainly on a north-east–south-west axis centred on Birmingham. Network South East businesses operated high-intensity commuter services into major London termini. Regional Railways businesses operated a wide mix of inter-urban commuter and rural services.

The main overlap in the operations of different profit centre businesses occurred on major radial routes into London termini, which were typically served by both InterCity and a Network South East business unit. There were also significant overlaps around other conurbations, such as Birmingham, either between InterCity and Regional Railway operations, or between different Regional Rail profit centres.

Under BR ownership, the business policy decisions of profit centres with overlapping territories were set to maximize corporate benefit. This dictated that tickets were sold on a fully interavailable basis and service patterns coordinated, so that, for example, non-stop or limited-stop InterCity services operated alongside stopping services provided by other profit centres. Breaking up BR into a multiplicity of franchise units would, in principle, alter these incentives, leading to changes in price and output.

The nature of the changes can be assessed by noting that the process is essentially one of demerging two or more suppliers of differentiated products previously under common ownership. Prior to demerger, prices and outputs will have been set taking account of the interactions between the two lines of business. Focusing on price-setting behaviour, business units i and j will each set prices to maximize a corporate profit function $(TT_i + TT_j)$ where:

$$TT_i = p_i q_i (p_i, p_j) - c_i(q_i) \text{ and } TT_j = p_j q_j (p_j, p_i) - c_j(q_j)$$

The first order condition for i's price setting is then:

$$\frac{\partial TT_i}{\partial p_i} = p_i \frac{\partial q_i}{\partial p_i} + q_i - \frac{\partial c_i}{\partial q_i}\frac{\partial q_i}{\partial p_i} + p_j \frac{\partial q_j}{\partial p_i} - \frac{\partial c_j}{\partial q_j}\frac{\partial q_j}{\partial p_i} = 0$$

This yields, after rearrangement,

$$MR_i = MC_i + X_{ij},$$

where X_{ij} is positive and reflects the market interaction between i and j. Other things equal, X_{ij} is higher, the higher the price-marginal cost margin in j and the higher (more positive) the cross-elasticity between j and i.

Following demerger, prices p_i and p_j will be set by independent profit-seeking businesses. Assuming that the parties act non-collaboratively, the first order condition for i reduces to the more familiar equality of marginal revenue and cost in activity i, implying some reduction in price or expansion of output on the part of both i and j.

The Effects of On-rail Competition: Some Empirical Results

The effects of on-rail competition in practice have been examined by comparing changes in outputs (service frequencies) and fares across a sample of point-to-point flows on routes served by more than one operator with outcomes across the rail network as a whole. The sample of flows is given in Table 6.3, which also shows the number of competing operators, their shares of weekday departures, and the Herfindahl measures of market concentration derived from the 'market share' data. Eleven of the flows are duopolistic, the remainder triopolistic. All would be characterized as 'highly concentrated' according to criteria employed by competition policy agencies in the USA and Europe.

Table 6.3   The sample of competitive routes

Route	Operators	Services*	Share of departures (%)	Herfindahl
London–Peterborough	GNER	42	51	0.50
	WAGN	41	49	
London–Ipswich	Anglia	30	51	0.50
	Great Eastern	29	49	
London–Birmingham	Virgin	36	45	0.36
	Silverlink	22	28	
	Chiltern	22	28	
London–Glasgow	Virgin	10	59	0.52
	GNER	7	41	
London–Milton Keynes	Silverlink	91	63	0.53
	Virgin	53	37	
London–Rugby	Virgin	28	54	0.50
	Silverlink	24	46	
York–Newcastle	GNER	32	53	0.39
	Virgin	12	20	
	Northern Spirit	16	27	
London–Gatwick	Connex	118	45	0.36
	Thameslink	65	25	
	Gatwick Express	82	31	
London–Bedford	MML	24	21	0.67
	Thameslink	92	79	
York–Leeds	Northern Spirit	67	87	0.77
	Virgin	10	13	
Liverpool–Manchester	North Western	51	61	0.44
	Northern Spirit	16	19	
	Central Trains	16	19	
London–Oxford	Virgin	4	7	0.77
	GWT	4	7	
	Thames	53	87	
Exeter–Plymouth	GWT	15	44	0.35
	Virgin	11	32	
	Wales and West	8	24	
Gatwick–Brighton	Thameslink	57	67	0.56
	Connex	28	33	

Route	Operators	Services*	Share of departures (%)	Herfindahl
London–Exeter	South West	8	28	0.60
	GWT	21	72	
Newcastle–Edinburgh	GNER	23	88	0.79
	Virgin	3	12	
Cardiff–Newport	Wales and West	71	72	0.56
	Central Trains	7	7	
	GWT	20	20	
London–Southend	Great Eastern	64	37	0.53
	LTS Rail	110	63	
Sheffield–Manchester	Central Trains	15	34	0.35
	Northern Spirit	19	43	
	North Western	10	23	

Note: * May 1999 timetable.

The results for changes in service frequency are shown in Table 6.4, which compares changes in the number of direct services on the flows with the increase in total train miles on comparable types of service across the network as a whole. It is striking that the average increase in each category in the sample of competed flows is higher than the corresponding change in network frequencies. The average increase in frequency on the sample flows is nearly 50 per cent higher than the average network-wide increase.

Assessment of the way on-rail competition has affected fares is handicapped by a lack of published data on changes in the average fare paid on the sample of competed flows with which to compare network-wide changes in fares. Instead, a simple comparison has been carried out of the

Table 6.4   Changes in service frequencies, 1995-9 (per cent increase)

Type of flow	NERA sample of competed flows	Network average increase in train miles[1]
London-based InterCity	29.2	24.3
London Commuter/InterCity	22.3[2]	13.6[3]
Regional Interurban	14.9	13.4[4]

Notes:
1. Taken from ATOC briefing, May 1999.
2. Includes London–Gatwick services.
3. Train miles weighted average of London InterCity and Commuting.
4. Average of urban/Passenger Transport Executive (PTE) and interurban flows.

change in average unregulated ordinary (that is, non-season ticket) fares on sample flows with the change in passenger revenues per kilometre on all journeys on ordinary fares across the network. The results, which are shown in Table 6.5, suggest that, on average, fares across the sample of competed flows rose by approximately two-thirds as much as the increase in average revenue per passenger kilometre across the network. Because the sample data exclude certain types of dedicated ticket, which have generally been more strongly discounted on competed routes than interavailable or standard tickets, this result probably underestimates the true difference between experience on the competed and non-competed flows. Even if this omission is ignored, however, the difference is sufficiently marked to suggest that the presence of on-rail competition has put downward pressure on fares.

Table 6.5   Changes in fares, 1995-9 (per cent increases)

Type of flow	NERA sample of competed flows[1]	Network average ordinary tickets[2]
All flows	11.8	18.6
London InterCity flows	11.3	

Notes:
1. Unweighted average change in unregulated fares (Standard Open, Super Advance, Network Awayday and Network Stayaway), May–September 1995 to May–September 1999.
2. The table shows the change in average revenue per passenger kilometre on ordinary tickets as a proxy for the average change in fares. The data used to compute this are taken from Tables 1 and 3 of the *Bulletin of Rail Statistics*, Quarter 1 1999/2000. Table 3 gives estimates of revenues from ordinary (that is, non-season ticket sales). Table 1 gives estimated passenger kilometres. The percentage increase is computed over the period between the second quarter of 1995/6 and the first quarter of 1999/2000. A footnote to Table 1 indicates that the volume of passenger kilometres may be underestimated because journeys on certain types of dedicated ticket may not be fully captured in the database used to generate the series. If correct, the percentage increase in revenue per passenger kilometre shown in the table may also be biased upwards. However, as noted in the text, the NERA data exclude certain types of dedicated tickets which have been extensively introduced on competitive flows; this omission would tend to bias upwards the estimated increase in 'average' fares.

CONCLUSIONS

In my remarks as a discussant in the 1994 Lecture Series (Jones, 1995), I suggested that resolving the tensions between franchising and open access might ultimately require further evolution of the industry *structure*, either towards a full open-access model, with TOCs paying marginal cost-reflective track access charges, or towards a more vertically integrated structure with little or no on-rail competition. In fact, the tensions between open-access competition and economy in public expenditure have been resolved within the vertically separated structure by the 'Moderation of Competition' policy. A heavily regulated form of on-rail competition only persists where franchises overlap.[9]

The franchise renegotiation process initiated by the shadow SRA under Sir Alistair Morton could see the already limited extent of on-rail competition reduced even further. It will be surprising if the SRA is not confronted by proposals for reducing the number of franchise units, especially on lines of route served by more than one operator. Proponents of such mergers will point to the potential benefits they offer from greater coordination of services and ticketing, economies in fleet management, and reductions in market uncertainty, all of which would be reflected in reduced demand for subsidy support to maintain given levels of output and fares.

What other factors should be taken into account in determining the public policy stance on such proposals and on the implementation of the second stage of the 'Moderation of Competition' framework? First, the results presented in the previous section suggest that the presence of competition on a route has led to somewhat higher outputs and lower fares by comparison with single-operator routes, although we cannot draw firm conclusions about the welfare consequences. To do so we would need fuller information on whether the increased outputs reflected lower costs or lower profitability, and on how consumers valued the increased outputs.

Second, experience in other liberalized transport markets, such as the European air transport market, demonstrates that market liberalization may be an important spur to service innovation. In aviation, this has taken the form primarily of carriers like easyJet and Ryanair offering low-cost, no frills services, which have greatly expanded the range of consumer choice and are now beginning to exert real pressures on incumbent flag carriers. In the rail sector, the scope for innovations of this kind may be less. However, there may also be more scope for developing new services across London, or improving public transport access to major airports. This experience links with remarks made by the previous rail regulator that the very restrictive stance of policy under the first stage of 'Moderation of Competition' has discouraged innovatory services.

In the light of this discussion, my principal conclusions are, first, that the shift in the underlying stance of policy towards on-rail competition discussed earlier represents a realistic assessment of its role under current market conditions. Second, however, there is no case for not proceeding with the strictly limited extension of open access proposed by the previous rail regulator. Finally, I would suggest that the SRA takes a highly sceptical view of any proposals emerging from the franchise renegotiation process involving reductions in existing on-rail competition through mergers, and resists demands for exclusivity in return for investment. Such a mix of policies would recognize that the primary instrument for securing better outcomes for consumers and taxpayers will be competition for the market through the franchising process. However, an element of on-rail competition will be a useful adjunct, and may, indeed, come to play a more important role if the industry's fortunes continue to improve.

NOTES

1. The author wishes to thank Juliet Young (University of Warwick) for research assistance, and Stuart Holder (NERA) for constructive comments.
2. Until recently, the Office of Passenger Rail Franchising (OPRAF), but following the passage of the Railways Bill, 1999, the Strategic Rail Authority (SRA). Until the legislation is passed, OPRAF operates as the *shadow* SRA.
3. Glaister (1999).
4. See, in particular, the *Passenger Demand Forecasting Handbook* (PDFH). The handbook contains an executive summary of the available evidence on key demand parameters and contains recommended values for different sectors of the railway passenger business.
5. Perhaps because of some weakening in politicians' resolve to impose continuing real increases in fuel taxation, a failure of the rail industry to respond to public concerns about rail safety, or increasing congestion on the rail network leading to a reduction in service quality.
6. This was especially likely if charges were set as a rate per vehicle, rather than as a rate per train.
7. Office of the Rail Regulator (1994b, para. 4.28).
8. For a discussion of possible types of on-rail competition, see Preston *et al.* (1999).
9. The arrangements for upgrading the West Coast Main Line offer an interesting example of vertical integration through contractual mechanisms.

REFERENCES

Department of Environment, Transport and the Regions (1998a), *A New Deal for Railways*, London: HMSO.
Department of Environment, Transport and the Regions (1998b), *A New Deal for Transport - Better for Everyone, The Government White Paper on the Future of Transport*, London: HMSO.
Department of Transport (1992), *New Opportunities for Railways*, London: HMSO.
Department of Transport (1993), *Gaining Access to the Railways Network - the Government's Proposals*, London: Department of Transport.
Glaister, S. (1999), 'Integrated Transport: A Future for Rail', in M.E. Beesley (ed.), *Regulating Utilities: A New Era?*, IEA Readings, no. 49.
Jones, Ian (1995), 'Regulatory Relationships in the Re-structured Railway Industry; Comment', in M.E. Beesley (ed.), *Utility Regulation: Challenge and Response*, IEA Readings, no. 42.
O'Donnell, P. (1997), 'Competitive Access to the Railway Network', paper presented to a Seminar on Privatisation and Deregulation in Transport, Centre for Regulatory Policy, University of Oxford.
Office of Passenger Rail Franchising (1996), *Passenger Rail Industry Overview*, London: HMSO.

Office of Passenger Rail Franchising (1997), *Appraisal of Support for Passenger Rail Services. Planning Criteria: an interim guide*, London: OPRAF.

Office of the Rail Regulator (1994a), *Competition for Railway Passenger Services. A Consultation Document*, London: ORR.

Office of the Rail Regulator (1994b), *Competition for Railway Passenger Services. A Policy Statement*, London: ORR.

Office of the Rail Regulator (1995), *Criteria and Procedures for the Approval of Moderation of Competition Proposals from the Passenger Train Operating Companies*, London: ORR.

Office of the Rail Regulator (1997a), *New Service Opportunities for Passengers. A Consultation Document on the Competitive Framework of Passenger Rail Services*, London: ORR.

Office of the Rail Regulator (1997b), *Regulatory Objectives for Passenger and Station Operators*, London: ORR.

Office of the Rail Regulator (1998a), *New Service Opportunities for Passengers. A Policy Statement*, London: ORR.

Office of the Rail Regulator (1998b), *New Service Opportunities for Passengers. Criteria for Evaluation. A Consultation Document*, London: ORR.

Preston, John, Gerard Whelan and Mark Wardman (1999), 'An Analysis of the Potential for On-track Competition in the British Passenger Rail Industry', *Journal of Transport Economics and Policy*, 33(1), 77–94.

Welsby, John and Alan Nichols (1999), 'The Privatisation of Britain's Railways', *Journal of Transport Economics and Policy*, 33(1), 55–76.

CHAIRMAN'S COMMENTS

Tom Winsor

Thank you very much indeed Ian. You make a very good case for allowing more rail competition and there are a number of important issues which you have discussed which it is not only for me but also for the Strategic Rail Authority to contemplate in franchise replacement. We need to get the terminology right; it is not renegotiation, it is replacement. These are new contracts, new structures. They are not just a few more years on the old terms. The franchise replacement programme is getting under way. There are undeniably serious pitfalls of open access. They are well known: cherry picking, as in the deregulated bus industry. We have to avoid this. We can avoid it under the existing structure through licence conditions and through the Regulator's power to approve or not to approve new access contracts or amendments of existing access contracts. We have seen the development of quality partnerships in other industries which incentivize investment in exchange for security of tenure, and security of tenure is what the railway companies most want to have.

I have only been in this job for four months. My policy so far has been that new open-access services under 'Moderation of Competition' phase 2 can be helpful provided they are controlled and there is no duplication of services, provided one operator does not raid the revenue of another and provided that they bring real passenger benefits. (After all, it is the passenger that pays my wages, not the railway companies!) We want to see passenger benefits through innovation, through quality and through new services such as Anglia's proposed service from Ipswich to Basingstoke.

In these matters it is extremely important that I and my office work very closely with the Strategic Rail Authority on new service proposals and I am already doing so. The Railways Bill presently before Parliament, and about to be reintroduced, makes explicit what was already implicit. It is going to give me a new duty – or rather amend an existing statutory duty – to promote competition by adding that what counts is not competition for the sake of competition alone: it must be for the benefit of passengers. That was the case already. I am to be given a new statutory requirement to take account of the strategies which the Strategic Rail Authority has formulated as part of its process, and to facilitate their achievement in making decisions in the things that I do. That is the need to balance the desire for a planned national railway which delivers public goods and services with the ability to allow innovative services which are derived in response to market forces.

As Ian says, phase 2 of Moderation of Competition loosens the contractual constraints on Railtrack on selling new access rights for competitive services, but it does not in any way loosen my public interest duties under the Railways Act and therefore there is still always a control. I am working closely and consulting with the SRA in the franchise replacement programme to ensure that open access does not take place at the expense of the public interest or at the expense of franchise value.

Ian mentioned that open access is thought to sit easily with the franchising process. But there are voices, which must be listened to, which say that open access sits uneasily with the franchise replacement process. I suggest that, if you have not already done so, you send a copy of your paper to my fellow regulator, Sir Alistair Morton, who I think will read it with great interest.

A key requirement is to establish and examine the relationship between competition and capacity, particularly in relation to investment. The new franchisees will not invest if they are exposed to material revenue risk from open-access operators and, as Ian said, 'investment – investment – investment' are the catchwords. So it is important to ensure that, where operators are allowed to introduce competitive services, there are protections for the public. It is important also to ensure that, where operators are protected from competitive entry, the interest of the captive passenger is also protected. The future of the moderation of competition policy is inextricably linked with the franchise replacement process, but I have to say that so far the evidence is that there is not much appetite for additional competitive services. The railway companies are concentrating all their time and efforts now on getting their franchises replaced by longer ones and not upsetting the Strategic Rail Authority by bringing in troublesome competitive services which just make life difficult. That is the reality so far.

All this is in a matrix of quite considerable change in public policy for the railway. These are very different considerations in a number of respects from what was being desired of the railway industry in 1994/5/6. A lot has changed in these public policy areas in relation to the railways, flowing from the change of government on 1 May 1997. We are to have a new railway institution, the Strategic Rail Authority (SRA), OPRAF reborn, but much more than that. We have new occupants of the offices of franchising director (which still exists until the Bill is passed) and the Rail Regulator, my job. Indeed, the last 12 months have seen three regulators.

We have a new regulatory agenda of more proactive regulation: greater use of the powers of the Regulator where the circumstances warrant it, but they must be exercised honestly, openly, proportionately and fairly. It is already showing benefits in Railtrack's performance and will probably show more benefits. I believe real benefits have already been found in relation to the recent enforcement action on Railtrack's progress on the West Coast main line. But it is not a policy of enforcement for enforcement's sake. The government came in on a policy of tougher and more effective regulation, and that is the basis on which I was appointed. The key word there is 'effective'. What we are trying to do is get a better railway. It is a different approach. My predecessors had one style; I have a different one. There are many things which are occupying my time and the time of my colleagues. As I have mentioned, they include Railtrack's network performance on the West Coast main line upgrade, Railtrack's knowledge of its assets and their condition, the sufficiency of their investment programme, and of course the periodic review of access charges.

We are rather busy with the periodic review. Next month we will announce provisional conclusions on a number of aspects of the structure of Railtrack's charges, including the incentive regime, and one of the issues we have had to think about is whether or not Railtrack should have an effective right of appeal to the Competition Commission. At the moment it does not. Other regulated industries like water, electricity, gas and telecommunications have appeal rights, but Railtrack does not because the price controls are in Railtrack's access contracts with its customers and not in its licence. In 1996, Railtrack stated publicly that it was quite unconcerned with the absence of the right of appeal and was quite content to have the right only to have the Regulator judicially reviewed if they disliked his conclusions. Indeed, the chairman of Railtrack stated publicly that not only was he unconcerned with it but that he positively welcomed the absence of the right of appeal. Well, I disagree with Sir Robert Horton and I support, in principle, Railtrack being given in the railways legislation the right of appeal to the Competition Commission against my decisions on the periodic review of access charges. There are, however, very real practical difficulties in implementing this right, including the roles of other parties in the process. This is a matter of a policy decision by the government and by Parliament, not by the Rail Regulator.

7.   A new deal for airports?

David Starkie[1]

INTRODUCTION

Airports are different from the other regulated utilities, or so it would seem. The debate on the fundamentals of the UK approach to regulating its privatized utilities has focused on electricity, gas, telecommunications and water, but airports tend to receive a passing mention, if that. This low profile has particularly suited BAA and, when it has run the risk of being pigeon-holed with the other utilities, it has itself argued that it is different. It did so, for example, when the windfall tax was on the cards. It was not successful, however, in ducking the tax and it also received a shock at the time of this year's budget when the chancellor announced a special review of the competition issues surrounding BAA's ownership of most of London's airports.

But there is some justification to the claim that airports are different and it was these inherent differences that led to Michael Beesley, in last year's series, suggesting a very different approach to regulating airports. This evening I want to continue with this theme. I, too, want to point to some important differences that set airports aside from the other utilities and I will argue that, to a degree, this reflects some curious or less common economic characteristics of airports. This will lead me to propose significant changes to the present regulatory regime and, perhaps, *in extremis*, to proposals not too different from those put forward by Michael Beesley. But, before doing so, let me sketch out the regulatory approach to airports. This too is different from the approach adopted for the other utilities and associated with it are a number of issues which I will outline.

AN OUTLINE OF ECONOMIC REGULATION

General Powers

The economic regulation of UK airports is governed by the 1986 Airports Act, but this legislation also includes more general powers that have the potential to impact significantly upon the business of the airport companies. For example, the government is able to direct different types of air traffic to different airports within a 'single system' and, under these powers, until the early 1990s, aircraft carrying only charter passengers were not permitted to use Heathrow Airport. Other provisions in the Act enable limits to be placed on the number of air transport movements at congested airports. This might seem uncontroversial, but airports long since considered congested have shown a remarkable capacity to handle, over time, increasing numbers of aircraft (assisted by improvements in techniques of capacity management). The government, therefore, has powers under the 1986 Act (should it wish to use them) to restrict both the volume and type of business handled by an airport company. Arguably, these powers allow for greater intervention in the airport industry than in any of the other regulated utilities.[2]

Price Controls

It is section 40 of the 1986 Act which provides, crucially, for the designation of an airport. Designation (which is done by statutory order) imposes on the airport an RPI-x price-cap regime. Four airports have been designated: BAA's three London airports, and Manchester plc. These four airports are normally subject to a five-yearly review of specified charges, with the review of Manchester taking place one year later than the London review. The last round of reviews was conducted between 1995 and 1997. It is only selected 'airport charges' that are subject to explicit regulation (limiting the maximum amount that may be levied) and these are defined as those charges connected with the landing, take-off, and parking of aircraft, and with the handling of passengers through terminals. Individual charges as such are not subject to a price cap, but the latter is applied to the overall revenue yield per passenger; the airport operator, therefore, has a degree of discretion with respect to the level of each individual charge and the relationship between them (although, in practice, this discretion is limited by the pressures that airlines can, and do, exert on the airport operator through their powerful trade associations and sometimes through governments making representations on their behalf).

By statute, the regulator is obliged to perform his economic regulation function in a manner which furthers the reasonable interests of users (as well as promoting efficiency, economic and profitable operation of airports, and encouraging investment). Partly for this reason, but also because of past treaty obligations and custom in the international air transport industry, the determination of X during the quinquennial review is much influenced by what is commonly referred to as the *single till* approach. Importantly, the regulator's judgment regarding an appropriate level for the price cap takes into account not only the revenue generated by airport charges but, in addition, the revenues generated by activities such as retailing within terminals and the provision of rental property and other services to tenants and licensees (airline companies, car hire operators and so on) the fees and charges for which are not subject to a price-cap formula.[3] The revenue from retailing and property, which can dominate the revenues from price-capped airport charges (see Table 7.1)[4], are combined with the latter into a single till as a prerequisite for judging whether the forecast of total revenue net of operating expenditure provides a rate of return consistent with the firm's cost of capital and whether the projected cash flow is sufficient to sustain the prospective investment programme. The expectation of an inadequate return, or an insufficient cash flow, will lead to a less stringent price cap, and vice versa.

Much of this price-cap review process is common to those reviews undertaken for other utilities. However, the single till, in the airports case, is an important difference. As Michael Beesley pointed out last year, while the other utility regulators have sought to isolate and bear down upon the natural monopoly elements, because of the single till such focusing has not occurred in the case of airports.

Table 7.1   Revenue sources at BAA regulated airports, 1998/9

	Retail	Airport and other traffic charges	Property and operational facilities	Other	Total by airport
Revenue	(£m)	(£m)	(£m)	(£m)	(£m)
Airports:					
Heathrow	398	317	153	22	890
Gatwick	199	112	42	7	360
Stansted	53	28	15	3	99
Total	650	457	210	32	1349
(and per cent) by revenue source	(48.1)	(33.9)	(15.6)	(2.4)	(100)

Source: BAA Annual Report.

Framework Reviews

Since the 1986 Act a couple of reviews of the legislative framework have taken place. The first, in 1994, essentially considered the *process* applied to economic regulation and resulted in proposals for 'streamlining' the approach, the most significant being an intention to adopt the standard utility model with a single economic regulator. Thus far the review process applied to airports by the 1986 Act has been unusual; it has been the Monopolies and Mergers

Commission (MMC) that has conducted the initial review and made recommendations to the regulator. This differs from the usual approach where the industry regulator conducts the review and a reference is made to the Commission only in the event of a utility challenging the regulator's conclusion.

The second review, in 1998, formed part of the government's general review of utility regulation. The thrust of this review was to continue aligning the process applying to airports with that applying to the other utilities. The proposals include: placing a primary duty on the Civil Aviation Authority (CAA) to further the interests of airport users; enabling the CAA to intervene when standards of performance have not been met or have led to disagreement with airport users; and providing the CAA with concurrent powers with the director-general of fair trading, under the Fair Trading Act of 1973, to refer possible monopoly situations to the Competition Commission for investigation (currently the CAA does not enjoy concurrent powers in this area). These changes will bring the CAA more in line with the other utility regulators.

These proposals aim to tidy the edges of the existing regulatory framework. As a consequence, they are essentially conservative and they either choose to ignore, or fail to get to grips with, deeper problems inherent within the current framework. It is to these that I now turn.

ISSUES ARISING FROM THE REGULATORY FRAMEWORK

The Nature of the Airport User

One element in the package of proposed measures aligning airport regulation with the standard utility model is the placing of a primary duty on the regulator to *further* the interests of the airport user. But this proposal contains a subtle, but potentially significant, difference from the government's proposal for the other utilities, which is to require regulators to *protect* the interests of consumers. Furthering interests is not the same as protecting interests and, if the object is consistency, it is not clear why the duty to be placed on the CAA is not also one of protecting the user.

This touches upon important developments in some of the regulated industries which have a bearing on how we might define the user in the case of airports. In the initial post-privatization periods, most regulators were faced with a priority of setting price-caps for services provided to millions of small customers. Subsequent deregulation in telecoms and energy has meant price cap regulation shrinking to focus on intermediate products (interconnection services in telecoms, transmission and distribution services in electricity and in gas). In these intermediate 'access' markets the demand side is characterized by much smaller numbers of relatively large buyers, some of which are, in global terms, much larger than the access provider. These are not 'consumers' in the sense usually meant by politicians. (Airports regulation is ahead of the pack in this area, in that the large user issue has been prominent from the outset, although it should be noted that the activities of the airport companies also have a direct impact on large numbers of individual travellers.)

Given these circumstances, the utilities bill, by placing a duty on the utility regulators to protect the interests of *consumers*, is, arguably, somewhat backward looking in its conceptual framework, and might also be criticized for its lack of clear thinking on the duties of regulators in respect of the relevant intermediate markets. It is, for example, by no means obvious that the primary aim of regulation should be to 'protect' or, even less obviously, to 'further' the interests of users, not least since, as competitors in downstream markets, there should be no presumption that such users have common interests. For example, in many, but not all, aviation markets there are the complications of bilateral air service agreements which often incorporate various barriers to entry.

In respect of congested airports, there is a further consideration. At an airport like Heathrow there are considerable scarcity rents which lead to rent-seeking behaviour on the part of the different economic agents involved in the supply of air services. Such behaviour is constrained in the case of BAA by economic regulation, but why should a regulator be given a duty to allocate a higher weight to the rents of users than to the rents of suppliers, such as BAA, which is what an unqualified application of the principle furthering the interest of users would imply?

There are, therefore, important distribution issues to address which, in this case, take on an added significance, partly because of the size of the scarcity rents and partly because non-UK/EU users of the airport utility are a sizeable part of the market.[5]

Airport Designation Criteria

An airport to be subject to a price cap has to be designated under section 40 of the 1986 Act and, as pointed out above, four airports are designated, the same four that were designated at the outset of regulation. Why these four, and why others have not been added, remains unclear, which is perhaps surprising given that designation is the crucial trigger for economic regulation. But economic regulation does not come without (sometimes considerable) disadvantages. Therefore one might have expected airports to be treated on the basis of consistent and perhaps self-evident criteria when the decision is made upon which ones to designate.

In my 1994 lecture in this series[6], I questioned why, at the outset, the Scottish airports of BAA were not designated. As a group, they dominated the

Scottish airport market and in scale terms were similar to Manchester, which was designated. Subsequently, the government reviewed the case for designating them and, at the same time and for the first time, set out criteria which it considered relevant to designation generally. These criteria include the extent of competition from other airports/transport modes and *prima facie* evidence of excessive profitability *or* abuse of monopoly position. To include both abuse of a monopoly position and evidence of excessive profitability as alternative criteria is curious and appears contrary to the thrust of competition law with its focus on abuse. At what point profits become excessive is arguable and the danger is that any profits in excess of normal will be judged excessive. There is, after all, nothing inherently wrong with above-normal levels of profit; such levels could indicate, for example, superior organizational efficiency and cost control and signal opportunities for profitable entry.

In the event, the government concluded that there was no case for designating the two principal Scottish airports, Glasgow and Edinburgh, because there was no evidence of abuse of monopoly position or inefficiency. However, both airports had achieved high levels of profit and rates of return. This suggests that, in spite of having included profitability in the list of designation criteria, in practice the government was inclined (correctly) to disregard it as a singular reason for designation. When announcing its decision, the government added that it believed the threat of designation provided a strong incentive for BAA to control its charges. Possibly reflecting this, BAA did cap its charges on a voluntary basis (initially with the formula of RPI-3) at both Glasgow and Edinburgh.

This outcome begs the obvious question of whether this approach in Scotland is not a more appropriate way of approaching the economic regulation of airports generally. Rather than link the implementation of economic regulation to evidence that market power exists (which appears to be the basis upon which the four airports were originally designated), would it not be preferable to hold reserve powers which are put into effect only when there is evidence that market power is being exploited and no voluntary agreement can be reached?

Service Quality

Whatever the merits of the current price cap applied to the major UK airports, it does mean that the focus of the regulatory system is upon charges *per se*. But should service standards be brought within the ambit of regulation as well, because of the incentives that price controls give for degrading service quality? If demand with respect to service quality is inelastic (that is, a unit decrease in quality leads to a proportionately smaller decrease in demand) then it is possible that the cost savings from degrading the quality of service will exceed revenues forgone; profits will be enhanced as a consequence. For example, the quality of airside activities such as baggage handling, trolley services and holding lounges, can probably be degraded (perhaps severely) without any consequence for short-term passenger demand (in the long term, adverse reputation may have an impact). On the other hand, demand for some commercial activities at an airport is probably (highly) sensitive to quality of service. Queuing by passengers will have a marked effect on demand for duty-free goods and food and drink purchases, for example. Does this suggest that quality could be degraded in some activities to increase net profits, but not in others? Not necessarily. The willingness of passengers to undertake discretionary spending could very well depend on their treatment airside, so that this interdependence of demand may reduce incentives to degrade quality in *any* element of the airport service.

Although not subject to formal regulation of its quality of service by statute, BAA has for some time produced a quality of service index and provided specific service guarantees to airline passengers and to tenants; it also has consultation procedures with airlines and shares the results of market research with airlines, concessionaires and others involved in service delivery at its airports. The MMC has also taken into account complaints made by airlines and consumers when reviewing the price cap for the regulator.

Emphasis is now switching to the establishment of formal agreements between the airport companies and the airlines, known as 'service level agreements'. After a period of experimentation, these are being introduced, although not without controversy. The main area of contention is whether the airport company should be penalized when performance falls below agreed standards. BAA considers that the processes covered by 'service level agreements' are shared between the airport and the airlines and that penalties should apply potentially to both parties. The airlines, on the other hand, believe that penalties should be payable by the airport alone; they argue that it is the airport that is the monopoly supplier, while airlines operate in a competitive market and poor performance by an individual airline leads to passengers transferring to other airlines.

Clearly, from a practical point of view, there are a number of difficulties if service quality is to be formally regulated. Judging the appropriate quality of service is difficult and it would be uneconomic to overprovide quality and inefficient to underprovide. The quality of service to aim for is that which would exist in a competitive market for the services in question. Bearing in mind that different airlines have different (sometimes very different) requirements, it is probable that in a competitive market there would exist a variety of service qualities attached to which would be different prices. The user would then choose the quality/price package which most suited its requirements. Unfortunately, the emphasis on service level agreements tends to focus the debate on a uniform (and possibly too high) standard and, thus, on a lower level of welfare than is potentially achievable.

The Structure of Charges

As Michael Beesley remarked last year, little serious attention seems to be given nowadays to peak load pricing. This is perhaps regrettable given the pioneering role in this field of BAA's predecessor, the British Airports Authority. The Authority introduced a policy of pricing peak demand at Heathrow and Gatwick in the early 1970s and, although the implementation left much to be desired, it was the first attempt to introduce, on a large scale, efficient pricing signals for the use of airports. The rudiments of the policy still exist, albeit substantially modified, and now focus upon runways and the utilization of space for parking aircraft. There has also been an overlay of environmental charges whereby noisier aircraft pay more, sometimes much more, than quieter aircraft. The policy has come under fierce attack in the past from US aviation interests that felt that the peak passenger charge for the use of terminals unfairly penalized the early morning trans-Atlantic arrivals traffic at Heathrow.

What is particularly regrettable is that the structure of charges, and its implications for economic efficiency, have not received more attention in the regulatory reviews. In fact, on the evidence of the three MMC reports reviewing Manchester, the Commission seemed to alter its position from positively encouraging the adoption of peak load pricing (1987) to mild encouragement (1992) and then to indifference (1997), with no mention being made in the latter review of the earlier recommendations on the subject, in spite of their apparent neglect. It could be argued that by 1997 the cause was in fact lost; proposals to construct a second runway and provide substantial additional capacity were, by that time, well advanced. The time to have pressed the issue would have been in 1992, when a well-considered peak load pricing scheme would have tested the case for a second runway and informed a decision on its optimal timing.

That apart, we have a situation at London airports where demand greatly exceeds supply at the current level of charges. There is a commonly held view that to clear the current London market requires a substantial hike in charges. This, of course, would run contrary to the current paradigm which results in a continual reduction in the real level of charge in spite of the congestion, so that, as a consequence, a balance between supply and demand is achieved through quantity rationing. But there is an argurnent that *some* increase in charges would probably improve the situation even if it were not large enough to actually clear the market. This arises from the importance of the *structure* of charges regardless of whcthcr the average *level* of charge clears the market.

The underlying point is that total demand can be broken down into a number of sub-demands (by routes, scheduled/charter traffic, transfer/originating traffic, etc.) each of which will have its own elasticity of demand. With excess demand, quantity rationing, will tend to lead to inefficiencies in the allocation of capacity between these sub-markets. An increase in charges will, however, induce different substitutions among the sub-markets (there will be a greater reduction of demand where price sensitivities are higher). This will affect the rationing of the (now smaller) demand in ways that might be expected to improve efficiency a little. For example, if low-value users are priced out, there will be more capacity available for higher-value users. Thus, although the overall allocation will tend to be inefficient, there will at least have been some movement in the desired direction (that is, some reallocation from lower- to higher-value users).

It may also be possible to devise an approach to charges which clears, or more nearly clears, the market without greatly affecting the average charge. Suppose, for example, the passenger facilities charge (for the use of terminals) was abolished and the emphasis was placed entirely upon a fixed charge for landing aircraft (which might apply throughout the day if demand is at a constantly high level). This would bear more heavily upon smaller jets with fewer passengers, so that demand is reduced significantly in this part of the market, thus leaving runway demand and supply more balanced, but with an increase in the average size of aircraft.

A similar outcome in efficiency terms can be achieved by the introduction of a secondary market in take-off and landing 'slots' (entitlements for use of the runway at particular times). If incumbent airlines are free to trade their entitlements, the consequence will be that slots will be transferred to those airlines that place a higher value on their use. However, the allocation of slots is governed by European legislation and the Commission has so far opposed the trading of slots. This has not stopped a 'grey' market developing at both Gatwick and Heathrow, but in my view it would be better to legitimize the process and make it transparent. Nevertheless, a secondary market is not without its disadvantages; in particular, it involves a lump sum financial transfer from entrants to incumbents with consequences for the balance sheets and financial strength of often competing airlines. Reducing the discrepancy between market-clearing prices and the prices actually charged for the use of runways remains the preferred course of action.

The Single Till

I have already outlined the unusual but central role of the single till in the overall approach to the price regulation of airports. It is an approach that has been criticized especially for forcing down charges at congested airports below market-clearing levels and sometimes below the (resource) costs of providing airside services. Given the total revenue requirement, the amount of revenue from airport charges (and thus the average level of those charges) is determined by the anticipated level of profits from retailing and property activities. As more volume is squeezed out of a congested facility, retail revenues are increased and, if forecast to continue, the price-cap review will (all other things being equal) increase X, thus reducing charges at a time when economic efficiency requires these to increase. Indeed, if the price-capped airside activities contribute a minor share of total revenues, the gearing effect means that modest changes in revenue requirements give rise to large changes in (price-capped) charges.

This is the most evident distortion resulting from the single-till approach, but there are others. Although the retail and property activities are formally excluded from the scope of the price cap, nevertheless the approach, by taking into account these revenues when determining the price cap, implicitly extends the range of activities subject to regulation. It means, for example, that the retailing activities are possibly subject to inefficient investment incentives. A further complication is that the overall regulatory approach requires the regulator to assess the airport company's cost of capital and an incorrect assessment will further distort investment incentives. The incorporation of retailing and property activities into the assessment inevitably complicates this exercise and increases the potential scope for error. Their incorporation requires, for example, the regulator to take a view on the cost of capital for retailing activities but this is not an area in which regulators generally have much, or indeed any, experience.

In spite of the distortions that the single till imparts to the overall process, it is, nevertheless, an approach which focuses upon the important complementary nature of the relationship between the airside and retailing activities; an increase in the demand for flights from a particular airport will increase the demand for related goods and services and for rented property at that airport.[7] But there is a twist to this relationship that is particularly important. The retailing and property activities enjoy locational rents due to the fact that superior locations have an enhanced value (in just the same way that retailing properties in, say, Bond Street or Oxford Street enjoy similar economic rents from their own unique location).[8] And because the retailing and property activities gain these locational rents, increases in traffic volumes at an airport will often produce significant increases in their profitability.[9] For a profit-maximizing airport company with market power, selling in both markets, the effect of the demand complementarity linked to the locational rents is to attenuate the normal, downward pressure on profits which would arise when increased air traffic volumes have to be bought at the expense of lower prices (see Figure 7.1). This means that, as long as an airport combines both

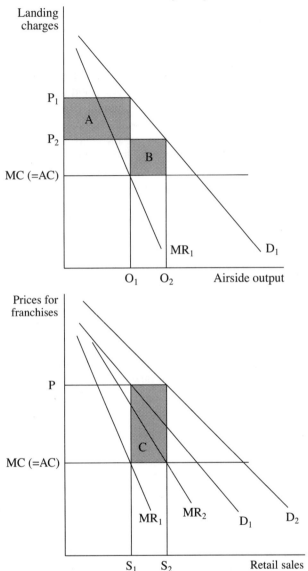

Figure 7.1: The effect of location rents on airport charges. A profit-maximizing airport business, if considering only airside activities, will produce O_1 output and price at P_1 (top diagram). However, increasing airside output raises demand for the complementary good (airport retailing), thus increasing location rents for the latter (bottom diagram). A business with an interest in both markets will expand airside output providing that $B + C > A$, that is, up to output O_2

activities, the incentive will be to set charges lower than if runways were a stand-alone facility.

This outcome has some potentially efficient properties. For example, if an airport is operating with excess capacity, efficient pricing of runways and terminals implies a level of charge that will fall short of cost recovery (including a reasonable return on capital employed). Absent the retailing activities, these efficient prices would not be achieved. If, however, there are economic rents from retailing activities, the complementary relationship will encourage the airport to increase these rents by lowering airside charges. That is, the returns from retailing may support a more efficient level of charges (although it is also possible that this situation could actually give rise to charges for airside activities that are below marginal cost).

Once the capacity of an airport is reached, however, the pattern of incentives will change. There is now nothing to be gained in not pricing the use of runways and terminals at market-clearing levels; increased turnover in and profits from retailing cannot in the short term be secured by reducing charges for runways and terminals below the level which equates demand with the capacity available. In these capacity-constrained circumstances, the prices charged for the use of airside activities by an efficient airport business which combines these with retailing will be the same as the prices charged by an efficient airport business wherein runways and terminals are a stand-alone facility. Of course, once sufficient capacity is added, the situation will revert; the pricing of runways and terminals will take into account the contributory revenues from retailing and property.

REFORM OPTIONS

More Focused Regulation

In the light of these important economic characteristics, there are various options for regulatory reform which suggest themselves. The more obvious option would be to remove the single-till constraint while retaining price-cap regulation. In other words, maximum airport charges would be determined by a requirement to allow an appropriate return on airside assets, disregarding the revenues and costs of retailing and property activities. This might be referred to as more 'focused' regulation.

More focused regulation should bring about improvements in economic efficiency, since it would have the effect of reducing the distorted investment incentives previously outlined. In terms of its impact on charges, the effects here are contingent upon circumstances. At congested airports it is to be expected that average charges will increase, perhaps significantly, but, to the extent that charges have been held by regulation below marginal cost, the effects of the increase in economic terms will be beneficial. At uncongested airports it is more difficult to judge the impact of more focused regulation on charges. This will depend upon whether the existing price cap is actually binding on the airport company's charging decisions. The powerful economic incentives I have noted, whereby an airport company with significant earnings from retailing and with spare capacity has an incentive to keep charges lower than would otherwise be the case, mean that the maximum allowable average charge may exceed what the company wishes to charge. If this is the case, charges will not increase once the single-till constraint is removed. Alternatively, the price cap may be binding, in which case charges will rise, but not necessarily to inefficient levels.

There will also be longer-term impacts. Removal of retailing and property from the regulatory assessments can be expected to affect both the pricing of, and investment in, these activities. As these sectors adjust, factors such as their price–cost margin will change, and these changes will have feedback effects on pricing and investment in these sectors. For example, if price–cost margins in retailing increase over time, the marginal profitability of extra demand will increase, and this will tend to increase incentives to price lower and invest more in (complementary) runways and terminal facilities. These incentives apply equally to congested and uncongested airports.

Overall, it would seem that, from an economic viewpoint, there is probably much to be gained by doing away with the single-till approach when undertaking the price-cap review. The risks from doing so are reduced substantially by the complementary nature of airport activities, and the incentives that these complementarities impart for efficient behaviour. However, if the regulatory framework was to be altered in this way, it would be expedient to encourage airport companies to develop commercial activities that depend for their profitability upon the number of passengers using the airport. Less desirable would be moves to demerge, or hive off, these activities into companies separate from those owning and operating the runway and terminal infrastructure. Although a separate retailing or property company would continue to benefit from airport growth, the company retaining the airside assets might have less incentive to increase output. This is because the owners of such assets would no longer have a shared interest in the performance of the retailing and property assets (an interest which does exist if the company has an integrated structure). If the airport is operating at capacity, this is perhaps of less significance, but in the longer term it is likely to affect the incentives to invest. There might then be a requirement for greater regulatory scrutiny of the investment plans of the airport company to ensure that investment was at an appropriate level.

An alternative view is that, as a consequence of the demand complementarities, there would be incentives for separate companies to enter into contractual relationships that compensated the airport company for the beneficial effects that any expansion in its activities would have on the retailing company. To the extent that this was successful, we can note that all that would happen is that the effects of common ownership (integration) would be replicated by contractual arrangements, and the economic effects of demerger would be insubstantial. That is, demerger would only have significant effects if the contractual alternative was infeasible or costly (for example because of transactions costs) in which case these effects would not be beneficial.

Abolition of the Price Cap

A further option to consider is full deregulation of both airport services and retailing activities. This involves the classic trade-off between the economic effects of market power and the distortions introduced by regulatory intervention. The option is, therefore, more/less attractive the greater/lesser the degree of competition among airports, and it raises associated questions concerning, for example, the common ownership of the three London airports.

But putting these questions aside for the time being, the economic factors that have led me to argue for the abolition of the single-till approach to regulation also lend weight to an argument for doing away with a permanent price cap. The existence of economic rents from complementary retailing and property activities has the effect of reducing some of the adverse effects of market power. It provides incentives for lower pricing and higher investment in airside activities because the extra air traffic will generate higher rents in retailing and property. The bundling of both types of activity is, therefore, a factor that, at least in terms of its effects on the market for runway and terminal services, tilts the balance of advantage towards deregulation more than would be the case if runways were operated on a stand-alone basis.

There is yet another factor associated with the economic characteristics of the industry which tilts the argument towards deregulation. Compared with the more traditional 'natural' monopoly examples, supply in the airport industry is probably characterized by increasing, rather than decreasing, long-run costs at quite moderate levels of output. That is to say, if we double the output of a sizeable airport by doubling the capacity available for use, total costs will more than double. This observation was made, somewhat in passing, in MMC2 (1991) and, although there is not the hard, statistical evidence to support the proposition, it is, as I argued with David Thompson in 1985,[10] a likely outcome of the complex way in which airports grow in size. The source of the airport monopoly, therefore, is not the usual economies of scale in the long-run production function, but the fixity of 'locational' inputs (that is, good sites) and economies of scope associated with established air service networks

The significance of this increasing cost argument is twofold. First, even in the absence of congestion, prices in excess of average costs are not necessarily inappropriate. And second, in increasing-cost industries, regulation of prices based on allowances for normal or reasonable rates of return on capital may lead to inefficiently low prices. Thus, even though deregulation may, in spite of the moderating factors previously mentioned, lead to inefficiently high prices, the outcome is not necessarily worse than the regulatory outcome.

In addition to these economic arguments supporting the case for deregulation, there is a further argument which derives from the earlier observations made regarding the nature of the airport user. As we observed, the airport user from a regulatory standpoint is not so much the individual airline passenger but rather a relatively small number of airlines providing services in downstream markets. These airlines, when represented through their trade associations, are relatively large and sophisticated customers more than capable of challenging the airport operators. They have often done so and frequently have used the courts to put their case. Arguably, therefore, the airlines have a measure of countervailing power. However, the countervailing power of airlines would clearly be greater if the London airports were all in separate ownership. For example, it is likely that Ryanair's recent threat to leave Stansted unless a proposed increase in charges was ameliorated, would have carried more weight if Stansted had not been in common ownership with Gatwick and Heathrow.

This suggests that there is a trade-off worth contemplating between abolishing or reducing the level of price control and separating the ownership of proximate airports. To achieve the level of restructuring required to advance airport competition and to ease the regulatory burden might not be too difficult a task. As the voluntary divestment of generating capacity in the electricity supply industry and the voluntary separation of Centrica from British Gas indicate, it does not necessarily require considerable political will (in the gas case, the government had rejected the MMC's divestment proposals but the company decided that restructuring was in the best interests of the shareholders). If BAA were confronted with the possibility of a much reduced regulatory burden in the event of divestment, it might be a trade-off that the company was willing to take seriously.

Taking into account the high level of existing demand relative to available capacity at both Heathrow and Gatwick, in the event of separate ownership, competition will centre less on prices and more on the second of the two competitive dimensions set out by George Yarrow in Chapter 3. Separate ownership in this airports case is more likely to spur product development and innovation, especially with a view to adding more capacity to the congested infrastructure. Although, as I have argued, BAA currently has an incentive to pursue the same end, competition is likely to sharpen creativity.

Consequently, it might be argued that for the capital markets there might be little to lose by BAA being broken up into potentially competing parts (the sum of the profitable parts might even exceed the sum of the existing profitable whole) and everything to gain from a less regulated environment.

The principal difficulty with deregulation is likely to be associated with distributional issues (rather than issues of economic efficiency). At *congested* airports, removal of the price cap can be expected to lead to user detriments in the form of higher prices to users and to significant increases in the profits of the airport companies. Consequently, even if efficiency is improved (if profit gains to the airport company exceed loss of profits to incumbent airlines and loss of consumers' surplus to passengers), the weighting given to the user interest may be decisive and make deregulation difficult, if not impossible, to achieve. Increased competition between airports could help to mitigate such distributional effects, but, if deregulation was to be pursued as a serious option, it might be necessary to consider it alongside other measures designed to offset the adverse effects on users.

One such measure would be to allow the airlines to take a stake in the airport. In Australia and New Zealand, for example, some domestic airlines own their own terminals and have thus vertically integrated some of the service functions typically provided by the airport company. However, such developments provide opportunities for foreclosing entry into the air services market and new entrants, particularly in Australia, have faced this situation. Although access rules could be formulated to try to ease this problem, an alternative (structural) approach would be to demerge airport *retailing* into a separate company which is then established as a joint venture between the owners of the runway and terminal assets, and the (downstream) airline companies.[11]

A joint venture of this type would maintain existing incentives for the airport company to increase output and, in addition, provide incumbent airlines with similar incentives which they do not necessarily have at the present time (given the strategic competition among airlines for landing slots at congested airports). Such a company structure could provide a means of compensating the airlines for losses following deregulation. Whether the required amount of compensation could be achieved would depend upon the willingness of the airport company to provide incumbent airlines with enough equity in a joint venture. This might be possible. Increased charges at congested airports could be expected to lead to an increase in the average number of passengers per aircraft movement and, because of this, there would be an increase in total retailing turnover and profits which both parties to the joint venture could share; there could conceivably be a net overall gain to the airport company after allowing for the lump sum transfer of enough equity to compensate the airlines for any increase in charges.

CONCLUSIONS

Overall, I believe the balance of the argument is against a continuation of the single-till approach to the regulation of airport charges. In the longer term, the approach introduces distorted investment incentives, particularly by extending the scope of regulation; it requires the regulator to make difficult judgments regarding the cost of capital not only for the air transport sector but also for retailing and property. In the shorter term, at congested airports, it also leads to distorted pricing signals. These distorted economic incentives are probably reason enough to abolish the single-till approach. But a more telling reason for its abolition is that it is an unnecessary complication. A business which combines the landing of aircraft with retailing will have, without the intervention of a regulator, an incentive to reduce charges to airlines and to expand output. The special factors in this favourable situation is the union of strong demand complementarities (the demand for the use of the runway and the demand for retailing and property facilities) with location rents (from retailing and property).

The added significance of the demand complementarities combined with economic rents is that they also make it less likely, and possibly *much* less likely, that any market power that does exist in the market for landing aircraft and handling passengers will be abused. In fact, because the airport company has incentives to maximize throughput, the problem is more likely to be one of excessive use and congestion (rather than the classical problem of a monopolist restricting output).[12] It is important, therefore, not to jump from the proposition that the operator of, say, Heathrow has significant market power (which is certainly the case) to the proposition that the operator can be expected to abuse that market power. Consequently, the special economic circumstances in the airport case tip the balance of the argument not only towards the abolition of the single-till approach to price-cap regulation, but also towards the abolition of price cap regulation *per se*.

In addition to the underlying pattern of economic incentives there are other aspects to take into account which lead to the conclusion that serious consideration should be given to removing the formal price cap at airports currently designated. Foremost among these is the new Competition Act, which will give the CAA considerable powers to police and punish abuse of a dominant position, thereby establishing *ex ante* incentives not to abuse market power. With this in mind, if designation was set aside, it might be appropriate if this was accompanied by undertakings in respect of pricing at Heathrow (and possibly Gatwick and Manchester) given under general competition law; such undertakings might have an economic effect similar to the imposition of a relatively loose price cap at Heathrow.

The overall thrust of such moves would be to shift airport regulation in the direction of the approach adopted in New Zealand, where the privatized airports are subject to reserve powers of price control under the Commerce Act, and, importantly, towards the approach now adopted for BAA's main Scottish airports. At the latter, charges are capped on an informal basis following an agreement with the CAA. This establishes an important precedent broadly along the lines of the approach I am suggesting here.

Finally, there is the question of timing if radical change is to take place. One necessary step is to notify the US authorities of any proposal to abolish the single till, as is required under the 1994 amendment to article 10 of the Bermuda II Agreement (article 10 was amended so that there is no longer a requirement for the UK to maintain a single till approach). A further consideration is how change can be introduced within the timetable of the regulatory review process. The next review (of BAA) was due to take place, starting in 2000, with completion expected in 2001, but the timetable has been put back a year to allow time for a decision on Terminal 5 and to allow for completion of the general review of aviation policy that the present government has set in train. This delay provides an opportunity to undertake an appraisal of the regulatory framework as a whole, the outcome of which may make a further quinquennial review unnecessary.

NOTES

1. This paper is based on joint work with Professor George Yarrow, to whom I am indebted. I am also grateful to David Thompson for his comments. All views expressed here, however, are entirely my own.
2. Because of externalities associated with airports the planning control system is also onerous and the government is heavily involved in the decisions regarding the scale and location of new capacity.
3. These fees and charges have, nevertheless, been considered by the MMC during the quinquennial review process with a view to judging whether their level was contrary to the public interest.
4. Table 7.1 shows an *ex post* situation; the balance of revenue sources after the regulation of airport charges.
5. We can note here attempts by US negotiators to shift the scarcity rents of Heathrow to US airlines, foreign ownership and control of which remains foreclosed.
6. David Starkie, 'Regulating Airports and Airlines' in *Regulating Utilities: The Way Forward*, IEA Readings 41, 37–51, 1994.
7. Reductions in *real* air fares can be expected to lead to additional demand for the complementary good because of changes in the cross-price elasticities; that is, besides there being more passengers, a lower real air fare will encourage each passenger to spend more in airport shops.
8. As Martin Kunz ('Airport Regulation: The Policy Framework', in W. Pfähler *et al.* (eds), *Airports and Air Traffic*, Frankfurt am Main: Peter Lang, 1999) points out (p.14) these locational rents are part of the process of allocating limited space efficiently.
9. These related activities are not always undertaken directly by the airport companies, but are frequently franchised. The terms of the franchise normally enable the airport to extract much of the rent. Note, however, that section 41 of the 1986 Act potentially constrains the ability of the airport companies to increase these rents by limiting the number of franchisees.

10. David Starkie and David Thompson (1985), '*Privatising London's Airports*', Institute for Fiscal Studies, Report Series 16, London.

11. The 'deal' put forward last year by Michael Beesley was essentially one between the government and BAA (with the airlines offered the comfort of charges being pegged in real terms). However, in paragraph 49 of his paper he also hinted at the possibility of a joint venture between BAA and the airlines in relation to the development of Terminal 5. It would seem, though, that he viewed this 'joint venture' in terms of airlines bidding for access rights to the new terminal.

12. On this issue, see Peter Forsyth (1997), 'Price Regulation of Airports: Principles with Australian Applications', *Transport Research - E*, 33(4), 297–309.

CHAIRMAN'S COMMENTS
Sir Malcolm Field

This lecture last year was given by Michael Beesley. Michael broke new territory in a way which was both controversial and thought-provoking; he delivered his views in a most vigorous and appealing manner. He, of course, invited our speaker this evening, David Starkie, to give this lecture, and that in itself is the best possible recommendation.

I plan to comment very briefly upon the key areas that David has covered. As was to be expected, David has built on the views developed by Michael Beesley last year and the debate is particularly important in the light of the government's review of airport competition and airport policy.

I think the main points are the following:

- airports and airspace in the south east are, and will continue to be, under pressure;
- the RPI model is not as well suited to the regulation of airports as it is to utilities;
- economic regulation by the Competition Commission and the CAA has continued to push prices down at congested facilities;
- the RPI-x has uncertain effects upon investment.

The questions for discussion are as follows:

1. Should the single till remain?
2. Is the single till an unnecessary complication?
3. What would be necessary to get the airlines to accept abolition of the single till?
4. Are the distorted economic incentives sufficient reason to abolish the single till?
5. Because of the single till principle, it has not been possible to develop RPI-x in the way that utility regulators have, but the system has delivered reducing prices to the airlines in real terms. So, I ask, what improvements would there be for BAA's customers, passengers, airlines and others which would result from the greater commercial freedom proposed for BAA? David places considerable weight on the power of the airlines to counterbalance airport market power. I wonder if this is really credible?

A further key issue is whether serious consideration should be given to removing the formal price cap at airports currently designated. For example, the Competition Act would give the CAA considerable powers to police and punish the abuse of dominant position. Why not let the Competiton Act, albeit as yet untested, do the work?

David raised the question of designation of airports. My question for discussion is this: if airports were dedesignated, would the potential threat of redesignation be a sufficient weapon to avoid abuse of dominant position?

I now throw these key questions open to the discussion.

8. Gas: regulatory response to social needs

Catherine Waddams Price[1]

INTRODUCTION

The role of social needs in economic regulation of the utilities has changed significantly over the last decade. The original model of privatization and regulation focused on efficiency rather than equity or distributional issues, but this model has been challenged by public perceptions of the utilities as services necessary for life, and the interaction has been reinterpreted by the current government. This paper follows the development of regulatory response to social needs with special reference to gas, particularly in the light of developing competition, and focuses on the debates surrounding prepayment consumers. It ends with an assessment of current proposals and the interaction between efficiency and equity.

The framework established for regulating privatized industries assumed that they would behave just like any other companies. Monopoly power was constrained by caps on price levels, and regulators were given general responsibilities for some specific groups, but not for low-income households. The fundamental model was of a textbook profit-maximizing company, supplying a commodity just like any other, responding to market forces where these existed and constrained by regulation where they did not. There was little recognition or debate about social needs which the nationalized corporations had implicitly undertaken, for example through their policies on disconnection for bad debt, or cross-subsidies incorporated in their price structure. Many managers within the nationalized industries had felt themselves to be in 'special' industries, with different responsibilities from those in the private sector (Mulholland, 1998). The privatization process did little to acknowledge these differences, and critics often saw them as excuses for slack and inefficient procedures. Flanders and Swann even wrote a song about inefficient working practices, with the Gas Man as the eponymous 'hero'. Privatization was to streamline and commercialize the industries.

During the 1990s, the policy's success was accompanied by growing public concern about the behaviour of the privatized utilities and their responsibilities for broader social welfare, exacerbated by an unfortunate coincidence of rising prices and share values in the water industry. In the public perception, at least, these industries were not just like any other private company, supplying a commodity which consumers could choose to buy or not as they wished; but as monopolies, supplying services regarded as essential to live in a civilized society, they were expected to take a broader responsibility for social welfare, and especially for 'vulnerable' households. In particular, there was concern over changes which were perceived simultaneously to increase the profits of the companies and disadvantage low-income or vulnerable households. In gas, the introduction of competition exposed many of the cross-subsidies which had been operating, and was the catalyst for closer inspection of the effect of regulation on low-income households. These developments have confronted the original efficiency-focused model, and opened new challenges to the industries and their regulators. The next section elaborates the initial regulatory vision and framework while the third section identifies the role of cross-subsidies. The fourth section explains the gas regulator's response, while the fifth section outlines the current government framework and its interpretation in other utilities. The final section assesses the proposals in gas and electricity at the beginning of the new century.

REGULATING FOR EFFICIENCY

To say that the nationalized industries did not enjoy a good reputation for efficiency when they were privatized would be an understatement, and it was no surprise that the Conservative Government placed much of the emphasis of the privatization and regulatory reform on improving efficiency, paying very little attention to equity and the distribution of any benefits which the system would generate. Such a model is consistent with traditional economic approaches of separating analysis of efficiency and distribution; that is, the size of the cake and how it is divided. In many ways the original UK regulation system could be regarded as an economist's dream. The statutory duties of regulators were primarily to ensure adequate financing for the industries' regulated activities, with only secondary duties to protect consumers, through the introduction of competition, or price controls, or both. The original Gas Act (1986) specified that the regulator should have regard to the needs of those of pensionable age and the disabled, and the Utilities Act (1992) added the chronically sick to the list. Electricity and water regulators were also to have special regard to the needs of consumers living in rural areas. But there was no guidance about the nature of 'regard' for such groups, which did not include those on low incomes.

All the regulators (or the industries) inherited from their nationalized predecessors a duty not to show undue discrimination or preference between any consumers or groups of consumers. Again there was no guidance, and very little precedent, on interpreting this requirement. The debate centred on how to regulate the companies efficiently, rather than the distributional effects of such regulation. The role of consumer representation itself was somewhat confused. Gas was unique in having a separately established Gas Consumers Council, independent of the regulator, rather than sharing its staff, as in other industries. This separation proved to be influential in the development of a broader agenda for the role of social needs in gas regulation, or at least in opening the debate to public scrutiny.

The regulation model, applied to all the utilities (and the British Airports Authority), provided high-powered incentives to the companies to increase both productive and allocative efficiency. A price cap, originally designed by Stephen Littlechild (1983) for British Telecommunications, placed a maximum limit on the average price which could be charged for a basket of services for which the company still held monopoly power. Unlike the cost of service regulation based on allowed rate of return, which had been applied in the USA for many years, this gave the company incentives to produce as efficiently as possible to lower its costs, since it could keep any realized savings, at least in the short term. In this way the system encouraged productive efficiency. At the same time the regulator could design the basket and set the allowed price cap at a level which would ensure that consumer prices reflected these costs in the best possible way, so ensuring allocative efficiency (Bradley and Price, 1988). Compared with the US system, this strong incentive scheme required much less information for the regulator, and was therefore cheaper to operate. The anticipated nature of the regulatory burden is illustrated by the initial appointment of a part-time regulator for gas, with an established staff of less than 20 (which included no economist). The mechanism seemed at a stroke to establish incentives for the previously 'sluggish' nationalized industries to become more efficient, and to provide clear protection for consumers against monopoly exploitation through direct control of price levels.

Discussion of distributional issues was largely restricted to the level of the cap, which would determine what proportion of any cost savings made by the company would be passed on to consumers as a whole in the form of lower average prices. Initial price caps were set as part of the privatization deal, and tended (at least with the benefit of hindsight) to be rather lax; this is not surprising since the government still owned the companies and had an interest in the flotation proceeds. However, the need to reset the limits considerably weakened the incentive properties of the price-cap system, since realized cost reductions would be passed on to consumers by tightening the cap at the next review. For the capital-intensive operations typical of the network sectors which would need long-term regulation, it was difficult to identify any sensible determinant of revenue other than return on capital, and this raised all the difficulties familiar from the US system. The incentives therefore proved to be effective within the price-cap period, but only for a myopic company which did not foresee the roles which lower costs or an inflated capital base might play in determining the next cap. However, the incentive is strengthened by the comparatively high discount rate of the private sector compared with the public sector. Companies will be keen to lower costs within the price-cap period to secure immediate gains, even though eventually these will be passed on to consumers in the form of tighter price controls when the cap is reviewed; meanwhile, regulators and consumers should be relatively patient in waiting for their share of these benefits in the form of these lower prices.

Efficiency gains were evident around the time of privatization in many companies, some undoubtedly motivated by the change in ownership. Managers were liberated both from borrowing restrictions and from government oversight, and found such freedom a heady mixture, anticipating that the newly privatized utilities could behave like other private companies, so long as they complied with regulatory financial requirements. Changes in labour legislation made it much easier to shed jobs (Foreman-Peck and Millward, 1994), and labour productivity soared through voluntary redundancy and revised working practices. Some of these cost reductions were passed on to consumers, and real prices fell in all the utility industries except water, where demands for higher quality drove prices up (for a review of these changes, see Markou and Waddams Price, 1999). But in gas, increasing numbers of disconnections for non-payment of bills immediately after privatization raised concerns about the distribution of gains from the reform, and highlighted fundamental issues about the nature of the utility industries. After regulatory intervention, disconnection levels fell, but were counterbalanced by an increase in the installation of prepayment meters. These prepayment meters became central to later debates about social concerns in the industry.

The first questions about distribution concerned two large groups: shareholders and consumers (Young, 1998). The original share sale mechanism had led to large gains for shareholders[2], and the incentives given to senior managers in the form of share options yielded especially dramatic gains for some executives. Some of the increased pay reflected the move of companies from the public to the private sector, where rewards to senior staff have traditionally been greater to reflect higher risks. But how far were these industries truly high risk? They were virtually guaranteed a return on capital employed, and their shares bear similarities to government bonds. British Gas came in for particular public criticism over the rewards to its chief executive, Cedric Brown, in 1994, with the visit of Cedric the pig to the shareholders' annual general meeting. Trade unions were also concerned about the loss of jobs, particularly at a time of high unemployment. Even though there were few compulsory redundancies, many of those who left the industries took early retirement, and so made little direct contribution to the economy. It seems likely that the financial gains for the companies from their saved salaries overestimated the saved resources to the economy, at least in the short term. Many of the continuing jobs were 'contracted out', with previous employees being moved to a more casual arrangement, so productivity gains were partially at the expense of employee welfare.

The incentives to reduce costs provided by price-cap regulation and the new private sector freedom were regarded as 'too powerful' in one respect, because they led to degradation in the quality of service provided. This became apparent soon after the flotation of the first utility, British Telecom (BT), in 1984. BT allowed the provision of public call boxes to deteriorate, and the regulator intervened to protect consumer interests, just as the gas regulator later acted against increased disconnection levels.

CROSS-SUBSIDIES AND RELATIVE PRICES

While there was some debate about the division of benefits between large groups of stakeholders, including the consumer population, there was little initial change in relative prices between consumers in markets like domestic gas where monopoly was maintained, despite the potentially higher profits which such rebalancing could yield. This opportunity arose from the inherited pattern of prices, which contained considerable cross-subsidy, despite a non-discrimination requirement similar to that inherited from their nationalized predecessors. Although rarely challenged, such cross-subsidy would probably have been justified on the basis of a 'universal service ethos', indicating that these services should be made available to all consumers at a similar price, even if the costs of supply differed.

Cross-subsidy in the residential gas market was typical. Apart from a small surcharge for prepayment meters, uniform prices were levied across England, Wales and Scotland, despite considerable variations in the costs of supplying different customers. In particular, the lower costs for the company of payment by direct debit and the higher costs of prepayment meter use were not fully reflected in the tariffs. Prepayment is more expensive for companies to operate for two reasons: the meters themselves are more costly to provide and maintain, especially the 'quantum' meters used in gas; and prepayment users typically charge their cards by making frequent small payments, which are more expensive to handle than regular monthly bank debits. Many prepayment meter users have a history of gas debt (indeed, at times incurring debt has been the only means of acquiring a prepayment meter) and so most prepayment consumers have incurred debt recovery costs in the past, though this is not a cost of using the meters themselves. Nevertheless, both the capital and recurrent costs associated with prepayment meters have been issues for regulation, although the instruments available to the regulator are rather different in each case.

Transco, the pipeline operator, retains an effective monopoly of the network system, enabling it to continue cross-subsidizing. Traditionally, Transco has charged the same price for delivery of gas to rural and urban areas, despite differences in cost, and for the provision of credit and prepayment meters, even though the latter are more expensive. Within a monopoly structure such cross-subsidy is sustainable, though it is unlikely to be efficient. However, it clearly has distributional effects: urban users subsidize rural consumers, credit consumers subsidize prepayers. Given the pervasiveness of such cross-subsidies in the utilities, the political economy of unwinding them is rather different from the deliberate introduction of new redistributive subsidies.

Failure to rebalance prices in other monopoly parts of the utilities may have been because the companies had insufficient information about relative costs to identify appropriate changes; or, more cynically, it may have been a deliberate policy to maintain monopoly status, because that would be the only way to maintain the cross-subsidies inherited from the nationalized industry. Such a political motive is consistent with the behaviour of British Gas when it knew that its residential markets would be opened to competition. Unlike telecoms and electricity, where a competition timetable was planned from the date of privatization, British Gas was privatized with a statutory monopoly in the residential market, which could only be removed by primary legislation. It was not certain that the necessary legislation would be tabled until the Queen's speech in November 1994; the next day, British Gas announced the introduction of discounts for households settling their bills by direct debit. Since the *average* of prices charged to the residential sector was subject to a price cap, such discounts would enable higher charges for other consumers, particularly those using prepayment meters. The timing of British Gas's announcement was clearly political, but the changes were inevitable in a competitive market. If the incumbent company had maintained a uniform price structure with different costs of supply, the (low-cost) markets with the highest mark-ups were vulnerable to 'cherry picking' by entrants. Unlike monopoly parts of the industry, British Gas was unable to maintain the cross-subsidies even if it wished to do so, because the profitable consumers who provided the subsidy would be seduced away by other suppliers.

The rebalancing caused concern because of the socioeconomic characteristics of those using different payment methods. Direct debit was more commonly used by the better off, and a disproportionate number of low-income households used prepayment meters (see Table 8.1), while the

Table 8.1   Analysis of payment methods for gas and electricity by income decile for equivalized income, 1995/6

Income decile	Lowest (%)	2nd (%)	3rd (%)	4th (%)	5th (%)	6th (%)	7th (%)	8th (%)	9th (%)	Highest (%)	Total 1995/6 (%)
Gas method of payment											
Direct debit	27	31	37	38	43	48	51	54	54	47	43
Quarterly credit	40	49	50	51	49	46	44	42	43	50	46
Prepayment meter	22	15	11	9	6	3	3	2	1	0	7
Fuel direct	6	2	1	1	0	–	–	–	–	–	1
Other method	4	3	1	2	2	2	2	2	2	2	2
Electricity method of payment											
Direct debit	18	18	23	29	34	38	38	48	47	38	33
Quarterly credit	35	55	57	53	52	50	51	45	45	59	50
Prepayment meter	43	25	18	16	12	10	9	5	6	1	14
Fuel direct	2	1	1	0	–	–	–	–	–	–	2
Other method	3	1	2	2	2	2	2	1	2	1	2
Fuel exp./weekly exp. (%)	6.8	8.3	6.7	5.5	4.8	4.5	4.0	3.7	3.5	2.8	4.4
Numbers	680	680	680	680	680	680	680	679	679	679	6797

Source: Waddams Price and Biermann (1998).

cheapest method of payment, direct debit, was unavailable, or too expensive for many who most needed lower-price energy[3]. The issue was therefore a broad one of social exclusion, of which the utilities were a comparatively small part. However, simultaneous changes across the utilities meant that effects were to some extent cumulative (Waddams Price and Hancock, 1998). Moreover, potential competition was as powerful as realized entry in unwinding cross-subsidies. From the date of privatization the telecoms line rental had been raised within the price cap by the maximum amount permitted by its separate constraint, adversely affecting those who used the telephone little, especially pensioner households. Direct debit discounts were introduced gradually into the electricity industry from the time of privatization up to and after competition was introduced in 1998, with similar effects to those in gas. While regulators did have some unspecified responsibilities for protecting the interests of those of pensionable age, we have seen that they had no remit to protect the poor before the Utilities Act, 2000, and such concerns were clearly outside the intentions of the original privatization acts which had established the regulatory offices and defined their duties.

Protection of certain groups posed a direct conflict with one of the regulator's duties, to encourage competition, and with another of her objectives: to encourage cost-reflective pricing, raising questions of how to achieve an appropriate balance. The most obvious route was to provide adequate safeguards directly to target households, but acting through the social security system may distort other markets, and both Conservative and Labour administrations have been loath to use such tools because of their reluctance to raise direct taxes. Cross-subsidies were possible via the monopoly networks as a second-best tool. Direct constraints could be placed on operators in competitive markets, but this would distort the development of competition, and might harm in the long term the very groups for whom short-term protection is sought. A consumer survey undertaken at the end of 1997 showed a clear preference for supporting low-income consumers via the tax and benefits system, as well as a marked difference between utilities in the perceived merit of providing subsidies (Table 8.2). It is against this background of consumer opinion in favour of direct methods of support, and government reluctance to implement them, that successive gas regulators have had to exercise judgment on social needs.

REGULATORY RESPONSE

The focus on cost-reflective pricing, and the higher costs of providing and maintaining prepayment meters, led the owner of the pipes and meters, Transco, to suggest a higher charge for suppliers using prepayment meters.

Table 8.2   Which of the following services should be provided at a subsidized cost to households genuinely not able to afford them, and how should this be funded?

Group	No. of respondents	Percentage supporting subsidy for:				Cross-subsidies	Percentage of sample		
		Water	Electric	Gas	Tel. line		Increased vat	Increased income tax	Some other way
All	1685	73	67	53	12	7	11	41	41
Income < £4K	421	66	61	48	15	9	11	33	47
Elderly	445	63	55	40	15	11	8	44	37
Elderly and income < £4K	139	55	45	36	16	13	10	41	36
Long-term sick or disabled	84	66	56	43	14	8	8	42	42
Lone parent and dependent child	124	75	72	66	13	4	10	35	47

Note: Percentages do not add up to 100 per cent as the choices are not mutually exclusive.

Source: Doble *et al.* (1998).

Transco was concerned at the increase in installation of prepayment meters following privatization and the reaction against the increasing disconnection rates, and feared that the advent of competition in gas retailing would lead to further demands for prepayment provision by entrants who had little experience in utility debt management. Given that the costs of such meters were higher, and Transco was revenue-capped, it was in their interests to reflect the higher costs in charges to shippers to discourage use. This is an example of the efficiency effects of the price-cap regulation system in encouraging cost-reflective pricing in the intermediate market. These higher charges would not necessarily be passed on to prepayment end consumers, but in a competitive market that would be the likely outcome. Moreover, there might be some scepticism if the regulator allowed the increases, since raising costs for all the competitors downstream increases industry profitability.

The regulator was faced with a dilemma: the current quantum technology was certainly more expensive for Transco to provide and operate than a regular credit meter, but allowing higher charges would be vociferously challenged by consumer groups who were concerned about its effect on low-income households. However, the continuation of equal charging for all forms of meters clearly constituted cross-subsidy of prepayment meters by other gas users. Although the regulator steadfastly declined to play an active role in encouraging cross-subsidies to particular social groups, it was quite a different matter to condone the removal of historical cross-subsidies where this was not enforced by the competitive market.

In the event, Transco did not differentiate its charges for prepayment and credit meters until October 1998, when it was allowed to introduce a surcharge of £10 for each prepayment meter. This was less than the £20 it then requested, and a request to raise the charge to £30 in October 1999 was refused. The regulator contested Transco's cost allocations, maintaining that the equipment should be depreciated over 20 years, as was standard Transco practice for other meters, and that maintenance costs should reflect efficient forward-looking costs, which are considerably lower than the quantum technology currently employed. These two arguments seem somewhat inconsistent, since transferring to a new technology entailed retiring the existing meters early.

While Transco's relative prices are a question of cost-reflectivity, a much more acute issue arose from the presence of cross-subsidy downstream in the residential market, as it was to be opened to competition, where the effect on low-income households was of particular public concern. It was in this context that the independent Gas Consumers Council (GCC) referred the new structure of residential gas prices to the gas regulator in early 1995, alleging undue discrimination against consumers who did not enjoy the new discounts, and undue preference towards those who did. The referrals triggered three reports, and an eventual restructuring both of the regulation price cap and of British Gas tariffs.

The referral was made on the basis of undue discrimination, a requirement common to the privatized industries. One reason why it was tested in gas rather than in other industries was the existence of an independent consumer council; in other industries, such issues would more likely be mediated internally within the regulatory office, where consumer representatives and the regulator shared resources. Testing this issue in gas arose from the particular political economy and institutional setting of regulation and consumer representation, suggesting that current proposals for more independent consumer councils throughout the privatized industries will probably give rise to more such references in the future.

The requirement not to discriminate unduly had not been tested robustly in a court room – the closest legal precedent referred to local government and dated from 1912. The gas regulator therefore had to find her own interpretation, and determined that non-discriminatory prices should be related to the costs of supplying different markets. She had to determine, first, the relation of prices to costs, and then whether the mark-ups were unduly discriminatory. In his excellent review of the issue of undue discrimination in these lectures two years ago, John Vickers pointed out that, from an economic perspective, basing prices only on costs is not usually the most efficient outcome (Vickers, 1998). In particular, where a company has market power and cannot cover its costs by putting all prices equal to marginal costs, economic efficiency may be maximized by charging prices which incur higher mark-ups over marginal costs in markets where demand is less responsive to price. This is clearly discriminatory, since relative prices depend on demand conditions as well as cost levels. However, in the case of the GCC referrals, there was an implicit issue of the distributive effect of British Gas's discounts, the potential conflict between non-discrimination and economic efficiency was exacerbated by concerns about social impact. The opening of the market put pressure on the incumbent to reflect the different costs of supply more closely in price structures, but this meant relative increases for consumers who could not or would not take advantage of direct debit payment, and particular concern for prepayment consumers. In any event the GCC referral led the gas regulator deep into questions of cost and price structure which were far removed from the original 'arm's-length' regulation vision.

The regulator produced two reports in direct response to the GCC's referrals (OFGAS 1995, 1996), under the 1986 Gas Act, and the issues were further resolved in a report on the structure of domestic gas tariffs published two years later (OFGAS, 1998). Although the final report followed a change of government and the publication of a Green Paper on utility regulation (discussed in the next section), the conclusions were broadly consistent with the regulator's earlier rulings.

The company maintained that direct debit consumers were cheaper and prepayment more expensive to supply, and provided accounting cost data to support their case. The regulator ruled that undue discrimination was not present if all classes of consumers met their attributable costs,[4] and none bore an undue burden of joint costs. A 'due' burden seemed to be interpreted as one proportional to the attributable costs for that group. So prices should, by implication, be proportional to attributable costs. This focused attention on the process and outcome of cost attribution. The regulator consistently argued for lower prepayment and higher direct debit costs than the company in an attempt to reduce the prices charged to prepayment customers. If OFGAS were right in its cost allocations, the only incentive for the company to 'talk up' the costs of prepayment meter supply would be if the profit-maximizing balance between prices involved higher mark-ups over the lower 'true [OFGAS-calculated] costs' in this market than in others. This is consistent with demand being less price-responsive for prepayment consumers than for others. But such a pattern seems unlikely, both intuitively and from econometric evidence (for example, Baker *et al.*, 1989), indicating that energy demand is *more* price-elastic for low-income users. Instead it appears that the regulator was arguing for lower prepayment costs and prices for distributional ends. Eventually, the regulator argued for a single tariff for prepayment and some (slow) credit payers, while allowing discounts for prompt credit payers. This clearly benefits prepayment meter users in the short term, by capping their prices at a lower level.

Moreover, as competition developed, the cap on average prices had been replaced in 1997 by individual caps on each element of each tariff; that is, all standing charges and running rates. This prevented British Gas from responding to competitive pressure in one part of the market by lowering prices to those consumers, and recouping lost revenue by increasing prices to others, who were not so eagerly sought by competitors. These individual caps made any rebalancing between tariffs much less likely, so preserving the inherited price structure.

However, new entrants seem to agree with the incumbent that the margins for prepayment meter consumers are much lower, since they are offering very little, if any, discount against the incumbent price compared with other markets (Otero and Waddams Price, 1999a).[5] The regulator has provided short-term protection, presumably on grounds of social needs, but at the cost of discouraging active market entry for these consumers.

The issues addressed by the gas regulator clearly raised a number of problems which were of wider concern, in particular where the responsibility for resolving questions of social need should properly lie. The next section takes a broader view of regulating for social needs, both in the energy and other regulated utilities, and the implications of current proposals in the gas and electricity markets are explored in the final section.

INITIATIVES FROM GOVERNMENT AND INTERPRETATION IN OTHER UTILITIES

The present government launched a major review of utility regulation within three months of taking office. The Green Paper (Department of Trade and Industry, 1998) confirmed the incoming Labour Government's general support for the model of regulation which it had inherited, but shifted the emphasis considerably towards distributional issues. The government proposed changing the primary statutory duty of regulators to one of consumer protection,[6] in recognition of the special nature of these industries. The title itself, 'A Fair Deal for Consumers', confirmed this new emphasis, and considerable attention was paid to just those issues which had concerned the gas regulator; in particular, the conflict between increasing competition in energy and the impact on prepayment meter users. The Green Paper declared as the government's objective that 'the economic benefits of liberalisation are spread fairly amongst everyone, including the most vulnerable consumers' (Department of Trade and Industry, 1998, p.35). Where regulatory action with financial effects on companies or consumer groups was required on grounds of social (or environmental) need, the government undertook to provide specific guidance or legislation. In the meantime the annual Department of Trade and Industry (DTI) energy review included a comprehensive annexe on fuel poverty, reviewing and bringing together recent work in the area (Hutton, 1998).

In its Utilities Act, enacted in the summer of 2000, the government changed the energy regulator's primary duty to protection of consumer interests. To the consumer groups for which he has special responsibility has been added those with low incomes, shifting the regulatory role decisively towards distributional issues and away from efficiency-focused control. The government may either issue compulsory guidance to the regulator, or more general advice which is not binding.

Guidance has already been issued in the water industry, where response to social needs is affected by the provision in the 1999 Water Act that no domestic consumer may have their supply disconnected for reasons of non-payment. The government provided advice to the companies on more flexible payment options for 'less well-off households', and draft guidance to the regulator on approval of tariffs. In October 1999, specific regulations were issued to protect low-income families with three or more children, and those with certain medical conditions, from high charges if their water is metered. The Department of the Environment, Transport and the Regions (1999) estimates that these measures may add about £1 to the average annual domestic water bill. However, while the regulator welcomes specific regulations, he is reluctant to allow companies revenue in consideration of social tariffs beyond these requirements (OFWAT, 1999). This highlights the question of how much discretion the regulator should retain in addressing social needs, and how far this should solely be at the direction of government. The water regulator seemed to be taking a somewhat narrower view than the current energy regulator, an area of comparison explored further in the next section.

Social needs pose a slightly different issue in telecommunications. The telecoms regulator has recently launched a review of universal service (Oftel, 2000); the consultation paper recognizes both the importance of telephony for social inclusion, and that the market may require intervention to ensure that all groups, including those on low incomes, have access to 'affordable telephony'. The last review imposed some obligations (such as a requirement to supply, geographically averaged prices, maintenance of public call boxes and provision of a low-user tariff) on the incumbent, and required that it meet the cost of this package without additional revenue.

There have been fewer developments on social needs in electricity regulation than in gas, but the merging of the regulatory offices for the two industries has brought convergence of policy across the industries. The next section deals with these more recent developments, and the prospects for future regulation for social needs in energy in the light of current proposals from both the government and the regulator.

CURRENT PROPOSALS

The original model of economic regulation, reaffirmed by this government, is not well suited to delivering social objectives, and regulators differ in their response to the general exhortation to consider distributional concerns. The government has reaffirmed its intention to incorporate distributional as well as efficiency concerns in utility regulation, but is not yet very explicit about the mechanism. It is in this context that the two most recent gas regulators have developed a Social Action Plan over the last 18 months, and revised price caps were implemented in April 2000.

The original government call for development of a social action plan by the (then separate) gas and electricity regulators was contained in the 1998 Green Paper; but the regulators were given very little time for its preparation, and the document was inevitably somewhat superficial (OFFER and OFGAS, 1998).

However, Callum McCarthy has developed this policy much more proactively since he took over as director-general for both industries. Four significant documents were published between May and November 1999. A Social Action Plan discussion document in May and a framework document in October (OFFER and OFGAS, 1998; OFGEM, 1999(a)); a document on prepayment meters (OFGEM, 1999b) in October; and proposed revised price limits for British Gas Trading (OFGEM, 1999c) in November. These reflect considerable development of the regulator's own policies towards social needs. The consultation paper and framework clearly anticipate more proactive guidance from the government, and accept that there should indeed be a 'social' aspect to energy regulation. Potential conflicts between social needs and development of competition, and the undesirability of the plan distorting competition, are acknowledged, but not fully resolved.

The clearest guidelines are contained in the framework for action and the consultation on prepayment meters, both published in October 1999, with proposals to amend supplier obligations, make some structural changes to regulation and initiate a programme of research activity. Some of this framework coordinates the work and monitoring of the gas and electricity industries, but some new requirements are introduced. The regulator clearly sees the rising numbers of prepayment customers as a problem, and expresses firm support for transferring prepayment consumers to credit tariffs wherever possible, while stating that he 'has no wish to prevent customers from using prepayment meters'.

OFGEM's priorities can be classified as falling under a number of headings. The main one is to lower barriers to consumers in choosing between alternative payment methods and suppliers, through improving consumer information, ensuring broader options and removing current barriers to switching for those in debt.[7] Suppliers are expected to develop and offer a broader range of payment methods, enter 'effective' dialogues with consumers in debt, develop innovative schemes to improve energy efficiency and undertake a range of research activities. Offering a range of payment methods might facilitate product or consumer differentiation in the market to 'soften' competition to the detriment of consumers. There are calls for increased transparency to help consumers choose in changing suppliers. Here there is some tension between helping consumers to make better informed choices and the danger of encouraging tacit collusion among suppliers. Such a possibility makes even more crucial an impartial monitoring of the competitive process, including the pattern and sequencing of price changes within the industry, to detect any collusive activity.

Probably the most significant requirement is the apparently innocuous request for supply companies to report on their social programmes. Even without specifying exactly how the information will be used, collecting such data will affect behaviour. In monitoring the information, the regulator is highlighting its significance, and implying that reward or punishment may follow. These steps are likely to increase the cost of supplying 'disadvantaged' customers, and so might prejudice development of competition for this group. However, the reporting requirements both ensure that these costs are reasonably evenly spread across suppliers and offer them the hope of some regulatory reward for serving low-income households. The response of the Electricity Association and the gas industry in setting up a fuel poverty task force to address these issues and fund independent research suggests that this is exactly how the messages are being read within the industries themselves. Such cooperation, together with calls for increased transparency, may run a risk of collusion in the longer term, and behaviour in the market will need to be carefully monitored to detect and deter any moves in this direction.

The prepayment document distinguishes the capital and revenue costs of prepayment provision. The cap on surcharges which electricity distribution companies may levy for prepayment meters recalls debates about Transco surcharges. Here in the network companies, at least, cross-subsidies can be maintained without distorting competition, albeit at the expense of some misallocation of resources. This will, ironically, encourage overprovision of prepayment meters at a time when the regulator would prefer to see their numbers decline.

More direct action on prices was taken in the review of British Gas Trading's controls, published in November 1999. The direct debit market was judged sufficiently competitive to be 'deregulated', and caps were retained on prepayment and credit prices for one further year, in the expectation that there would be sufficient entry to these markets for caps to be removed from 2001. However, this seems somewhat ambitious in the light of OFGEM's own cost estimates. These are lower than British Gas's estimates of prepayment costs, but still imply that the incumbent would make an average loss of nearly £10 a year on each prepayment customer, compared with a similar profit for each standard payer (Table 8.3). This is not an encouraging omen for more vigorous entry in the prepayment market, even if suppliers' right to object to the transfer of consumers is removed.

The regulator and the secretary of state for energy have also signalled concern about the level of standing charges. Because energy use increases with income in absolute terms (but not proportionately), high standing charges may disadvantage low income consumers. This is a similar concern to that for low users of telephony. However, like prepayment meters, low use is an imperfect surrogate for low income, and high use may correlate with some forms of disadvantage, such as unemployment, disability and chronic sickness

Table 8.3   OFGEM's estimate of costs and revenues of supplying residential gas markets (£ per consumer per annum, based on average consumption for each payment method)

Payment method	Prompt pay	Standard	Prepayment
Costs	234.40	256.12	243.79
Allowed revenue	229.99	234.19	234.15
Average profit	−4.42	+9.32	−9.64

Source: Based on OFGEM (1999c): consumption figures from table 2; cost figures from table 19; proposed caps from table 20.

(see, for example, Sharratt, 1999). In January 2000, British Gas Trading announced a major restructuring of tariffs, replacing the traditionally unpopular standing charge with block tariffs (British Gas Trading, 2000). The main beneficiaries are those who use little gas. These include some low-income households, but very few of the 'fuel poor' who, by definition, have high consumption, at least relative to their incomes. A study of an earlier standing charge rebate system, forced on the nationalized gas and electricity industries in the early 1980s, concluded that it was 'both mean and wasteful' (Gibson and Price, 1986). As Table 8.4 shows, it failed to reach many of those in need, and helped many who were not (for example, owners of second homes). Using tariff structures as a redistributive tool is likely to run into similar difficulties, exacerbated by the pressures of the competitive market.

The energy regulator's Social Action Plan makes an interesting comparison with codes of practice which have developed in the water industry. Where there are differences these reflect both variations in exposure to competition and the particular characteristics of and public attitude to the industries. For example, budget payment units, the equivalent of prepayment meters, and all disconnections for non-payment have been made illegal in water. Water companies are required to provide frequent payment options free of charge, while discounts are offered for energy payment methods which are cheaper for companies to operate. Water companies do not differentiate charges according to payment method, so they are continuing cross-subsidies between consumer groups. Customer service levels, including those for disadvantaged customers, are already part of OFWAT's comparative statistics. In many ways, OFGEM's Social Action Plan is proposing measures already operating in water. Some of these are more complex to introduce in markets open to competition, but there is clearly a degree of convergence on practical measures. Perhaps it is the lack of competition in his industry which makes the water regulator reluctant to approve further social tariffs unless he is so directed by the government. The

Table 8.4   Percentage of households subsidized by standing charge rebate scheme, by income (fully analysed records only)

Household income level (£ per week)	Percentage with rebate	Percentage income distribution of households with rebates*
Under 25	20	1
25 and under 50	18	21
50 and under 75	14	20
75 and under 100	9	11
100 and under 150	8	22
150 and under 200	7	13
200 and under 250	6	7
250 and under 300	6	3
Over 300	5	3

Note: *Figures do not add to 100 owing to rounding.

Source: Gibson and Price (1986).

scope for such measures in gas is limited by the constraints of the market itself.

It is perhaps surprising that the regulators, who have recently identified a number of areas where cooperation would be desirable, have not included social needs, the very area where cross-industry cooperation and consistency might seem most desirable. Perhaps this is to avoid exposing different views on how far such regulatory action should be discretionary, and how far enforced by central government. But it is clearly an area where 'joined-up regulation' would seem particularly appropriate, and where inconsistencies might have some very perverse implications for disadvantaged households. The whole issue of fuel poverty, the inability to afford adequate warmth, is a complex interaction of income, housing conditions and conditions of fuel supply (including price). If the government is serious about its eradication the agencies concerned need to work closely together.

Gas regulation has moved a long way from the original efficiency-based model – the economist's dream. Government policy has reflected public opinion that these are not ordinary private companies supplying commodities just like any other. The current regulator has accepted, indeed embraced, the need to address social needs as part of the regulatory process. This raises questions of how far utility markets should be used to deliver social objectives, which can be much more effectively addressed through the tax and benefits system; and concerns of unintended consequences, both in the short term for the households themselves and in encouraging cooperation between supplying companies, which may not always be in consumers' longer-term interests. These developments have certainly multiplied the cost of the regulatory office by many times that of a part-time director-general and 18 staff, and may have turned the economist's dream into a regulator's nightmare.

NOTES

1. I am grateful to Sue Cox of OFWAT for a comparison of the 1999 water and energy regulatory mechanisms and to Patrick Law, Diane Sharratt, Alison Young and participants at the IEA/LBS lectures for helpful comments on an earlier draft of this paper; none bears any responsibility for the final outcome.
2. Shares were sold at what seem, in retrospect, to be rather low prices for two reasons. First, the government was keen to encourage individuals who had not traditionally held shares to purchase utility issues, perhaps in part to create a 'share-owning democracy' where large numbers of voters would have an interest in preventing the return of the Labour Party, which remained committed to renationalization until the mid-1990s. Secondly, the extent of inefficiencies within the nationalized industries was not realized until after they were privatized and improved their productivity – one vindication for their incentive regulation scheme.
3. The problem for low-income households may not be lack of *access* to a current bank account and direct debit payments, but the high costs levied by banks if a direct debit payment results in the account becoming overdrawn (Doble, 1998). Households on very tight budgets are more likely to run the risk of such an event, and to avoid direct debit mandates as a result.
4. Attributable costs are not the same as marginal costs, but may be a reasonable surrogate for 'incremental' costs in the sense used by Faulhaber (1975).
5. A similar pattern is evident in electricity (Otero and Waddams Price, 1999b).
6. Changing the primary duty to one of consumer protection is unlikely to be very significant in itself, since medium-term consumer interests will only be served if the regulator allows adequate financing to companies for the service.
7. At present, suppliers of consumers with debt can object to their transfer to another supplier.

REFERENCES

Baker, P., R. Blundell and J. Micklewright (1989), 'Modelling household energy expenditure using micro-data', *Economic Journal*, 99, 220–38.
Bradley, Ian and Catherine Price (1988), 'The economic regulation of private industries by price constraints', *Journal of Industrial Economics*, 37, 99–106.
British Gas Trading (2000), 'British Gas to revolutionise energy bills', press release, 13 January.
Department of the Environment, Transport and the Regions (1999), *Water Industry Act 1999, Consultation on Regulations*, October.
Department of Trade and Industry (1998), *A Fair Deal for Consumers*, March.
Department of Trade and Industry (1999b), *A Fair Deal for Consumers, Regulatory, Environmental and Equal Treatment Appraisals*, October.
Doble, Michael (1998), 'Low Income Consumers in the Competitive Gas Market: Why Don't Prepayment Users Switch to Cheaper Methods?', Centre for

Management under Regulation, research paper 98/4, University of Warwick.

Doble, Michael, Eleni Markou and Catherine Waddams Price (1998), 'Utility Regulation: Fairness for All? Responses to the Government's Green Paper', Centre for Management under Regulation, research paper 98/2, University of Warwick.

Faulhaber, Gerry (1975), 'Cross-subsidization: pricing in public enterprises', *American Economic Review*, 65, 966–77.

Foreman-Peck, James and Robert Millward (1994), *Public and Private Ownership of British Industry*, Oxford: Clarendon Press.

Gibson, Michael and Catherine Price (1986), 'Standing charge rebates', *Energy Policy*, 262–71.

Hutton, Sandra (1998), 'The Energy Report' in Department of Trade and Industry (ed.), *Energy Trends*, p.72–116, London.

Littlechild, Stephen (1983), *Regulation of British Telecommunications Profitablity*, London: HMSO.

Markou, Eleni and Catherine Waddams Price (1999), 'UK utilities: past reform and current proposals', *Annals of Public and Co-operative Economics*, 70(3), 371–416.

Mulholland, Kate (1998), '"Survivors" vs "Movers and Shakers": the reconstitution of management and careers in the privatised utilities', in Paul Thompson and Chris Warhurst (eds), *Workplaces of the Future*, London: Macmillan.

OFFER and OFGAS (1998), 'The Social Dimension: Action Plan', June.

OFFER and OFGAS (1999), 'Social Action Plan: Discussion document', May.

OFGAS (1995), 'Referral by the Gas Consumers Council relating to discounts for customers paying by direct debit: the Director General's Decision'.

OFGAS (1996), 'Investigation into discounts for British Gas Supply's tariff customers paying promptly or by direct debit: the Director General's Decision'.

OFGAS (1998), 'Review of British Gas Trading's domestic supply tariffs: a decision document'.

OFGEM (1999a), 'Social action plan framework document', October.

OFGEM (1999b), 'Prepayment meters: a consultation document', October.

OFGEM (1999c), 'Review of British Gas Trading's Price Regulation: Initial Proposals', November.

OFTEL (2000), 'Universal Telecommunication Services, consultative document issued by the Director General of Telecommunications', Review of September.

OFWAT (1999), 'MD152, letter to all managing directors of water and sewerage companies and water only companies', 13 September.

Otero, Jesus and Catherine Waddams Price (1999a), 'Incumbent and Entrant Response to Regulated Competition: Signalling with Accounting Costs and Market Prices', Centre for Management under Regulation, research paper 99/3, University of Warwick.

Otero, Jesus and Catherine Waddams Price (1999b), 'Price Discrimination, Regulation and Entry in the UK Residential Electricity Market', Centre for Management under Regulation, research paper 99/4, University of Warwick.

Sharratt, Diane (1999), 'Fuel Direct – Help or Hindrance? Users' Experiences', Centre for Management under Regulation, research paper 99/5, University of Warwick.

Vickers, John (1998), 'When is discrimination undue?', in M.E. Beesley (ed.), *Regulating Utilities: Understanding the Issues*, London: Institute for Economic Affairs.

Waddams Price, Catherine and Andreas Biermann (1998), *Fuel Poverty in Britain: Expenditure on Fuels 1993-94 to 1995-96*, London: Gas Consumers Council.

Waddams Price, Catherine and Ruth Hancock (1998), 'Distributional effects of liberalising UK residential utility markets', *Fiscal Studies*, 19(3), 295–320.

Young, Alison (1998), 'Consumer Choice? Social Obligations, Cross Subsidies and Competition in the Privatised Utilities', Centre for Management under Regulation, research paper 98/7, University of Warwick.

CHAIRMAN'S COMMENTS
Callum McCarthy

I understand that tradition requires the Chairman to start the discussion by making some comments on the paper. I should like to start by endorsing the general thesis of Professor Waddams Price's paper, namely that regulation has become more complex as it embraces distributional as well as efficiency aspects. The additional complexity that this brings certainly makes the agenda of regulation a significantly different one from the original regulatory agenda. I should add that there is a further set of questions, namely the environmental questions, which are also coming to the fore, with their own complexities. I doubt whether any of the original utility regulators would have described their life as a dream. I certainly do not regard mine as a nightmare, but I do regard it as significantly more complex than that of original regulators.

Against this general background there are a number of points I would like to make. The first I should like to develop is the point made by Professor Waddams Price about accurately defining those in need for whom there is a social case for providing special assistance. I strongly endorse what she has said, namely the difficulty of identifying those who really need help as distinct from using a proxy which provides accuracy – perhaps spurious accuracy – but is only an approximation for those in real need. I think this is particularly a problem in terms of the correlation often made between the fuel poor and those who use repayment meters. I was interested to see from her own analysis of payment method against income decile that in every decile those who use prepayment meters are in a minority for both electricity and gas. For gas the figures are particularly striking, in that in every income decile, including the lowest income decile, a smaller percentage use prepayment meters than use direct debit.

There is real danger that an attempt to use a proxy such as a payment method to define the fuel poor will actually result in an additional burden being placed on the very group that the policy is designed to aid.

Second, I also agree strongly with Professor Waddams Price on the tension she identifies between an attempt to avoid price discrimination against a particular grouping, namely customers who pay via prepayment meters, and the spread of competition. More generally, I would say that a central concern of OFGEM in our proposals for the electricity and the supply price controls has been to establish a balance between promoting competition, on the one hand, and, on the other, establishing a safety net for those sectors where competition is not yet effective. You know our proposals for electricity, which involve taking one sector – the business and industrial sector – out of control and establishing for those sectors which remain subject to control a level of price control which is not intended to bite but rather to be a complement to competition. We shall be coming forward later this week with specific proposals for gas, but it would be strange if we adopted any different principle there.

I am conscious of a regulatory obstacle to competition affecting prepayment meter customers other than price control, namely the right to object to the transfer of customers who have debts. This right, designed to prevent fraudulent debtors from skipping from their debts, means that the marketing expenditure in pursuing prepayment meter customers, many of whom use their prepayment as an expensive way of managing debt, is unjustified, and is I believe one of the main reasons why companies are choosing not to market strongly to this class of customers. It will be very interesting to see, once there are arrangements to transfer debts on the basis which has been suggested in the Social Action Plan proposed by OFGEM, whether prepayment customers become more attractive to competing suppliers. We clearly hope they will.

The last point I would like to make is organizational. I am not sure whether in practice the pressure brought to bear by the GCC, as a body separate from OFGAS, has been more independent than that brought to bear by the Electricity Consumer Councils in relation to OFFER. By definition, since the GCC was separate its communication needed to be more public. I do not think that from that one can simply make the leap to believe that it has actually been more independent or more effective. That said, I do not support the principle of the regulator appointing those who comment upon regulation from the consumers' point of view, and believe that the electricity model is incorrect in that respect – though I do not argue that the results of this model were necessarily ineffective or less effective than the gas results.

9. The Competition Commission: prospects and problems

Dan Goyder

INTRODUCTION

On 1 April 1999, the Competition Commission came into existence. On the same day the Monopolies and Mergers Commission, after 50 years of service, ceased to exist and its role was taken over by the new body pursuant to the abrupt command of the 1998 Competition Act (Commencement Order No. 3) Order 1999 SI 1999/505. Moreover, on the same day, another statutory instrument ensured that, in at least a metaphorical sense, the removal men could take all the assets, tangible and intangible, belonging to the MMC, as well as the conduct of various reports still in train, metaphorically over from their old home to their new. In reality, I am sure things continued much as before under the new title.

Yet this transformation was, of course, an incomplete one, since it only affected one half of the new Competition Commission, and for the other half we have to wait until 1 March 2000, when its other part, the Appeal Tribunal, comes legally into existence, thereby creating the Competition Commission in its full authority. As authority for its creation we have to look at schedule 7 of the Competition Act, which provides for the following:

- the appointment of a president of the Appeal Tribunal, whom we now know to be Judge Christopher Bellamy;
- the appointment of a Council, the management board for the Commission;
- the appointment by the president of specific appeal tribunals under a number of legally qualified chairmen (in addition to himself) to deal with notices of appeal received against OFT decisions under the Competition Act;
- procedural rules for the appeal tribunals, which recently were published in draft for consultation purposes.

So much, then, for the mechanics of the creation of the new body, but of course you have not come principally to hear me talk about legal technicalities of this kind. What is far more interesting is the contribution that this new body is likely to make towards providing an effective and appropriate competition law for the UK: that is, whether these new institutions will be able to 'make a difference'. I am going to deal with the subject under four headings.

First, we have to begin with the single most important influence on the future of the Commission, which is the Competition Act itself. We need to look briefly at both its structure and content. It creates new laws (modelled on articles 81 and 82 of the Treaty of Rome); also new procedures and strengthened institutions to enforce those laws through those procedures. There are rather unusual features of the legislation, which provides that the legal basis for the application in the UK to matters of domestic competition law will be established EU principles of competition law. This will have major and direct influence on the work of the tribunal and also possibly indirect effect on the work of the reporting side of the Commission.

Second, we shall look at how, within the new statutory framework, the two parts of the Commission are intended to operate, given their different tasks and characteristics. Different criteria may well be applicable to measure the role to be played by each of them.

Third, we should consider the actual prospects for the Commission and also a number of problems that appear to face it. I will indicate how these may need to be dealt with if the Commission is to fulfil the hopes of its creators.

Fourth, and finally, I draw some brief conclusions about the likely development of the Commission over the next few years.

THE COMPETITION ACT 1998

Let us first get a clear picture of the Competition Act itself. The Act seeks to mimic articles 81 and 82 of the Treaty of Rome and to utilize the experience of the European Community in their application over the last 40 years. The move from our previous complex, and somewhat eccentric, Restrictive Trade Practices Acts of 1976 and 1977 to the new, relatively straightforward system of prohibition and exemption based on these well-known articles of the Treaty is undoubtedly a major and welcome change. It requires the creation of new institutions to enforce them and also the adaption of existing institutions for new purposes, to ensure that the new Chapters I and II reflecting articles 81 and 82, respectively, are enforced alongside the existing well-known Fair Trading Act, 1973. A new competition law based on principles of prohibition, backed up with substantial fines imposed for breach, as well as by the risk that relevant commercial agreements will be declared void and unenforceable, and where the prohibition is to be actively enforced by public bodies newly resourced to do so, should in theory at least bring about major changes in attitude, and practice.

The framework of articles 81 and 82, formally articles 85 and 86, is undoubtedly familiar to you. Article 81 deals broadly with the prohibition of agreements that both restrict competition and affect trade between member states, while article 82 prohibits the abuse by one or more undertakings of a dominant position within the Common Market or some substantial part of it, again insofar as it affects trade between member states. They are concerned for the EC essentially with the same objects that UK domestic competition law has concerned itself with, but they focus more effectively on economic principles and issues and upon the effect of the agreements and practices in question, rather than with formal legal definitions. UK undertakings have, of course, been subject to these EU rules from 1 January 1958 and later to a greater degree once the UK had joined the Community in 1973, and they became subject to the broad terms of the European Communities Act. It is unrealistic, notwithstanding the contrary comments of some politicians, to pretend that UK businesses are still in some way unfamiliar with these concepts. There have already been a large number of UK companies, large and small, which have had to pay fines for breach of one of the articles or had otherwise become involved in cases involving these rules. Moreover, the phrase 'that may affect trade with Member States' in article 81 has been very broadly interpreted by the European Courts (and therefore also by the European Commission) as covering even activities with a highly marginal effect on such trade.

The Act makes major changes in UK competition law. The director-general of fair trading (DGFT) remains in office, but with greatly enhanced powers, resources and responsibilities. He is now primarily responsible with his office for administering new substantive prohibitions to replace the old RTPA legislation, as well as the comparatively ineffective 1980 Competition Act. As I have mentioned, the new prohibitions are referred to broadly as 'Chapter I' and 'Chapter II' prohibitions in the new Act. The DGFT has also been given extra procedural powers to investigate alleged breaches of these obligations which are equivalent to, indeed marginally stronger than, those possessed by DG IV. For the first time, the director general will be able to levy fines on undertakings found to have engaged in prohibited activities or agreements, as well as issuing prohibitions against the continuation of them.

Once the possibility of fines is introduced to competition law, as a matter of due process and human rights law, there has also to be introduced a mechanism for reviewing the fairness of their imposition. This means that the legal aspects of the whole process, in terms of the greater involvement of lawyers and a more adversarial atmosphere, are increased; it also puts additional emphasis on the definition of those transactions which do fall within the prohibition: 'concerted practices' as well as 'agreements' between companies. Publicity for parties engaged in high-profile cases under Chapters I or II will undoubtedly, at least in the early stages, be greater than in the past. For the first time, therefore, in the UK we will have an Appeal Tribunal, in the sphere of competition law, which becomes one part of the new Competition Commission, dealing solely with appeals from the decisions of the director-general, but cohabiting with the 'reporting side' of the Commission. This latter body is the old Monopolies and Mergers Commission in its new form, which will still have its responsibility for investigating monopoly and merger references under the Fair Trading Act as well as dealing with utility licence appeals and price review cases under the various regulatory statutes and some other statutory jurisdiction (for example, under the Broadcasting Act 1990).

If the rules which the European Community applied to Chapters I and II situations were by now in all respects clearly established, so that a high degree of legal certainty prevailed as to their application in the UK to domestic practices and agreements, the new task of the UK authorities might appear quite straightforward. Unfortunately, while in some areas it is true to say that the EC substantive law is well established, in others, notably the area of vertical agreements, the Commission is in the process at this very moment of rethinking its whole approach and of sweeping away much of the existing structures of block exemption (that is, legislative exemption by category for particular agreements). It is replacing them with other rules designed to focus the Commission's attentions on those markets where the supplier[1] has more than 30 per cent of the relevant product in a recognized geographical market. The object of the Commission's reforms, which are anticipated as likely to take effect from 1 June 2000, is that there will be a single broad block exemption covering the great majority of vertical distribution agreements, in order that the Commission can focus their attention, and consider requests for individual exemption, in those cases involving a substantial market share of above the 30 per cent figure. It is important, however, to note that these reforms do not affect licences for the transfer of technology, which have their own special block exemption (No. 240/96); nor do they apply to the thorny topic of motor vehicle distribution, where the existing block exemption 1475/95 will expire in 2002 and at present looks unlikely to be renewed after that date, and if renewed, certainly not in the same form as at present.

What the Commission has been saying in its reform proposals, and it has much to commend it, is that, while in the early years of the European Community, with only six member states, it may have been good policy to focus on vertical agreements with a block exemption that provided a very tight framework for distribution and limited availability of individual exemption, this makes far less sense in a mature Community of 15 member states (numbers likely to increase substantially in future years) and with much of the single market integration now achieved. It is of course interesting that our own Restrictive Trade Practice Acts themselves have always largely excluded vertical agreements relating to conventional distribution of goods from their scope, and to that extent UK and EC practice appears to be converging. The difficulty, however, will lie in the assessment at both EC and UK level of those vertical agreements operated by companies which do have arguably a market share breaching the 30 per cent barrier in specific products in defined geographical areas. Here the European Community will still seek to impose individual control, but the UK's response to the same issue is far from clear; in fact section 50 of the Act appears to give the secretary of state a complete 'blank cheque', either to exclude such restrictions from the scope of the Chapter I prohibition or to 'claw them back' at a later date, if it appears necessary. Further serious complications for the UK are raised by the proposals contained in the April 1999 White Paper of the European Commission on modernization of the rules affecting all article 81 agreements, under which it is proposed that notification would itself cease to be available, and treating the prohibition in article 81 as one which would be dealt with *ex post* by national competition authorities and national courts, rather than *ex ante*, much as applies already in the EC to article 82 practices and generally, under US antitrust law.[2]

One of the most important sections in the Act (and of considerable significance to the new tribunal in particular) is section 60, which sets out the so-called 'general principles' clause. Subsection 1 states that the object of this section is to ensure 'so far as is possible (having regard to any relevant differences between the provisions concerned) that questions arising in relation to competition within the United Kingdom are dealt with in a manner consistent with a treatment of corresponding questions arising under EC law in relation to competition within the Community'. This in turn leads on to subsection 2, which contains the main substantive provision of the section. This requires the court, when it determines any competition law question, to act, so far as is compatible with the provisions of the Act, to preserve consistency between the principles applied by it and its decisions with those laid down by the Treaty of Rome and the European Court as applicable at the relevant time in determining a 'corresponding question' arising in Community law. Moreover, under subsection 3, UK courts and tribunals must also 'have regard' to any relevant decision or statement of the European Commission itself; these requirements of consistency apply also to the director-general of fair trading and to any court hearing claims under UK law for damages or injunctions in respect of breaches of UK competition law, though not to the reporting side of the Competition Commission, which at least so far has never been regarded in law as a 'court' or 'tribunal'.[3]

It is a notable feature of the Act, therefore, that it is not legislation that stands firmly on its own feet, but in some sense 'shadow legislation' seeking to apply equivalent provisions of EC competition law (whatever they may be at a particular time) to the UK situation. There have been other examples of this kind of legislation, notably in the European Communities Act itself. More recently, and of particular interest, we find the same phenomenon in the Human Rights Act (given Royal Assent on the same day in 1998 as the Competition Act) which will not, however, come into effect until well after the operative date of the Competition Act. In the latter case, of course, the reference point for the Act is the European Convention on Human Rights, rather than the Treaty of Rome, but in the same way courts, tribunals and public bodies will have under the Act to take into account principles laid down by the relevant treaty and also operative decisions of Community or European courts applying to a wide variety of situations.

The Competition Act is in some ways a deceptive piece of work; it has, after all, only 76 short sections and 14 quite short appendices. One might think that, compared with a normal Finance Bill or Companies Act, it is brief and fairly straightforward. The Act itself, however, is only the starting point for the new competition law regime. Upon its structure is in the near future to be erected under section 60 a further 'superstructure' to incorporate Community principles of competition law already decided in several thousand cases by the ECJ, the CFI (Court of First Instance) and the Commission itself since 1 January 1958. In addition there are to be a large number of official 'guidelines', many already published by the Office of Fair Trading which seek (in some cases controversially) to distil the content of all this case law, as well as much secondary legislation to supply some of the details which the Act itself lacks.

The process of drafting primary and secondary legislation in this country, so as to apply EC law (whether contained in the Treaty of Rome or in one or more Community directives made under the treaty,) is not a new one; the process has caused difficulties for all UK governments since 1973 which have on occasion demonstrably fallen short of implementing the full and accurate content of directives, while on other occasions civil servants have been accused of being guilty of 'overkill' in overenthusiastic implementation of EC principles. The introduction of the Competition Act, however, was not of course required by any EC directive but was a voluntary decision of the UK government to embody in our domestic law so far as possible the entire EC law of competition, consisting of the relevant articles of the Treaty of Rome as interpreted and applied in all these past cases or spelled out in regulations and notices of the Commission. To perform this task with complete fidelity, even if desirable, would have been difficult even if all the relevant rules had been certain or in a condition that one might describe as 'solid state', to misuse a scientific term. In fact a characteristic of EC competition law has been that, while some principles are well established, many are still not finally resolved, even 40 years after the Treaty of Rome, so that the substantive and procedural framework for the applications of articles 81 and 82 is in some respects far from certain.

The draftsmen of the bill (and those now seeking to implement the Act) have been in the unenviable position, therefore, of a ship's crew trying to moor a new craft alongside a wharf, which they find to their horror is not solidly set on firm foundations but is itself floating away slowly but inexorably in a different direction. I refer of course to the Commission's proposals both on vertical restraints and on the modernization of the implementation of article 81. Even if some of these radical Commission proposals may not come into effect for some years, they raise important questions about the way in which EC competition law should be enforced in the UK and therefore will have an effect upon national competition authorities such as the Competition Commission as well as, of course, on the director-general of fair trading and his Office.

Finally, it is important to emphasize what the Act does not do. It does not repeal, or even substantially amend, the Fair Trading Act. The former 'mergers and monopoly jurisdiction' of the MMC remains in statutory terms unchanged, and the procedure for reviewing and dealing with mergers remains the shared responsibility of the secretary of state, the director-general of fair trading and the Commission. The 1999 (July) Consultation Paper on UK Merger Forms indeed casts some doubt on whether the Competition Commission will continue to be the competition authority charged with detailed examination of mergers, and this problem is dealt with at a later point in this paper. Both 'scale' and 'complex' monopoly reference can still be made to the Competition Commission, although it appears from published statements of the government that 'scale monopoly' references may be made less often than in the past. This is an issue to which I will return when examining some of the problems that may confront the Commission. While therefore a major new influence will be entering UK domestic law as the result of the Act's adoption of EC principles in this area, we shall continue nevertheless to retain a number of familiar elements in our competition law. Indeed, there is much in the 'monopoly' jurisdiction of the Fair Trading Act that Brussels may well envy, given the demonstrable inadequacy of article 82 to handle the problems arising in many sectors threatened by oligopolistic tendencies and joint dominance, even though the European Community Merger Regulation has recently been held applicable to situations of joint dominance (of which the recent *Airtours/First Choice* decision[4] is the most striking and radical example).

THE TWO PARTS OF THE COMPETITION COMMISSION

The Commission will therefore have two quite distinct functions. Let us first look at the working of the tribunal, which is a statutory creation of the seventh schedule of the 1998 Act. Tribunals have become a familiar institution in our legal system, as statutory bodies given jurisdiction to deal with particular categories of claim. They have their own rules of procedure which must meet the minimum requirements laid down by the Council on Tribunals; their decisions are subject ultimately to appeal to either the High Court or in some cases direct to the Court of Appeal on matters of law. They have the advantage of becoming specialists in particular areas of law, whether social security, agricultural drainage disputes, equal opportunities or employment matters. They combine judicial and lay membership in a way appropriate to their subject matter. All tribunals are therefore in some respects alike, but each develops its own practices and style in order to cope with the particular demands of its caseload in its specialist area.

The Appeal Tribunal that forms part of the Competition Commission will have to fit into this mould. It will have a full-time chairman, Judge Christopher Bellamy, who has for the last five years been the UK judge at the Court of First Instance in Luxembourg, together with a number of part-time members, some of whom will be legally qualified and entitled to chair appeal tribunals themselves. The secretary of state will issue rules covering the operation of the tribunal, and the chairman of the tribunal is responsible for organizing hearing of appeals against any decision of the DGFT under Chapters I or II. These are not simply appeals against any fine that may be imposed by the DGFT but can concern other issues including the following:

1. Whether Chapters I or II have been infringed at all (this may involve a decision on fact, such as that there was no agreement or concerted practice at all, simply parallel conduct by the parties, with regard to, say, prices; alternatively it may be on a question of law, such as that an admitted agreement had no effect on competition in the UK and so was exempt from the Act).
2. Whether an exemption from the Act should have been refused or cancelled. This might involve an appeal by the parties to the agreement against the DGFT's decision on the grounds that it met all the criteria for individual exemption under section 9, but had nevertheless been rejected.
3. Whether an exemption from the Act should not have been given or should have been given only subject to conditions or obligations or for a different period of time. This, by contrast, might be brought by third parties.
4. Whether 'interim measures' orders should be made in a particular case, where there is urgency.

The tasks imposed upon the tribunal are similar to those which the Court of First Instance in Luxembourg has, since 1989, undertaken in hearing appeals from the European Commission under article 173 (now renumbered under the Treaty of Amsterdam as article 234) and the new president will be as familiar as anyone can be with that appeal process. A recent speech given by Koenraad Lenaerts, the Belgian judge at the CFI, emphasized the important contribution which the CFI has made over the last ten years to the quality of assessment of administrative decisions in this area, which surely will become also a priority for the new tribunal here. The official introduction to the draft Procedural Rules of the Tribunal states that it is to be primarily concerned with the correctness of the appealed decision, rather than with procedural issues.[5]

The experience of the CFI in these cases tends to suggest that there will be a large number of appeals, each of which is likely to raise, not just a single issue, but a large number of points often interrelated. It has been rare in fact for parties which have been fined by the European Commission for competition 'offences' not to appeal and, when they appeal, they tend to raise not only the substantive reasoning of the Commission but a number of procedural issues. The time taken for the disposal of appeals has, therefore, been substantial, running into many months and years. It is of course permissible that, under the rules of procedure (see schedule 8, para. 9e), the tribunal itself lay down time limits on all aspects of individual cases, including a time for oral presentation. It will be of interest to see how strict the tribunal will be both on time limits and on the length of oral hearings. My guess is that it will seek to be very strict indeed. It is likely that a number of appeal panels, possibly four or five, will have to sit simultaneously once the work of the tribunal is fully up and running. The president will have the difficult task of deciding which cases to take himself and which to allocate to other chairmen; this is of course no different from the responsibility of the Lord Chief Justice or the Master of the Rolls in the allocation of cases to their judicial brethren, although of course there is a difference here in that the other tribunal chairmen will not initially have the wide experience of the president in dealing with cases of this kind.

The decisions of the tribunal will themselves be both of critical significance to the parties and an important source of law generally; there are likely to be a large number of appeals to it from the decisions of the Office of Fair Trading. It is important, however, that the decisions of the DGFT under Chapters I and II are given in sufficient detail to enable the grounds underlying them to be clearly brought out. The Act itself is silent as to the content of the written decisions of the director-general. Decisions of the European Commission in competition cases have in many instances been extremely lengthy, partly because of the certainty that they will be scrutinized with great care by the parties to see if any fault in reasoning, substantive law or procedure can be extracted. Commission officials in Brussels are always greatly concerned to ensure that their findings of fact and law are set out in such detail as to reduce the risk that, as in some early cases such as *Continental Can*[6] or *Belgian Wallpaper*,[7] the Court will uphold the appeal simply on the grounds that the relevant market had not been adequately defined or that in other respects insufficiently convincing reasoning had been produced.

The parties to appeals to the tribunal will obviously want to give oral evidence as well as to submit legal arguments, and schedule 8, para. 9 of the Act makes express provision for this. This will undoubtedly mean that cases will last longer than if they were merely dealt with on affidavit evidence or on the basis of the written record of proceedings before the director-general. Appeals from the decision of the tribunal will go direct to the Court of Appeal and then on points of law to the House of Lords. The familiarity of our judges with issues of competition law will undoubtedly over time be increased.

There is an important distinction, however, between the work of the tribunal and that of the reporting side of the Commission. The tribunal will be essentially applying legal principles to specific appeals from the initial decision of the DGFT and determining whether it should either stand, be set aside or be remitted to the DGFT for further examination. If an exemption has been granted, the tribunal will be entitled to alter its terms and conditions. If an exemption has been refused, the tribunal can nevertheless grant it either unconditionally or on condition. It will have to exercise all these powers within the criteria laid down by section 60 of the Act. A ground of appeal in some cases is therefore likely to be 'that the decision was inconsistent with the treatment of the corresponding question under EC law', or equally 'that the decision of the DGFT was ostensibly but wrongly based on a requirement of Community law but that there were important and relevant differences in the circumstances of the UK and EC, respectively, which means that the EC precedent should not be followed in this case'. It is likely to be argued frequently that a particular EC decision in the past was largely influenced by the need to integrate the single market, rather than made on general economic and competitive grounds (especially in cases relating to market sharing and distribution) and need not therefore be followed.

Alongside this new institution with its new jurisdiction, the existing Fair Trading Act will continue to be administered by the 'reporting side' carrying out the functions previously dealt with by the MMC. An important element of course in the work of the MMC and its successor is that, as already noted, it is not a court or tribunal but an administrative body charged simply with preparing a report within the requirements of the Act to the secretary of state or industry regulator on the particular monopoly situation, merger or utility reference made to it. While it is required, like any other administrative agency or authority, to observe the rules of natural justice, and subject of course to the control of judicial review, it is nevertheless free, without formal restrictions that legal precedents may impose, (a) to reach whatever decisions it regards as appropriate to the reference and (b) where necessary, following a public interest finding, to put forward appropriate remedies which may involve legislative as well as administrative action. In reaching its decision it has (unlike a court or tribunal) the benefit of an experienced staff of administrators, accountants, economists and other specialists (sometimes supported by consultants) who not only collect the relevant facts and evidence but prepare draft material for consideration of the individual groups of members handling the case and give all the required administrative support necessary to enable the group to reach conclusions and prepare a full and relevant report within stringent time limits. Moreover, the task can be helped by taking into account existing published literature, either from official government sources or elsewhere.

By contrast, the Appeal Tribunal will not have the benefit of such staff assistance, since the only assistance likely to be allowed to its three man panels will be that of a registrar who will handle the details of scheduling of cases and so on; they will have to rely on the evidence presented to them by the DGFT and the parties as well as, in some cases, from third parties. Moreover, unless its rules are drawn up in a far more liberal way than those of existing tribunals, it will find difficulty in being able officially to take into account either MMC reports or government or academic publications on the relevant markets or industries. This may make it more difficult for extensive cross-membership between the two parts of the Commission to exist, as the respective working style and rules of the two may differ so widely. This is a point I will return to below.

To summarize, therefore, we have within the same Commission two separate components carrying out different tasks under very different ground rules and with contrasting staff resources. One could make the assumption initially, therefore, that the two bodies might have little to do with each other and little influence on each other. I think this would be a misjudgment. My view is that both the effect of section 60 of the Act and the close administrative relationship between the two bodies will in time have an important effect on the present approach of the reporting side. While the reporting side will remain largely an advisory body producing reports over a wide range of monopoly and competition issues in regulatory matters, it will necessarily begin in time to be influenced by the European context in which its decisions are to be rendered and by the decisions of the tribunal itself on similar issues or in similar markets. While it is clearly not desirable that the separate roles which they perform be blurred, it is equally important that each benefits from the experience of the other and a measure of consistency be achieved. Any degree of cross-membership that can be achieved, therefore, will be valuable.

PROSPECTS AND PROBLEMS FOR THE COMPETITION COMMISSION

Prospects

Competition law inevitably involves the creation or adaptation of institutions to enforce the substantive law affecting both restrictive agreements and abuse of monopoly (or dominant position). If the institutions are themselves for any reason ill-suited or underresourced for the tasks which the particular laws impose, their performance will be unsatisfactory. Examples of this can be found in the development of competition law both in the European Community and in the USA. Taking the USA first, it is well known that, while the passage of the Sherman Act in 1890 was an important step in the development of legal rules to control cartels and abuse of monopoly power between and by the oil, tobacco, sugar and sugar trusts, not until both federal judges and federal agencies began to take the application of the law seriously (and were given sufficient resources to implement them) did the principles set out in the legislation begin to have an effect on the industrial and commercial situation, as shown in the *Northern Securities*[8] and the *Standard Oil*[9] cases. Similarly, the original efforts of the European Commission in implementing both articles 81 and 82 and later the European Community Merger Regulation have been substantially affected (unfavourably and favourably, respectively) by the resources allocated to them over their early years.

How then are we to regard the prospects for the Competition Commission? On the whole, I am an optimist. First, because the introduction of the new substantive procedural and administrative arrangements have been carefully prepared over a period of nearly 18 months and every attempt has been made to ensure that, from 1 March 2000, the 'new' part of the Commission can get off to a smooth start in liaising with the Office of Fair Trading. Looking back at the implementation in Brussels ten years ago of the European Community Merger (ECMR), one reason for the immediate and continuing success of the Merger Task Force in handling the cases that came was that the Merger Regulation itself was the careful prior consultation and preparation over nearly a whole year. During this time the procedural arrangements (including the emphasis to be placed on the prenotification period) were carefully made; equally important, it enabled the careful choosing of appropriate teams and their leaders to enable the new jurisdiction to have a good start. The UK government has wisely also sought not to rush the implementation of this key institutional reform in the UK, and likewise has consulted widely in setting up the secondary documentation and procedures to support the Act.

A second reason for optimism is that I detect a strong political will behind the Act and the important changes that it brings. Our competition law has been defective in many respects for far too long, but our experience as a member of the European Community has taught us that there is much to be gained from a prohibition system containing real penalties for anti-competitive behaviour, even if there are still important gaps in the EC system of control which its further development (or the use in the UK of the Fair Trading Act) will still be needed to fill. There are clear signs from the nature of recent initiatives and policy statements that the government wants a radical look taken at pricing and other practices in a number of important markets. This may involve not only traditional investigations under the Fair Trading Act but also, for the first time, realistic sanctions to be applied for clear breaches of Chapters I or II. It is my expectation that fines will initially be larger than anticipated, in order to provide a firm element of deterrence.

Yet another reason for optimism is simple: that both the chairman of the Commission and the president of the Tribunal could not be better qualified for the tasks they are taking on. The chairman of the Commission, as an academic economist and practical consultant with 30 years' experience of regulatory and competition cases, is well suited to lead the implementation of the Fair Trading Act jurisdiction now having to be applied to ever more complex markets (often containing notably oligopolistic characteristics), where a clear grasp of the economic issues for and against will be crucial. Just how complex the Competition Commission's task has now become in particular cases is well illustrated, for example, by the technical detail contained in the *Mobile Telephone*[10] case, where the task was to assess the reasonableness of the charges made for calls from fixed to mobile phones. Moreover, the influence of section 60, as indicated above, will be felt in this respect not only in tribunal but also, in my view, in Fair Trading Act cases as we move generally to a more 'effects-based' system.

Nor could the experience of Judge Christopher Bellamy have been bettered for his new role, since in his five years as the UK judge at the Court of First Instance he has spent much of his time reviewing administrative decisions of the European Commission in competition cases and has earned in this role widespread respect for his pertinacity and eye for detail in the individual cases. Most of the fines imposed by the European Commission for breach of the competition rules are appealed, though in a large number of them these appeals are dismissed or merely marginally reduced. On occasion, however, the Commission has found (*European Night Services*[11] is a clear example of recent times) that the Court of First Instance can be merciless in overruling decisions lacking merit on essentially substantive grounds, quite apart from procedural deficiencies. There is no doubt that it will be a considerable advantage that the Office of Fair Trading will from the start realize itself subject to a similar strict approach when exercising the considerable discretion that the new Act provides.

Problems

But while the prospects for the Commission are, in my view, for these reasons good, I am also conscious that a number of problems lie ahead which could threaten the potential effectiveness of either or both parts of the Commission. The first two apply mainly or entirely to the 'reporting side' of the Commission, the third exclusively to the Tribunal. The remaining considerations apply to both parts of the Commission, though possibly they may affect them in different ways.

Dealing with the 'reporting side' of the Commission, the first problem is the degree to which greater 'visibility' now to be provided for its hearings is truly an advance, or instead risks damaging the quality of the work for the sake of what may prove a cosmetic change. It is noticeable that it is currently giving great emphasis to making its procedures more 'user-friendly'. Traditionally, the MMC conducted references almost entirely behind closed doors. When a particular reference was announced, advertisements would be inserted in certain newspapers requesting interested parties or members of the public to send in evidence. No other public announcement or publicity was thereafter made or sought, until publication of the report. Proceedings were inquisitorial, very much left in the hands of the particular group conducting the enquiry. The 'adversarial' approach of courts was avoided and confrontational cross-examination between different undertakings or interest groups did not occur. The practice of conducting all the hearings in private was believed to encourage frankness and the early illumination of the real issues.

Changes in the approach of the MMC were initially the result of the government's 1998 Green Paper, 'A Fair Deal for Consumers', modernizing the framework for 'utility regulation'. This suggested moving (in para. 29) to a more open approach in licence modification references, in which it was thought that greater transparency would reassure both the companies and the regulators because each would know exactly what was said about their proposals or operations. The procedural changes recommended included the introduction of open hearings, coupled with the disclosure of written evidence between parties and the requirement of the Commission to publish draft conclusions in advance of its final report. On 11 May 1999, the Commission announced that it would be consulting widely on possible measures to incorporate more transparency in enquiry procedures and practices, and in July of the same year it published its consultation paper, which set out possible ways of providing greater transparency, including (a) publication of a statement of issues for individual references, (b) publication of hypothetical remedies, (c) joint hearings of main and principal parties, not necessarily in public, and (d) the conduct of open hearings in public at which the interested parties could set forth their arguments.

This latter proposal was first implemented at a hearing on 20 July 1999 in the *New Cars*[12] reference, and further public hearings have since been held in the *Supermarkets* reference. Further changes are now proposed, including publishing outline timetables and requesting parties to provide written evidence in a form that would enable non-confidential sections to be made publicly available. The Commission also intends to publish the issues under consideration and a list of options for remedying possible public interest detriments. It seems likely that the majority of open hearings will take place in certain references where they feel they are likely to assist the enquiry process. This will obviously include those cases where there is a major public interest, rather than those involved with more technical or specialized markets. The Commission is already making substantial use of its website to give more information about its operations and references.

In general, the shift from 'private' procedures to a more open approach is to be welcomed, but there is always a danger that its emphasis will become too 'cosmetic', at the possible expense of the quality of the report, as well as possibly in lengthening the time taken for its delivery, if these additional steps have to be taken. I accept, however, that the fact that the Tribunal for its part will normally be sitting in public will itself create pressures for greater public transparency in the hearings also of the 'reporting side'.

The second problem for the reporting side which gives me concern is the statement in government publications and in the guidance documents being issued by the OFT that the use of scale monopoly references will be reduced. The official line of the OFT appears to be that scale monopoly references will not normally be made (except possibly in the utility sectors) until after Chapter I and II procedures have been tried. This would mean that a number of important sectors with a scale monopoly (sometimes amounting to 100 per cent) will avoid Fair Trading Act (FTA) investigations unless and until practices have been identified by the OFT which are sufficiently anti-competitive to enable cases to be brought under Chapters I or II, with the possibility of fines if to be imposed. This appears to eliminate from FTA consideration by the Commission a number of important markets which require consideration not primarily with a view to imposing fines for past anti-competitive conduct but with a view to legislative or administrative change to promote a better competitive situation for the future.

One can see, for example, that an enquiry such as that into the *Performing Rights Society* (1995) would never have taken place under such a rule, since the rules of the society were not such as would be likely to merit a fine under Chapters I or II, but nevertheless required substantial amendment in the interests of equity between the different members of the PRS. Another example would be the recent enquiry into the scale monopoly of *Milk Marque* in the supply of milk; the MMC's recent report (July 1999) produced proposals for structural reform of the milk auction function previously conducted by Milk Marque on behalf of dairy farmers nationwide; however, under the government's current proposals, such a scale monopoly enquiry would not have been made even though events in the industry showed that it was badly needed, and after all the OFT's attempts to find a solution for the problems of the industry over a number of years had failed. The only actions that could have been taken under the Competition Act, by contrast, would have produced possibly fines on Milk Marque for its anti-competitive practices as a dominant company, but no steps towards the needed structural reform. This undue limitation of the scale monopoly jurisdiction under the Fair Trading Act is not one compelled by the legislation; in my view it is an aspect of the new regime that requires reconsideration.

An aspect of the Tribunal's jurisdiction that may be a cause for concern is whether the resources to be provided for its operation will prove adequate. In my view, the workload of the Tribunal is likely in time to grow quite heavy and the hearing of cases, as already stated, likely to last weeks and months rather than simply days. This will require the appointment of tribunals consisting of members able to sit for a substantial number of consecutive days or weeks, rather than simply on one or two days a week, as is the normal requirement for members of the reporting side. This alone may make the possibility of cross-membership between the two parts of the Commission difficult. The resource requirements of the reporting side are well known, because of its long experience in the cost of carrying out particular categories of enquiry; but the cost of operating the Tribunal and providing adequate resources there may be a more difficult task and may lead to a risk of considerable delay in the hearing of cases if insufficient members are provided to deal with its caseload.

My final group of concerns affects both parts of the Commission. The first relates to the relationship between them. Will it be possible for the two parts to work closely together in the Commission Council, established by para. 5 of schedule 7? While on a personal level relationships should be excellent, there may be institutional strains if, for example, it appears that there may need to be 'Chinese walls'. Let us imagine the situation where, for example, the reporting side has recently completed a major investigation of the car industry, and the Tribunal is then faced with an appeal against a substantial fine imposed by the director-general of fair trading in respect of resale price maintenance in that market. Can the Tribunal's proceedings benefit from any of the information which the reporting side already possesses, or (as one might expect) will all relevant contact between the two parts of the Commission be banned on the basis that this would be unfair to the parties to the Tribunal appeal? There can be problems regarding cross-membership, for example whether a member who has sat on a previous FTA case involving a particular party or market can also sit on a subsequent Competition Act appeal being heard by the Tribunal, since it may be claimed that he may be influenced by his previous experience for or against one party, and may in his performance as a member of An Appeal Tribunal give weight to matters not dealt with by the parties actually in front of the Tribunal. Another potential problem is that of consistency, since the different nature of the two parts of the Commission could lead to different approaches being taken to similar economic and legal issues. The Tribunal will have to be extremely careful to observe the exact terms of section 60 in observing consistency with EC law, whereas the reporting side of the Commission may have greater scope for flexibility in its assessment of the effects of particular practices. There is also another need for consistency; that is, between the practices of the DGFT, on the one hand, and the utility regulators, on the other, since the latter will themselves have a major concurrent responsibility for investigating cases under Chapter I and Chapter II. It is far from clear how disputes will be resolved where each respectively takes a different view on a particular action, other than ultimately by appeal to the Tribunal (in case of a decision by the DGFT or other regulator) or possibly to the reporting side itself where a decision of another regulator leads to proposed changes in the licence. Many unanswered questions are still to be found in this difficult area of shared jurisdiction between DGFT and other sector regulators.

Another problem relates to the nature of the evidence that can be adduced in the Tribunal. Parties to a case may find that they are unable to refer to the content of earlier MMC or other government reports because of the findings of Scott J in the *MaCarthy*[13] case, in which he refused to allow the contents of a relevant MMC report to be treated as evidence. Notwithstanding that the Civil Evidence Act 1995 has since removed the doctrine of hearsay from the English law of evidence, it is by no means certain that the Tribunal will be as liberal in its approach to the acceptance of reports of the MMC (or now of the Competition Commission) or other government documents or other publications as the MMC itself has previously been, which was of course not bound by any rules of evidence, and can consult both experts and publications at its own discretion, provided only that the parties before it are then given proper opportunity of commenting on any arguments or issues which such consultations may bring up. Though there should be little difficulty for the Tribunal in referring to decisions of Community courts or to formal notices published by the European Commission, problems may arise for it with regard to less formal publications, for example policy speeches by the commissioner for competition which under section 60 may nevertheless be argued to be relevant to the hearing of the case.

Another important matter and potential problem relating to the Tribunal, and perhaps also to a lesser extent to the reporting side, is the extent to which the extensive guidance notes produced by the DGFT may be cited or relied upon. Is there any reason why they should of themselves have any more weight than, say, an MMC report? It may be argued that they deserve rather less weight since they have not necessarily been the product of a lengthy and exhaustive enquiry, but represent merely the views of UK officials themselves without necessarily having had considerable experience of the issues considered.

The complications introduced by section 60 of the Act will present problems, as already suggested, for both the reporting side and the Tribunal. While the general duty to bring UK competition law into a state consistent with EC competition law is clearly desirable, there are many practical problems about the detailed application of EC principles in a UK context. It may be thought that these are more likely to affect the Tribunal, which has to apply specific rules to disputes between appellants and the DGFT. On the other hand, it is likely that the existence of section 60 will also in the long run have its effect on the working of the reporting side. It may constrain it in some ways to seek solutions that clearly are consistent with Community jurisprudence, rather than feeling free to seek solutions for UK markets that make economic sense and common sense, without reference back to Community arguments, language or precedents. In other words, is it possible that the reporting side will find itself more inclined to be constrained by some form of a doctrine of precedent than is at present the case? The whole situation is now made more difficult by the fact that the 1999 EC White Paper on the modernization of the application of Article 81 now suggests that the whole application of that article be placed much more on the shoulders of national courts and national competition authorities. This changes in major respects the responsibilities of the European Commission, altering the whole basis upon which the Competition Act (particularly its treatment of exemptions in respect of Chapter I) has been based.

My final and probably main concern is that the success of the Competition Commission does not lie in its own hands alone, because much depends on which way other institutions carry out their responsibilities. With regard to the Tribunal, its role will be much influenced by the performance of the director-general of fair trading and his officials. If they are able to produce consistent and well-reasoned decisions within reasonable time limits, this will make the task of the Tribunal in handling the inevitable crop of appeals easier. While inevitably the OFT will take time to adapt to its new responsibilities, a consistent and confident performance of these will be itself a considerable support and encouragement to the Tribunal, whereas an uncertain or inconsistent element in its rulings could place the Tribunal itself in difficulties. It would be unfortunate if the initial decisions of the Tribunal involve a frequent repudiation of the reasoning or outcomes of early OFT decisions on fines or exemptions. It is obvious that the requirements of section 60 alone will not enable all the problems which will face the director-general and the OFT to be easily solved.

By contrast, the future of the reporting side of the Commission while obviously dependent, as in the past, on the performance by the DGFT of his statutory obligations with regard to mergers and monopolies, depends even more on the approach adopted by the secretary of state for trade and industry and the attitude that he will adopt to its decisions. Confusing signals have been emerging from the DTI in recent months. In July 1999, as already mentioned, an MMC monopoly report on the milk industry was deeply critical of Milk Marque, finding that it had repeatedly manipulated its auction selling system to keep milk prices high, to the disadvantage of the consumer. The MMC produced a lengthy report devoting far greater attention to the details of an appropriate structural remedy than had been the case under normal MMC practice. Nevertheless, the secretary of state saw fit to reject its recommendations for breaking up the Milk Marque and dividing responsibility for sales between several farmers' regional cooperatives. Without dealing with the issues set out in detail in the report, the basis for the suggestion by the secretary of state that a non-structural solution be adopted seemed purely political, influenced by the current difficulties of the agricultural community. Similar approaches to the MMC public interest assessment dominated by 'political' issues were also characteristic of some periods of the Conservative administration, particularly under Michael Heseltine during his period of office as secretary of state. However, within a month of his refusal to accept the Commission's findings in the Milk Marque case, the secretary of state had proceeded to issue a consultation document on proposals for reform in merger cases in which he stated that he believed that 'merger cases should be taken out of the political arena. The system would be significantly improved if the vast majority of decisions were taken by independent competition authority rather than politicians'. It seems difficult to reconcile the secretary of state's actions in the Milk Marque case with his statements in the consultation document.[14] If the new system is to work effectively, the authority of the Competition Commission needs to be enhanced, not interfered with on purely political grounds. Such a lack of consistency between stated principles and actual conduct is disturbing.

This merger consultation paper is disturbingly equivocal in a number of other respects. If the government was seriously committed to this principle, one would expect to find proposals such as the following:

1. other than in exceptional circumstances (a) the competition authorities taking responsibility for determining if any detailed investigation was

required and (b) also making, after such investigations, the final decisions in the cases;

2. retaining the right of competition authorities to apply a broad test (as under the existing public interest test of section 84 FTA) rather than simply a narrow one (competition criteria only) with any right to expand it reserved solely to the secretary of state and Parliament;

3. making the choice of body ('options 1 and 2') to carry out the full investigation of a merger on the basis of experience and resources, rather than simple administrative convenience; and

4. distinguishing between the 'independence' of an administrative body such as the OFT and that of the Competition Commission, which is of a quite distinct nature.

Though paragraphs 4.5 and 4.6 of the White Paper propose that, as regards (1) it shall be the accepted principle other than in exceptional circumstances, no mention is made in the White Paper of the need to ensure that the same principle applies in equal measure to newspaper mergers. These can occasionally raise important 'policy' decisions when it is better for the difficult judgments needed under sections 59 and 84 of the Fair Trading Act to be made by an independent body rather than by a politician. It suggests that the test under (2) should be narrow rather than broad, except when the secretary of state wishes to broaden it(!). As far as (3) is concerned, it gives no indication why it should be the Competition Commission or the OFT which carries out the detailed investigative process of mergers, not even stating the criteria for making such a choice. It places emphasis (para 2.5) on the importance of giving 'considerable greater responsibilities' to independent competition authorities, but appears to overlook the fact that the implementation of option 2 (giving the OFT responsibility for investigating mergers) would actually eliminate much of the current jurisdiction of the reporting side of the Competition Commission, which would be left simply with the responsibilities for utility licence appeals and 'complex monopoly' references under the Fair Trading Act, together with any additional jurisdiction which may be provided under current or pending legislation of a sectoral nature, such as that in broadcasting and financial services.

An underlying premise of the White Paper seems to be that the UK domestic grounds for intervening in a merger have to be harmonized precisely with those contained in Article 2 ECMR. The White Paper gives no real reasons for or against such harmonization, and fails to mention that important cases, such as *BP/Kuwait* (October 1988), have occurred in the past when the existing broad terms of section 84 proved extremely valuable not only to the MMC but also to the UK government in enabling a broad assessment of the public interest, in unusual circumstances admittedly, but which might recur! The secretary of state claims in the White Paper that he can specify additional 'public interest criteria' which *he* (not the competition authorities) can identify, though it is far from clear by what process he would do so. It seems likely that the existence of such a process would involve large-scale lobbying on the secretary of state in contentious cases – perhaps those involving a non-EC bidder proposing to take over some well-established and much-loved UK company. Is this better than allowing such responsibility based on objective grounds (whether competition criteria or broader public interest) to be applied by independent bodies, which are in any case rather better equipped than the DTI with the resources to make an objective (as opposed to a political) judgment in individual cases?

If the criteria for merger cases are limited to those of competition, there is no logical reason to maintain a broader test of 'public interest' for other Fair Trading Act cases. This will mean that the Competition Commission, if examining a complex monopoly such as cars or beer, would have to limit themselves to competition criteria, ignoring all other aspects of the public interests such as public health, safety considerations, employment or regional balance. This would reduce the value of the FTA monopoly jurisdiction, which has proved its worth in its application to a number of sectors (large and small) with anti-competitive elements, a jurisdiction incidentally which the European Commission would love to possess. It may be in any case quite difficult (and time-consuming) for the responsible competition authority to ensure that any finding it makes is based simply on competition criteria, without giving any weight to other elements.

The choices put forward in the consultation document by the secretary of state as models for merger investigation treat as equal options (a) one under which the *status quo* continues as at present with a well-understood division of responsibility between the OFT and the MMC, and (b) an alternative under which the OFT would take on responsibility for detailed examination of mergers, proceeding to give a clearance with or without conditions or to impose a prohibition, forcing the parties if dissatisfied with any decision to appeal to 'an Appeal Tribunal' within the Competition Commission. The premise of the White Paper seems to be that any merger is simply a form of 'agreement' whose effect can be analysed in the same way as any Chapter I case. This is of course a travesty of the actual position, which is that a proposed merger (normally still to be implemented) is a multifaceted proposal which cannot be dealt with satisfactorily either under article 81 or under article 82 (Chapters I and II) procedures. It needs rather to be examined in depth and in the context of both the past and the likely future of the sector, by an independent body without continuing administrative responsibility. The White Paper draws a comparison with the operation of the ECMR and the Merger Task Force, but it should be remembered that the

Merger Task Force itself has no sectoral or continuing administrative responsibilities (equivalent to those of the OFT) and simply handles a succession of merger cases under the discipline of tight time limits. If option 2 were adopted, the OFT would in effect have to create its own 'Merger Task Force' to take over responsibility of handling the detailed investigation of mergers. Even if a large number of the existing staff with the Competition Commission were then transferred for this purpose to OFT, its merger investigations would still lack the essential independent element provided by the membership of the MMC, which is quite different from the 'independence' of the OFT, with its continuing commitment for administration of the Competition Act and UK competition law generally.

A further problem about adopting option 2 is that in practice the OFT is likely to find it difficult to incorporate in its own procedures the protection to third party interests in merger cases given in the past by the MMC and now by the reporting side of the Competition Commission. The MMC had well-established procedures for ensuring that the many views of all third parties, major and minor, were solicited, collected, digested and further refined through group discussion and hearings. In the light of paragraphs 4.12 to 4.14 of the White Paper, it must be doubted just how seriously the OFT could or would undertake this responsibility, bearing in mind too that any dissatisfied third party has no remedy other than possibly through judicial review, which is normally of limited use in these circumstances.

Moreover, an even more fundamental argument against the secretary of state's proposals is one of principle, namely that the OFT, as an administrative body concerned with the prosecution of competition prohibitions under Chapters I and II should not also be engaged in a quasi-judicial capacity in assessing the detailed criteria applicable to mergers (as opposed to merely identifying those cases which require further examination by the Competition Commission).

CONCLUSIONS

It is a well-known characteristic of the British that we are much better at the gradual adaptation and moulding of existing institutions to meet the changing needs of society than we are at laying down general principles of universal application and founding new bodies to implement them. In the framing of the Competition Commission, our predilection for such compromise is very evident. Essentially, the new Commission will provide a combination of an existing well-established body (with a long track record tradition and a considerable reputation) with a totally untried new body, even if the concept of the tribunal is familiar from other areas of law. These two 'halves' in principle could have been kept completely separate, the MMC continuing to report on the Fair Trading Act and utility licence cases as in the past, while the Tribunal, as a self-standing body like the Employment Appeal Tribunal, dealt simply with appeals from the DGFT's decision under Chapters I and II of the new Act. There was no overwhelming logical principle for joining them in one body as the Competition Commission, though no doubt there were administrative advantages and even savings in public expenditure through bringing them together. I suspect, however, that in time the short-term advantages of joining them may turn out in fact to have possibly unanticipated long-term advantages, and the synergy of their close association may have productive results, to an extent not yet even contemplated by their present officers and members. I hope, therefore, that my optimism regarding their prospects will be realized and my quite serious concerns turn out to be unjustified.

To conclude on a lighter note, the new Competition Commission is in effect a marriage of one well-tried institution with a brand new one. Traditionally, the bride and groom in such a marriage are supposed to win good fortune for the future by wearing the following: something old – perhaps the MMC could be given this description; something new – perhaps the Tribunal deserves this appellation; something borrowed – definitely Chapters I and II, borrowed from the Treaty of Rome, as leading principles of EC competition law; something blue – the Oxford antecedents of both the chairman of the Commission and the president of the Tribunal.

NOTES

1. Although in the case of exclusive purchasing agreements the relevant market share figure is that of the exclusive purchaser, rather than the supplier.
2. Where of course there is no system of notification of agreement to an official agency or government department apart from a limited availability of 'business review letters'.
3. Though it is arguable that in those cases where the Commission's report is determinative, for example in water industry price review appeals, it is acting as a 'tribunal'.
4. A case now on appeal to the Court of First Instance.
5. The introduction also states that, by comparison, the CFI 'does not have the ability to examine the merits of the decision' (para. 14). This is misleading as, although the CFI cannot review a Commission decision *de novo*, it has annulled such decisions on occasion on the grounds of 'manifest errors of assessment'. See generally Nehl (1999), *Principles of Administrative Procedure in EC Law*, Hart Publishing, Oxford.
6. Case 6/72 (1973) ECR 215: CMLR 199.
7. Case 73/74 (1975) ECR 1491: (1976) I CMLR 589.
8. 193 US 197 (1904).
9. 221 US 1 (1911).
10. The *Cellnet/Vodafone* report, Dec. 1998, made under s. 13, Telecommunications Act 1984.
11. [1998] 5 CMLR 718.
12. A report due for delivery to the secretary of state in January 2000.
13. *MaCarthy* v. *Unichem* (an unreported decision of 24 November 1989); see also Goyder (1998), 'Reliance on Community Decisions in National Courts', in M. Andenas and F. Jacobs (eds), *Community Law in the English Courts*, Oxford University Press, pp.179-83.
14. Though ultimately the dairy farmers decided on a structural change to their industry incorporating many of the elements recommended in the Commission's report.

CHAIRMAN'S COMMENTS
Derek Morris

Dan, thank you very much for that. It is usual for the chairman to make some comments and observations, and I am going to be extremely brief . The reason for that is that I think that Dan has very successfully and very succinctly covered a substantial area and has raised a very significant number of issues and questions.

The main conclusion that I personally draw from what you said, remembering that the title is 'prospects and problems', is just how very uncertain the future is – that is both a prospect and a problem. There are a number of generalized uncertainties to which I think you have pointed; most obviously, how really in practice will the new Act operate? We do not really know what volume of business is going to come the way of the Appeal Tribunal; and we know still less about what the overall effect on UK industry is going to be. There are potentially very dramatic changes in Europe going on, not only the current initiative in relation to vertical restraints but also the proposed devolution in implementation of articles 81 and 82. Then there is the whole merger reform area about which you have spoken. So there are major areas of competition policy that really are very uncertain.

Within those areas, there are some very specific uncertainties. One that I might just pinpoint in relation to the Tribunal concerns what sorts of decisions it can make. It has the power to quash decisions by the director-general of the office of fair trading; it will also have the power to remit decisions. There are quite tricky issues involved regarding when it should remit an issue and when it should quash an issue. Another relates to scale monopoly which you mentioned. The reason that scale monopoly references are less likely in the future is the guidance which was given with the proposed Act, but this is not part of the Act, and guidance can be changed. You quoted past cases, and there may be cases in the future, where it might be felt that there is need for a scale monopoly reference, but it is not appropriate to go through Chapter I or Chapter II of the new Act first. If so, it is not clear what will happen. So, again, there is some uncertainty.

You have not talked so much about the regulatory field, but one has to remember that there is another whole area involved here for the work of the Commission. I do not know, and I do not think anyone really knows, at the moment to what extent the sector regulators are going to rely on licence amendments predominantly or on the new Act for dealing with issues of competition within their sectors.

Nor is this all. Will there be a new merger regime and, assuming there is, what will the new merger test be? How will it reflect competition and consumer interest? How will it be implemented? All these things are unclear at present.

So against this background, just two points. First, there are some broader themes here. There is an intense emphasis on competition and the consumer interest. There is a growing sense, I think, that the competition authorities in all sorts of ways – I am not just thinking of the merger test – should act in a more independent manner. And there is clearly a move towards greater transparency as an element of fairness and, ultimately, efficiency in the process, though you have raised questions as to whether greater transparency might inhibit efficiency in some ways. So anything that we discuss tonight has to reflect those broader tides that are sweeping though competition policy.

The last point is more parochial. It is just to focus on the two sides of the Commission. They will operate under different Acts. They reflect different types of process. One is a judicial process and the other is better described as quasi-judicial. They will for the most part have different personnel and they will have different procedures. There is, nonetheless, logic in combining them. The underlying economics is likely to be similar. You have raised the question of what weight should be attached to OFT guidance documents. That is something people here may want to pursue. I am struck by the fact that I am not aware of any past MMC report to which one could easily point and say that it is inconsistent with the new OFT guidance. I could see the reporting side finding it relatively easy to fit in with the underlying economic analysis of the Tribunal, stemming, as it will, from European jurisprudence. In other words, I do not see the Commission's work to date as being significantly at odds with its European counterpart. I believe therefore that the Competition Commission is well placed to deliver a sound, coherent and transparent approach as competition policy evolves in the future.

Index